Saints
Sinners
&
Sacred Ground

JILL MARIE MORRIS

DEDICATION

This book is dedicated to those that believe the truth will prevail in spite of adversity, ignorance, and intolerance.

CONTENTS

1. IN THE BEGINNING

"The farther backward you can look, the farther forward you are likely to see." Winston Churchill

It was a tough decision to end *207* as I had, however, it was done with good reason: it was *my personal story*. Uncovering a mounting pattern of historically unsavory events and coincidences in the course of a cursory search, it was evident that another book was needed to put it all into perspective. This book does just that, and is a compilation of research, investigative journalism, and anecdotes, accented with private occurrences involving paranormal phenomenon.

Dating back to a time that was both wild, and unsettled, *Saints* provides a multi-century timeline of historical, and spiritual happenings. Collectively, this information sheds light on residents, and key events that imprinted on the house formerly known as 207 19th Street, and the city of Watervliet, itself.

Upon commencement of my research for this book, I decided that it was best to go back as far as possible, in order to fully understand the history of the city. My gut intuition as a psychic and medium, combined with the desire to conduct as comprehensive of an investigation as possible, led me straight back to a time when the Native Americans roamed the region, well in advance of the state's, and even country's first settlers.

Making the decision to summarize the history of the city prior to delving into a more detailed story affords the reader a better background of Upstate New York; a land steeped in rich, and tragic account. It also reveals a deficiency relative to lessons learned in elementary and high school. Somehow, my education neglected to define the impact of history on to the spirit world.

* * * * * * * *

New York's pine-riddled forests, sparkling blue lakes, abundant farmland, and buzzing cityscapes are remarkably infused with the essence of many cultures; a collection, and reflection of years of growth, and change. Having faced harsh challenges primarily due to rapid development of settled areas and extreme weather conditions, it has survived, and evolved into its own empire.

As with other settled areas of its time, the state has been no stranger to illness. Diseases such as smallpox, measles, cholera and consumption once wiped-out close to entire populations, more so when the Native Americans began to coexist with their new neighbors. Watervliet, once known as *West Troy*, was just as prone to such epidemics, as were the more metropolitan areas of its time.

It was a wave of foreign adventurists who discovered Albany County, inclusive of Watervliet. The initial encounter was made by Henry Hudson, during late spring of 1609.

Hudson was an eager Englishman with a penchant for learning the ways of the sea, and developed a fondness for investigating the globe. Initially, Hudson embarked upon a short round of voyages that proved futile in effort. Shifting gears, he became an employee of the British owned *Muscovy Company,* which took his interests along a more westerly course.

After brief employ with the Muscovy Co., Hudson went to work for the Netherland's *Dutch East India Company.* Not too long after his joining the DEIC, Henry embarked upon the most famous voyage of his career, and set sail across treacherous waters, on the ship *Half Moon.*

After a change of plans relative to routes, Hudson and his crew managed to head towards America, where they stumbled upon Native Americans located in southern New York State. After a scuffle with the Indians, Hudson made a wise choice, and chartered his way north, up a large body of water, now known as the *Hudson River.*

Quite upon accident, Hudson landed in the general vicinity of modern day Watervliet, making it his final destination before turning around, and heading back to the Netherlands. A fruitful escapade, the ship captain found the land robust, and filled with promise.

While visiting the region, Hudson also made contact with the Algonquian Indians. The area had long been home to the Algonquians for centuries prior to his arrival.

For the duration of his stay in uncivilized New York, a productive Hudson established two separate forts: Fort Nassau, and Fort Orange. Although both were fur trading posts, Fort Orange, was the largest.

Thanks to Hudson, Fort Orange became a permanent Dutch settlement in the region. For sake of perspective, the settlement is said to have been located on the land now defined as *Albany.* For those unfamiliar, Albany is the capital of New York State.

Traveling back overseas to spread word of a new and favorable land, Hudson met with the consequences of his earlier decision to explore other countries; that was a big no-no, according to British law. As a result, the Half Moon, along with Hudson, were imprisoned in England.

Deemed a foolish venture, and in direct violation of English law, Hudson was booted from the Dutch East India Company, and jobless – at least for a short period of time.

In due course, Hudson's innate wanderlust resulted in his untimely death. Managing to fund another expedition, Hudson once more set sail. This time, a mutiny transpired, leading to many stories of Hudson being sent to waste-away aboard a tiny raft in the ocean. It is presumed that he died a horrific death.

Despite a tragic ending to his life, word of Hudson's unsanctioned, yet somewhat successful expedition to America (specifically Upstate New York), resulted in both the English and Dutch retracing the doomed explorer's westerly path. In turn, many other pioneers flooded to the wonderfully green land.

Hudson's endeavors led to the establishment of New Netherland. In the early 17th century, New Netherland was a province of the Seven United Netherlands, as located on along the Eastern Seaboard of America. The colonial Seven United Netherlands included Rhode Island, Massachusetts, Connecticut, New York, New Jersey, Pennsylvania and Delaware.

From late roughly 1609, until close to 1620, merchants from all over the world, most notably Amsterdam, fancied Hudson's findings and boldly directed their ships northward, up the 315-mile river for prospect of fur trade. At this time, the Dutch explored the interior portion of the country, often crossing paths with the natives.

Both the Native Americans and the settlers were unsure of the other, however, in spite of the tension the Dutch advanced with reckless abandon, trekking through the region, often arrogantly swiping the land from the Indians in the process. This is how the term *land thieves* was derived. It was, and still is, used to describe the selfish, frequently brutal exploits that the settlers unleashed upon the natives throughout the settlement, and colonization era.

In the early part of the 1600s, Kiliaen (Killian) van Rensselaer, a Dutch merchant, as well as founder of the Dutch East India Company, had been advised of Hudson's discovery. Not long after, van Rensselaer warranted representatives from the Dutch East India Company, to purchase close to *one million acres of land* from the Native Americans living in the region. After securing the property, he named it *Rensselaerswyck*.

Rensselaerswyck was a loosely defined territory along both the east and west banks of the Hudson River, and encompassed what are now known as Rensselaer, and Albany Counties. The western half of Rensselaerswyck, located in Albany County, included the villages of *Port Schuyler*, the *Washington Settlement*, *Gibbonsville*, and *West Troy* (Watervliet).

Intruding upon a well-established Native American population, settlers who resided on van Rensselaer's property encountered resistance, and frequently clashed with aggressive Indians. Today, this area is called northern Albany County, or, Watervliet.

After a few rounds of intense exchanges, coupled with strategic communication, the natives and settlers adjusted. Cooperation between the settlers and the Indians was imperative. The pioneers needed the natives to assist with other natives in the area, specifically the Iroquois.

With word of favorable lands yielding magnificent crops and prolific fur trade reaching halfway around the world, the ship *Unity* set sail from Amsterdam. The ship was chock-full of settlers who had been selected to be tenants of van Rensselaer's very own colony. This group established the settlement known as the *Manor of Rensselaerswyck*.

A man of great skill, van Rensselaer's connection to the *Directors of New Netherland* positioned him to send his Dutch East India Co. business associates, and his family, to the new world. These decisions are said to have laid the groundwork for the establishment of modern day New York. It also resulted in the formation of the *Dutch West India Company.*

It is said that van Rensselaer's strong support of the *Charter of Freedoms and Exemptions*, as written by the Dutch East India Company, groomed him to become one of the most successful landowners, known in the annals of history. Rensselaerswyck remained a legal entity until approximately the mid-to-late 1840s.

The Van Rensselaer Empire continued to grow, with one slight change to the family name: The surname was changed from *van* Rensselaer, to *Van* Rensselaer. Several locations in Upstate New York have paid homage to the family namesake including the Town of *Rensselaerville,* the *City of Rensselaer,* and *Rensselaer County.*

In the mid-1600s, van Rensselaer's nemesis, Peter Stuyvesant, come onto the scene. Stuyvesant wanted van Rensselaer's claims removed, and stopped at nothing to do realize his dream. In a rather hostile take-over, Stuyvesant's bold maneuver created the village of *Beverwyck.*

With an influx of settlers from different countries continuing to arrive in the vicinity of Watervliet by the boat load, the mid-17th century experienced cycles of stabilization, and destabilization. Relinquishing the land to the British, the Dutch surrendered New Netherland to the Duke of York. As a result, Fort Orange (Beverwyck), was renamed *Fort Albany.* Almost twenty years later, the land was named Albany County.

Governor Thomas Dongan granted Albany its city charter. This is known as the *Charter of Liberties.* Amidst a sea of cautious natives, Dongan made the crucial decision include them when drafting the proposal. By doing so, the Indians became allies.

At the time of the charter, Pieter (Peter) Schuyler was born in Beverwyck, and went on to serve as one of Albany's first mayors. Equally notable, Schuyler was also in charge of the *Albany Commissioners for Indian Affairs.*

The Schuyler family farm was located at *the flats,* north of the manor house located in northern Menands. This area is situated just south of Watervliet, and was originally part of Rensselaerswyk.

For over two hundred years, the Schuyler family occupied the farm locally known to many as *Schuyler Flats* (or *Schuyler Flatts*). Integral to local and state history, the flats served as both a camp, and hospital grounds for soldiers during the Revolutionary War.

As of the early 18th century, the town's main ferry was located on an expanse of *Bleecker Farm* (aka: Bleeker), near 16th Street, Watervliet. The landing was just south of 207 19th Street. The ferry was later used by soldiers crossing the Hudson River, in the Revolutionary War, more specifically for the Battle of Saratoga, as briefly noted in my first book.

A great deal of significant history continued to unfold in the Capital District during the 1700s. The *First Colonial Congress* was held in Albany. During the session, Benjamin Franklin introduced the *Albany Plan of Union for all Colonies.* The forward-thinking Franklin had an inkling that the instability of the region was best buffered if there was unity among the settlers, and colonists.

Within a year of Franklin's well-thought strategy, the *French and Indian War* erupted just north of Watervliet, in the Lake George region. French General Dieskau's troops were a fierce blend, consisting of Canadians, French troops, and Native American Indians. They were said to have been a ruthless lot.

It was during the *Battle of Lake George* that Colonel Johnson, Commander of the *Albany County Militia,* captured the French general. Despite the token capture, the French still managed to siege, and destroy, *Fort William Henry.* The fort is located at the southern end of Lake George.

The gory battle made an impression on author James Fenimore Cooper, and resulted in his famed novel, *The*

Last of the Mohicans (1826). Some state that Cooper's tale is a worthy timeline of the historical events that unfolded in the beautiful, Adirondack Mountains.

* * * * * * * *

Just as Cooper's book became a cherished read, the movie released with the same title (Morgan Creek Pictures, 1992), happens to be one of my all-time favorite films. Not only do I hold it in regard given the history of my native New York, but more so, in addition to something that transpired in my youth.

As a child and teenager, I fondly recall spending many summers camping in the Village of Lake George, as well as boating on the waters. From Roger's Rock, to Hearthstone Campground, many wonderful memories were made at the lake.

When I was approximately 12-years-old, my family went camping at the *Lake George Battleground State Campground.* This was the first time camping together at the location. This proved to be one of the more startling experiences I had as a child medium.

Aware of the history, and having visited Fort William Henry many times before, I was accustomed to tales of ghostly hauntings taking place at the fort, and battlefield. Discussing very little with family, I kept my personal spirit encounters safe, in the confidence of Marie, my maternal grandmother.

I had sensed different spirits in, and around the fort. Some were, and still are, stronger than others. In view of the amount of time that my family spent in Lake George, it had become common place for me to tune (or block) them out. So long as I did not stay in the area too long, I was able to manage the ambush of spectral beings.

To this day, the fort and grounds remain to be saturated with energies of those killed in the course of the clash. The overall feeling, even when blocking the communications, is one of excessive spiritual interference, coupled with chaos. The activity made my head buzz when I was much younger, however, as an adult, is much easier to contend with.

Needless to say, and relative to our original camping trip, I was not keen on spending an entire weekend at the battlefield campgrounds. The adventure meant exposure to the area, and for an extended period of time.

The area swarmed with spirits of soldiers, and Indians. Some hiding behind large rocks, and tall pine trees, while others were residually looping through their last minutes of life. The fort loomed in the distance with a quiet presence, but I could see raging flames; it was like looking at a massive bonfire. Even at a distance, I heard screams and shouts coming the direction of the large, wooden garrison.

The energy of the battlefield campground was speckled with pockets of sheer, and utter mayhem. I felt some Indian scouts observing the fort, while in a different location, could 'see' crude, cloth and wood stretchers carrying the wounded, and dead. It was completely overwhelming.

Inundated, it was a welcome relief to go into the village after pitching the family tent. The excitement of the shops along Canada Street afforded slight reprieve from the bedlam of the spirit world, located back at the campsite.

As the day drew to a close, my lack of enthusiasm for having to sleep at the site, combined with overwhelming emotion as a result of my abilities, had made me quite anxious. No matter what I tried to do, I could not turn off the *noise:* spirits were *everywhere.*

Campfire extinguished, we all plopped our stuffed selves into plaid, flannel-lined, musty-smelling sleeping bags, and called it a night – well, at least my brother, father, and stepmother did. I faced a barrage of spirit activity that lasted through the night.

Some spirits sought my help, while others were yelling, and screaming from sustained wounds. Nearby, and a short distance away, I heard the sound of gun fire, loud blasts, shattering glass and the roar of a fire. *There was so much screaming, and yelling.*

Those whom were gravely injured were the most difficult to sense. I picked up on pandemonium coming from the direction of the fort. Intelligent spirits, and residual imprints were scattered over the entire property.

Other spirits were quiet; strategically looking for a place to hide, be it for safety, or to out-maneuver, and attack the enemy. Some crawled around, some stumbled and fell, while others showed themselves; bloodied and gasping their last breath of life.

A few spirits provided glimpses of their fate from inside the fort. The violence and carnage was unprecedented. I had never seen anything like it. The fight was rage-filled. Anything, and everything in the path of a hostile enemy was destroyed. They set everything on fire!

I did see some soldiers being stripped of their scalps; their screams were difficult to ignore. It was a horrific mess, and something that my grandmother worked with me, to instill the significance of prayer for those left to die so horrifically. As a medium, my grandmother taught me how important it was to pray for those who lost their lives, regardless of why.

Most vividly, I still recall the essence of a young, male Indian sitting in the background, afraid to battle. He was terrified. I estimate his age to be approximately 15-years-old.

Located just behind our tent, he never once moved from his spot. Squatting low to the ground, he cowered, watching the slaughter unfold in the direction of Fort William Henry.

Discovered by the enemy, he screamed out, and died. He suffered a gunshot wound to the center of his back. He was a trapped spirit with a heavy imprint. It was like watching a movie-short: his final moments of life continued to loop back to just moments before his death.

Never interactive, it was a strong residual imprint that had a lasting impact on me. I felt helpless, and remember begging my grandmother to help him cross.

A young girl with abilities, I was not seasoned, nor mature enough to process everything that transpired. At least the day's busy activities afforded distraction to all of the spirit chatter, but the quiet of the night created the perfect setting for me to pick up on all of the dreadful drama that occurred nearly two centuries prior.

As dawn's mist fell over the Adirondacks, campsite fires fanned fragrantly delicious aromas of bacon and coffee through the damp, morning air. Watching nearby campers as they bustled about, I sat at our picnic table, exhausted and drained by the night's experience.

Surrounded by nature's beauty, only one thing ran through my mind: *I needed to get out of there!* I was on a mission to get as far away from the battlefield as my adolescent feet could take me. I was almost praying for a storm to drive us from the campground.

Unable to focus, I trotted down towards the base of the sloping battleground hill, where I sat and looked at the lake. It was a much needed diversion.

Finding a quiet spot in the cool, green grass, I stared at the glistening water as children frolicked, teens played Frisbee, and adults walked their dogs. In the distance, boat motors buzzed across the lake. It was surreal.

Such a beautiful space to behold, yet a terrifying place for a young medium. Even with all of the merriment going on around me, it didn't drown out the death that I saw, felt and heard. I sat and cried: I saw two, parallel worlds simultaneously overlapping. Nobody else saw it. No one else heard it; *only me.*

* * * * * * * *

No sooner had the French and Indian War ended, when the American Revolution erupted in 1775. With local volatility, a call to arms was made among the many local militias. Major Gen. Philip Schuyler, a descendant of Peter Schuyler, was one local resident who took charge, and led the fight.

As a result, the *1st New York Regiment of the Continental Line* was established. The regiment was based in Albany. Some documentation notes that a militia training house was built very close to the Price Chopper supermarket, nearby 19th Street and 2nd Avenue, in Watervliet. If this is correct, that building could have been seen if looking southeast from the second floor, living room window, at 207.

Within months, New York was all but crippled during the British invasion. The war resulted in a number of battles, inclusive of the area just north of Lake George.

In approximately 1782, General Washington, along with many of his soldiers, paid Albany a glorious visit. The *Treaty of Paris* was signed that September, and is hailed as having put an end to the very bloody, Revolutionary War. Subsequent to the war, and as most Americans are aware, General Washington went on to become the first President of the United States.

Indeed, the latter part of the 18th century resulted in quite a bit of change relative to Albany County, and impacted West Troy (Watervliet), in many ways. From militias, to ferries, and notable residents, northern Albany County was a busy place.

Nearing the end of the 18th century, John Bleecker's Farm (Broadway and 15th Street), ran up to the outer boundaries of the Oothout Farm, which was located in the approximate area of 25th St., Watervliet. This entire swath of land was renamed *West Troy*. Taking this information into account, 207 19th Street was in fact, once part of Bleecker's Farm.

* * * * * * * *

From a ghostly perspective, I have conducted two, remarkable house readings for current residents of Watervliet. Both cases are located within the confines of the old Bleecker Farm, and each has a unique set of characteristics relative to paranormal phenomenon. Additionally, each of the residents have reported spirit activity of individuals believed to have lived in the area throughout the mid-to-late 1700s.

The first case involved a house situated north of the *Watervliet Arsenal.* I had received a referral call from a set of parents whose child was "constantly" bothered by a "soldier wearing a funny uniform."

After assessing the situation with routine questions and a remote reading, I conducted a hands-on house reading during a visit to New York. Immediately after stepping out of the car, I felt the energy of two spirits: one male, the other female.

The parents were not concerned about their child's sensitivity to the spirit world, but were wanting to know who the soldier was, and if he was harmful. Luckily, after some research, we were able to identify the apparition, and the reason for his vigilance in the home. The soldier was looking after the child, and came to make his presence known at the exact time the youngster was being bullied at school.

Without giving away personal information relative to the clients, I can divulge that the spirit once had a home on the property. Channeling, followed by routine review of the family's property records, led us right to an actual name, and occupation that verified who was watching over their homestead.

Discussing a plan of action with the parents helped to extinguish the child's fears. In a matter of days, he was sleeping more soundly. As for the female that I picked up on; she was the soldier's wife, but was not an intelligent spirit. The family name dates back to having lived on property, in the mid-1700s, until the early 1800s.

The second case involved a Colonial specter who was a bit obnoxious. The location of this residence was two blocks south of 207, and close to Broadway.

I had received a call from a friend whom knows a family that has endured unusual events for almost *nine decades*. Never having had anyone to confide in, my friend asked me to help them.

The home had been in the family since the late 1800s, and according the family, had been on the receiving end of a rather unruly spirit's mischief. Descriptions of greyish apparitions dressed in colonial clothing, fast-moving shadows, shattered glasses, dishes, and even games of hide-go-seek with miscellaneous personal items, were passed down, and experienced by the residents for years.

My first impression while reading the house left me rather annoyed. There was a male spirit who evidently had a problem with liquor, prior to his passing. I am able to sense this by a 'spinning' feeling that I get while doing a reading. As with most spirits, their affect remains the same in this realm, as it did when they were alive. This ghostly hoodlum was no exception.

I visited the house three times before making a breakthrough. The homeowners were fed-up with the noise, and naughty-natured settler.

Giving the family two names to research, both came up as very distant relations from the Saratoga area. Sure enough, one was noted to have had a drinking problem, and frequently stayed in early Watervliet, at another family location – just a block away from the home. For some reason, he found it entertaining to visit his cousins, and annoy the snot out of them, doing so for generations.

Upon the last visit, the male homeowner confided in me that the two families had a long rivalry of sorts, and that the revenge on behalf of their houseguest, made a lot of sense. Stubborn to start, he quieted down after the family and I spoke to him about his rambunctious shenanigans.

This case taught all involved that sometimes grudges do last. Being that the hostilities date back to the late 1700s, shows just how bitter some kin can be.

Never one to divulge specific details without permission, what I am able to state is that the premise of this long-held supernatural spite, stems from a father's disdain for his daughter marrying her uncle. Shocking no, but interesting given the history.

* * * * * * * *

After undergoing quite a bit of change, on March 7, 1788, the entire state of New York was finally divided into a network of small towns. As a result, the township, or *Town of Watervliet*, was founded.

Just prior to the turn of the 19th Century, the *Industrial Revolution* began to boom along the Hudson River Valley corridor. It was a time of enormous growth for the Town of Watervliet.

The age of industrialization also led to the launch of many faith-based organizations. One year later, the first *Watervliet Shaker* meetinghouse was constructed, ushering in an era pivotal to the area's Shaker heritage. Simultaneously, work began on an intricate, and important series of canal waterways in western New York.

Respective to Watervliet's canal history is a little known fact that in 1795, one of the first attempted waterways was constructed, and completed as part of the *Western Inland Canal*. Some state that the Western Inland Canal served as a prototype for the *Erie Canal*. The canal was developed in the area of Little Falls, and extended into Watervliet, during the 1800s.

In an attempt to provide more efficient water transport along the Mohawk River, the *German Flatts Canal* was built. This canal was specifically built to coordinate transport from the Mohawk River, through the Cohoes Falls area. The falls are located slightly north of 207 19th Street. As you will find, the Cohoes Falls region is a very special place.

Around the same time as the completion of the German Flatts Canal, the Village of West Troy was divided into the following localities: *Port Shad, Temperance Hill, Shanghai, Durinsville, and Stone Hook.* Stone Hook is the most notable.

Records indicate that Stone Hook was an area near Broadway and 15th Street, of present-day Watervliet – probably at the ferry landing. The name Stone Hook was imparted because of large rocks that once demarcated the area, along the west bank of the Hudson River.

Notably, the lot of 207 19th Street, is situated between Stone Hook, and Durinsville. Many old maps show Stone Hook existing in the vicinity just south of the intersections of 19th Street and 2nd Avenue, while only one, or two, mark it slightly north. Either way, this was a well-traveled destination for many, making the general area of 207, a high-traffic area for ages.

By the close of the 18th century, Watervliet proved itself a beneficial location to befriend natives, as a means to better newly established settlements. The territory also proved itself as a strategic location for launching multiple war efforts, and was home to some of the state's most notable forefathers.

Most impressively, the small town was eyed as a tactical shipping venue. This attribute alone, resulted in the construction of the Erie Canal. In the long run, the canal endeavor presented as both a blessing, and a curse, for Watervliet during the 19th century.

* * * * * * * *

Case #1: L.F. Carrington, 1868
Location: Unknown

The Troy Whig, August 24, 1868 states: "Committed

Suicide . . . The Coroner's investigation of the circumstances at tending the death of L.F. Carrington, who was found dead in his bed at his residence in West Troy, on Friday morning, revealed the fact that the deceased committed suicide by taking an overdose of opium. He was a habitual opium-eater, and on retiring on Thursday evening, he took an unusually large dose, remarking at the same time to his son, that "this is the last." A verdict in accordance with these facts was rendered by the coroner's jury." (Troy Whig, 1868)

No other contributing factors are known relative to his death. The location of his home remains unknown.

2. SACRED GROUND

"When it comes time to die, be not like those whose hearts are filled with the fear of death, so when their time comes they weep and pray for a little more time to live their lives over again in a different way. Sing your death song, and die like a hero going home."

Chief Aupumut, Mohican (1725)

New York State's history can be traced back to approximately 10,000 BC. It is said that this is a fairly good estimate as to when the Native Americans first came into the state from Canada, as well as other neighboring lands.

For thousands of years, the indigenous people existed with little infringement by outsiders, aside from a wandering tribe, or territory war with another band of Indians. Winters were harsh and proved contest to the most skilled of hunters, while hot and stormy summers gave way to bountiful crop harvests in the fall. The terrain was both protective, and at times unkind to the indigenous people, but they managed to evolve, and survive.

Throughout the course of history, the state's tribes had developed into two primary cultures that were identified by their individual languages; the Algonquian, and the Iroquoian. The Algonquian tribes were the most widespread throughout uncivilized America, while the Iroquoian were fairly contained within southeastern Canada, northwest New York State, and a few Mid-Atlantic States.

At the time, New York was comprised of both Iroquoian and the Algonquian. Together, the two groups belonged under the umbrella of the *Eastern Woodland* group.

The Eastern Woodland Indians covered a territory that was distinctly marked by the geographic location directly east of the Mississippi. The Iroquois inhabited the north, and central regions of the state. These natives are referred to as the *Haudenosaunee*. The Mohawk, Cayuga, Seneca, Oneida and Onondaga were part of the Iroquois. Together, the five tribes formed the *League of the Five Nations*. The Tuscarora decided to join, thus making it the *League of Six Nations*.

The Iroquois were clever, fresh water fishermen. Relying on water as a means of transportation, they fashioned small, canoe-like vessels out of dead, or cut trees which were prefect for travel, and for fishing the rivers and lakes of Upstate New York. The Iroquois also assisted the earliest settlers with fur trade.

Unforgiving winters made the Iroquois expert gatherers. They also learned to tap plentiful maple trees for sap. This practice was passed onto the state's earliest settlers and in turn, is a method that has been implemented for centuries, despite some consideration pointing back to pioneers in neighboring, Vermont.

The other half of the Eastern Woodland group were comprised of the Algonquians. These natives tended to settle in areas along the ocean.

The Algonquians were known for their methods of clearing land to plant fruit and vegetables. A tell-tale trademark relative to Algonquian farming included hastily cut parcels of shrubs, small trees, and grass, followed by a burning of the land. This method made the soil optimal for planting, and farming. Their techniques also proved to be helpful to new settlers who ventured onto a former, Algonquian property, as it meant less arduous work to clear the land and plant crops for their own settlements.

Due to living in coastal areas, the Algonquians built much more substantial water-faring vessels. This gave them an advantage over the Iroquois, who were not accustomed to having to fish the larger bodies of water.

In view of their proximity to one another, the Iroquois not only suffered great in-fighting, but were at constant odds with the Algonquians. Over time, the Algonquians had managed to make their way up the Hudson, initially settling on the east side of the river, in Rensselaer County. In the winter, they migrated across the frozen river, to establish smaller villages in Port Schuyler, Watervliet, and Green Island.

Multiple sources state the Algonquians were encamped very close to Iroquois territory, just below the Cohoes Falls. Mohawks pillaged, and attacked small, Algonquian settlements. As a result, the Algonquians retreated back to their larger villages. This made Upstate New York an extremely dangerous place for incoming settlers.

On a rather unusual, yet interesting topic pertaining to the two groups, the Algonquians were said to have been heavily involved in witchcraft, and other magic, and spirit-related deeds. This was considered taboo to the Iroquois, and thought to be the work of devil spirits.

One Native American in particular, had a great vision, thus changing the wild behaviors of the Iroquois, and impacting the region in positive and profound ways. His name was *Skennenrahawi.*

Skennenrahawi, *the Peacemaker,* was a Native American born near Ontario, Canada. As an adult, Skennenrahawi confided in his mother that he had the gift of prophecy. Through message and vision, he believed that the *Great Spirit* was sending him on a mission of peace; something many thought a rather foolish venture.

There are a few different variations of the story, but most detail how Skennenrahawi took these spirit messages quite seriously. At some point, he asked his mother to go with him to a protruding summit. Most stories speak of a large tree at the peak.

Upon taking his mother to the location of the hilltop, he requested that she bring an axe with her to that exact spot, and take a swipe at the tree with the instrument. If blood dripped from the tree's wound, then it was a bad sign, however, if sap flowed from the tree, it meant her son was alive. He asked her to do this every year in the course of his absence.

In the midst of my research, I stumbled upon a lovely piece of information pertaining to this hill, and tree. Centuries after Skennenrahawi took his mother to the tree, the Chiefs from the *Six Nations Reserve* (Brantford, Ontario), still pay annual homage to the hill. Every year, they offer prayers, and repeat a special ritual in honor of their beloved Peacemaker, Skennenrahawi. What a beautiful gesture to the Great Spirit.

Taking to the task bestowed upon him by the Great Spirit, Skennenrahawi long-yearned to bring people together in peace, rather than war and conflict. Not only did the Iroquois battle with other groups of Indians, they had suffered tremendous fighting among their own tribes. Skennenrahawi's vision proved to be a noble undertaking.

He also had an interesting prophesy involving a white serpent, and a red serpent. The white one was interested in the land that the Native Americans called *home,* which in my opinion, equates to a vision of the earliest settlers coming to America. I believe the red serpent may indicate the Indians.

As history shows, the settlers (white serpent), often tricked the natives, and took away their homeland. In turn, Skennenrahawi's vision foretold of the red serpent making war with the white serpent. This loosely accounts for the fighting between the natives and settlers. At the time of the hostilities, a Native American with special powers (Skennenrahawi), was to become a well-respected leader, and share his revelation of peace.

Perhaps as envisioned, and coming to fruition as an even greater legacy, Skennenrahawi's philosophy led to the creation of the *Kaianerekowa,* or the *Great Law of Peace.* The Great Law of Peace helped the Iroquois reach out to other indigenous nations. As a result of these efforts, the *Haudenosaunee Confederacy* became the most powerful native organization in America. In time, it had a distinct impact on Watervliet, and its surrounding communities.

Relative to 207 19th Street, is a rather amazing fact pertaining to The Great Law of Peace. The Great Law of Peace established a series of *sacred grounds* within the northeast.

The first site designated as a sacred ground is Skennenrahawi's birthplace, located at *The Bay of Quinte.* The bay is positioned in Ontario, Canada.

The next site is *Ganondagan,* an area thought to be located in Ontario County, New York. Particulars associated to this designation indicate that this is the spot where Skennenrahawi met the female, Native American leader, *Jikonsaseh.*

The third sacred ground territory is located along the southern shore of *Onondaga Lake.* The special attributes of this site detail a meeting between Skennenrahawi, Jikonsaseh and *Hiawatha.* It is at this site that the three somehow managed to confront *Tadodaho.*

Tadodaho was a reprehensible chief, and violent warrior of the Onondaga nation, who was also known to work with demons. He was greatly feared throughout the region, and had a nefarious reputation, leaving many to die in his wake.

Together, the three managed to convince the chief to give up his magic, and convert to a peaceable life. After much deliberation and careful negotiation, Tadodaho yielded, and together, the four members raised what is now known in Iroquois culture, as the *Tree of Peace*.

The fourth sacred ground site, and the most critical to my research into Watervliet's history, is located in the area of the Cohoes Falls, just north of Watervliet. This sacred ground encompasses a rather large area, and stretches just north of the falls and waterway, southward, along the Hudson River, into Port Schuyler. This territory includes *all of Watervliet*.

The most fascinating aspect about this piece of history comes into play when the Mohawks put Skennenrahawi to a test at the Cohoes Falls. As many claim, the Mohawks forced him to stand in a tall tree protruding over the falls. The natives used some type of cutting tool, to split the branch Skennenrahawi was standing on. After completely cutting through the limb, Skennenrahawi plunged into the raging waters below, along with the severed branch.

Skennenrahawi was found downstream from the falls, evidently, sitting at a campfire. The direction of the water flow indicates he was found somewhere between Waterford, and Watervliet.

Since he reappeared unscathed, the Mohawks deemed Skennenrahawi a prophet. Even today, Mohawks and other tribes pay their respects to the Cohoes Falls, managing to sneak past barricades and fences in order to do so. For many generations this story has been part of the Iroquois and Mohawk culture, with the falls a widely revered sacred space.

Taking Skennenrahawi's survivability as a sign from the Great Spirit, the Mohawks joined the Confederacy. Sadly, as the colonists came to settle in the northeast, the lands that encompassed the sacred ground at the Cohoes Falls, (inclusive of Watervliet), were taken away from its people. The *land thieves* had no respect for what was holy to the indigenous people.

By the early 17th Century, the Algonquian Mahicans (aka: Mahikans), had also made the region, home. Always on the move and in search of a viable area to settle, the

Mahicans settled along the eastern, and western riverbanks of Upstate New York.

Modern-day Troy, Lansingburgh and Schodack, were initially Mahican villages, as were Watervliet, Port Schuyler, and Menands. Their territory grew, and later incorporated other areas north, and east of the Hudson River.

Author Dick Shovel states: "The original Mahican homeland was the Hudson River Valley from the Catskill Mountains north to the southern end of Lake Champlain. Bounded by the Schoharie River in the west, it extended east to the crest of the Berkshire Mountains in western Massachusetts from northwest Connecticut north to the Green Mountains in southern Vermont." (Shovel, 1997)

As time progressed, the Iroquois begin moving into the area, creating a conflict with the Algonquian Mahicans. This encroachment continued for roughly three hundred years. In some regions, the Iroquois and Algonquian overlapped, which is the case for much of Albany County, specifically in Watervliet.

Conducting research for *Saints* was often difficult due to conflicting, or missing information. One important aspect that I was able to clarify, has to do with the fact that *Mohican, Mahikan,* and *Mahican,* are the same type of Indian tribe. An interesting story about the evolution of their namesake is quite interesting, bearing in mind there at are least three correct, given names.

Shovel also states: "Both Mahican and Mohican are correct, but NOT Mohegan, a different tribe in eastern Connecticut who were related to the Pequot. In their own language, the Mahican referred to themselves collectively as the *"Muhhekunneuw," "people of the great river."* This name apparently was difficult for the Dutch to pronounce, so they settled on "Manhigan," the Mahican word for wolf and the name of one of their most important clans. . . In later years, the English altered this into the more-familiar Mahican or Mohican. The French name for the Mahican was Loup (French for wolf) and followed a similar reasoning." (Shovel, 1997)

Also included in Shovel's piece is a note about regional arrowheads. I was immediately fascinated by the article. As young children, my brother and I use to go exploring, in search of arrowheads during our trips to Lake George, or *Thacher State Park*, in nearby Voorheesville, New York.

As youngsters, we walked the woods, overturning rocks and leaves in hopes of finding an aged relic left hidden in the forest. One of our favorite findings, and more so in the region of Lake George, were arrowheads.

A discovery was almost magical; a real treasure. Never before, had I heard of copper arrowheads, and surely, one consisting of the material would have been a great find.

Shovel further states: "Copper, gotten from the Great Lakes through trade, was used extensively for ornaments and some of their arrowheads. Once they began trade with the Dutch, the Mahican abandoned many of their traditional weapons and quickly became very expert with their new firearms. Contrary to the usual stereotype, most Mahican warriors were deadly marksmen. The mother of the famous Miami chief Little Turtle was a Mahican." (Shovel, 1997)

Of particular interest to Native American history in Watervliet, the Mahicans were abundant in number and had a village in the area along the shore of the Hudson, specifically known as *Steen Hoeck* (Stone Hook, or Stony Point). As discussed in the previous chapter, Stone Hook was an elevated portion of rock that stuck out on the western banks of river, which became a small bay to anchor ships in the mid-1600s.

The camp covered several city blocks in Watervliet, stretching from approximately 15th Street, north to 23rd Street. Its western edge was established at the base of the hill, or as some say, "the tracks." This includes the area of the Watervliet High School, a building that many have reported to me as being haunted.

As for my quest of local ghost lore, several sources

made mention of spooky happenings at the high school, which is in direct line with the old Indian encampment. One individual showed me photographs taken from inside the high school auditorium, where something odd can be seen mid-frame. After discussing the photograph with the individual who took the shot, along with consulting with a few other paranormal investigators (for objectivity), the photograph is quite remarkable.

From my perspective, I do sense there to be a spirit of an adult female, along with a child, present in the photo. Unfortunately, the photographer did not give me permission to publish it for viewing.

* * * * * * * *

One common story relative to the high school has circulated since the 1970s. It initially involved a group of students who had befriended a former employee of the school. My sources wish to remain anonymous, as the students were not supposed to be on school property at the time of the events, nor was the employee allowed to let them in.

The abbreviated version states that a group of females went to visit their friend, who was an employee of the school. The incident took place after-hours.

Having heard the school was haunted (long before that evening), the group was rather skeptic. While the employee wrapped up his duties, the others sat in a nearby classroom, and chatted.

Heavy footsteps, flashes of light, and a dark shadow emerged at different times, sending the group to seek the worker. Thinking that the kids were feeding into 'silly accounts,' he ignored their pleas to investigate . . . until he heard the heavy footsteps for himself.

The group banded together to investigate, but could not find a source. The doors – and windows – remained locked.

Convinced someone had managed to find a way into the school and scare the employee and his guests, the worker became determined to hunt down the hoaxer. At some point, the lights in various sections of the school began to rapidly flash on, and then off. The entire group fled the high school.

The students ran to a nearby location, and phoned for a friend to go and help the worker. The employee had also left, but separated from the kids mid-flight. He made his way to a tavern, and called a friend to go back to the school with him, in order to subdue the intruder.

Shortly thereafter, the worker and his friend drove up to the high school and stated *all of the lights in the high school,* were flashing on, and off, upon approach. Alarmed, they returned to the tavern, and allegedly called the Watervliet Police Department, stating that someone had broken into the school and was causing mischief.

The employee and his friend agreed to meet the police at the school. According to the students (now adults), they were scared silly for days, and tried to contact their friend – the employee – to no avail.

Finally able to reach him, the school employee appeared to be completely changed by the events of the night, and told them he could not discuss anything with them. Despite repeated attempts, their friend did not relinquish any details, only making one statement about that night: the police saw the lights, and never found the cause, nor a trespasser.

Baffled by the strange change in their friend, the students spoke of the night with other friends and family members, some of whom had heard that the cops were spooked. I found this to be too coincidental relative to happenings at the commercial property behind 207's lot, as detailed in my first book. Just as years prior, the police were called to investigate unusual phenomenon, but did not find a source.

So many years later, one of the former students who

witnessed the events informed me that they ran into their old friend (the school employee), and tried to bring up that "crazy night." The man refused to discuss it, and blurted, "Forget about it. It never happened." He walked away, and has not spoken about it since.

* * * * * * * *

For those feeling adventurous, I highly recommend *googling* the *Bleecker Map of Rensselaerswyck - 1767*. The New York State Museum offers the map for online viewing. The reference point of the map is: "West side of the Manor," (New York State Museum, 2002).

According to the map and associated key, Stone Hook is identified on the 1767 map as "24." Reference to this point is named *Stonehook* (New York State Museum, 2002).

This numbered reference is just south of Green Island. For comparison, I suggest googling a map of present-day "207 19th Street, Watervliet."

Without a single doubt, "24," as drawn on the 1767 map of Rensselaerswyck, is extremely close to, if not right on top of the intersections of 19th Street and 2nd Avenue, Watervliet. Ironically, this places another Indian encampment almost on top of 207 19th Street's lot. This is a very important piece of information that needs to be tucked-away for future reference, and considered when weighing all of the evidence presented in this book.

Unfortunate to the Algonquian Mahicans, the Iroquoian Mohawks were known to be one of most aggressive Native American tribes. Slowly, the Mohawks filtered east and south, into Mahican territory, including the region of present-day Watervliet.

Relative to the Mahican population in the direct locality of Watervliet, Dick Shovel states: "Some estimates of the Mahican population in 1600 range as high as 35,000. However, when limited to the core tribes of the Mahican confederacy near Albany, New York, it was somewhere

around 8,000. By 1672 this had fallen to around 1,000. . . .
The Mahican Confederacy had a large population existing
on the eastern bank of the Hudson River and was
considered *Mahican Proper*. (Shovel, 1997).

The Mahican sub-tribe was located on the western
bank of the Hudson between Port Schuyler, and just below
the Cohoes Falls. Again, Watervliet falls between the two
points.

In the very early 1600s, fur trade remained a lucrative
industry for both the colonists and Indians of the region.
With Dutch settlers offering the Indians colored cloth and
glass beads in exchange for pelts, the Iroquois and
Algonquians learned rather quickly that the more land they
hunted for trade meant not only a high reward in payment,
but placed a deadly stake amongst the local tribes. Raids
and attacks on neighboring camps were taking place at a
fevered pitch.

Made on the banks of the Normanskill River, the *Treaty
of Tawasentha* proved to be another defining moment for
the Iroquois, and the colonists. Together, a group of
settlers, natives and chiefs, smoked a peace pipe, and
buried a tomahawk. The tomahawk represented war, and
the burial of the weapon symbolized peace. (Southworth,
1910)

Be it fact, or lore, it is said that the Dutch built a
church over the weapon in order to prevent it from being
excavated, thus breaking the symbolic treaty. Some stories
indicate that it was buried underneath the Dutch
Reformed Church. Regardless, and perhaps made with the
best of intentions, the Five Nations observed the peace
treaty until the American Revolution.

Nine years later, the Mahicans sought the support of
the Dutch against the Mohawks. Attacks on the
Algonquian tribes, inclusive of those located in Watervliet,
were brutal. Mahican numbers dwindled. Many were left
for dead, and did not receive a proper Indian burial. This
includes those that were killed within the boundaries of

Watervliet.

Much in the way the Mahicans were targeted, Fort Orange Commander Daniel Kriekebeck was killed by the Mohawks for assisting the Mahicans. Melee ensued. The Mahican-Mohawk war lasted a bit longer.

Some four years later, on August 6th, 1630, a huge tract of land was negotiated between the Dutch, and the Algonquian. This is noted as a *Contract of Sale of Land along the Hudson River from the Mahican Indians to Kiliean van Rensselaer*. The contract was a land title establishing the *Colony of Rensselaerswyck* within New Netherland. (New York State Library, 2012).

As previously mentioned, van Rensselaer was not physically present at the time of title. The above contract references the colonization under representation of the Dutch West India Company.

Since van Rensselaer owned Rensselaerswyck, he was responsible for his tenants, financially, and otherwise. Money was not an obstacle, and the business venture completed without a hitch. The title encompassed all of modern Albany and Rensselaer counties and was signed by Peter Minuit, Director General of New Netherland. (New York State Library, 2012).

Another important figure arrived on the scene, mid-17th century. There are many stories about Father Isaac Jogues, a French Jesuit priest.

Although there are some variations as to what actually transpired, the main story appears to be consistent. The major difference between accounts seems to be that of Jogues' death. That will be addressed after a brief synopsis on the events that led to his gruesome demise.

In August of 1642, Father Jogues, along with some of his protégés, were captured by a group of Mohawks while traveling in Upstate New York Indian territory. The group was taken to *Ossernenon*, a Mohawk village that was situated along the Mohawk River (Auriesville, New York). There, they were beaten, and tortured.

Even while imprisoned, Jogues attempted to teach the Mohawks about Christianity. After all, he was a missionary. This proved to be a dually brave, and tremendously risky undertaking, but Jogues had a task to fulfill, even in such a round-about, and horrific way.

Meanwhile, the Iroquois continued to kill hundreds. Apparently, while in one of the many battles, Jogues noticed his captors were distracted, and fled the village. On the run, he took refuge east, and found himself in Fort Orange (Albany).

While at the fort, Jogues was advised that the Mohawks were seeking revenge for his daring escape. It was here that Father *Johannes Megapolensis* came to Jogues' rescue, while hiding in a barn. The Mohawks were out for his blood.

Megapolensis cared for the priest for the duration of his refuge at Fort Orange. After successfully escaping the barn as the Indians circled closer, Jogues was smuggled to Manhattan, and from there, was placed on a ship, and sailed back to his native France. The saga did not end with Jogues' return to France.

Shortly after his return to Europe, the dedicated Jogues dove straight back into missionary work, and headed back to Canada. While in Canada, Indian wars raged with great ferocity. The Iroquois continued to invade New York as a means of gaining valuable hunting grounds for fur trade with the Dutch: no holds barred.

In 1646, Jogues returned to the infamous Mohawk territory west of Albany, with *Jean de Lalande*. Lalande was acting as Jogues' ambassador. He was but a mere teenager when he volunteered for such a courageous mission.

As to be expected, the Mohawks were still bitter, and not the least bit happy about Jogues' return. As a result, Jogues and Lalande became a sought-out objective of the Mohawks.

At the same time of Jogues' trip back into the territory, fur trade had created violent, inter-tribal warfare with the Iroquois. The region was embroiled with fighting.

It is said that Jogues met with the Iroquois for a peace treaty in early August of 1646, at *Lac du Saint Sacrement*. The lake was renamed: *Lake George*.

In August of 1646, Jogues and Lalande were attacked and *beheaded* when the Mohawks took a tomahawk to their throats. A handful of personal stories conflict with the method of execution, and cite that the two men were clubbed to death. However, according to others, their deaths are listed as decapitations, hence referencing any beatings as error.

A decade passed, and a second individual with ties to the Mohawk village of Ossernenon made history. I remember the story very well, as my maternal grandmother, Marie, told me about it several times.

Tekakwitha was born in mid-1600s, in the same village that Jogues had spent much of his captivity. In view of differing circumstances, both of their experiences left a lasting impression upon the Catholic, as well as the historical, communities.

Tekakwitha was an Algonquin-Mohawk. Her mother had been orphaned, and adopted by a family in Quebec. The Mohawks captured the young woman, and took her back to Ossernenon. There, she was taken as a wife by the Mohawk village chief, and in time, gave birth to Tekakwitha.

At a very young age, Tekakwitha succumbed to an outbreak of smallpox. Her immediate relatives, including a sibling and both parents, died. Although she rallied through the illness, she was left grossly disfigured, and practically blind. Fortunately, the little girl was adopted by a surviving family member, and raised within the same village.

By the mid-17th century, the settlements of Fort Orange and Beverwyck had been walled-off from the rest of the region by massive, wooden stockades. This was a necessary defense against the Indians. Continuing to assault the settlers and the Algonquians, the Iroquois showed little mercy. Fires raged, the stockades were nearly breached. Adding insult to injury, disease followed the fires.

The following year, yet another smallpox epidemic annihilated most of Fort Orange and Beverwyck, killing both colonists and Indians. Within a decade, the Mahican population had significantly declined, with disease listed as the main cause. This accounted for even lower numbers of Algonquians in the village of Watervliet.

A few Jesuit missionaries arrived in the area, reaching Tekakwitha's village. Their impression on the girl proved to be life-changing. After the missionaries left the village, Tekakwitha made the decision to convert to Catholicism. On Easter, 1676, the young girl was baptized Catholic, and given the name *Kateri Tekakwitha*. My grandmother always referred to her as "Little Lily."

An empowered, and very brave Kateri Tekakwitha, soon conducted her own missionary work. Unable to see, she traveled to Canada. Once in Montreal, she met a group of nuns. Her fondness for the nuns, combined with her devotion to her faith, led Kateri to offer the remainder of her short life to helping the infirmed, and impoverished in Canada.

Three years later, in 1680, Kateri Tekakwitha died in Montreal from an unknown illness. Some say that it was a fever, while others have recorded very little detail. She was just 24-years-old.

My grandmother often spoke of the miraculous transformation that several witnessed following Kateri's death. Many stories mention this aspect, noting that Kateri's scarred skin changed into an unblemished complexion.

Rather quickly, word spread of this remarkable happening, and in combination with her devotion to Catholicism, along with this amazing phenomenon, people began to make pilgrimage to her grave. Some even claimed their journey resulted in miraculous healings after paying respects to Kateri. A pattern of curative wonders continued, and in due course, paved the way for the Catholic Church to investigate the unusual claims.

* * * * * * * *

On an aside: ever since I was a little girl, my grandmother often spoke of Little Lily, commenting how she had the "face of a flower, and a heart of full of God." One to have several religious statues and objects in the home, she also had an indoor planter that separated the stairs, from the kitchen. She decorated the large box with plants, and miniature figurines.

In the greenery, she had a small statue of Jesus, which she called "Ditty" – a name adopted by us grandchildren who could not say "Jesus." I fondly cherish the time she allowed me to place my little, plastic *Fisher Price* person – a girl – in the planter, to play in the garden with Jesus. I named her *Little Lily* (in reference to Kateri).

* * * * * * * *

Ten years later, in a village due-northwest of present-day Watervliet, the nearby township of Schenectady fell under attack. On February 8th, 1690, the unprotected community was ravaged by Canadians, as well as various tribes, inclusive of the Mohawk. Out for blood, they sought justice for the *Lachine Massacre* of 1689.

Ruthlessly, the group stormed the village, and set almost every home and structure, on fire. Wounded, a man named Simon Schermerhorn escaped on horseback, and rode into the winter's night to warn the colonists in Albany. When the pandemonium ended, dozens of adults and children, were dead. This horrific tragedy will forever be known as the *Schenectady Massacre*.

As coincidence has it, the Schermerhorn surname is one I am familiar with, having known a family by the same

41

namesake in Rensselaer County. After sharing this tidbit of history with a very good, and dear friend of mine who attended my high school alma mater, and helped with a bit of research for the book (Attorney Cara Romanzo), she informed me that Simon Schermerhorn was a distant, paternal relative, and someone that her father had mentioned as part of their family heritage. What a small, small world.

As the Revolutionary War came to a close, the settlers sought to shamelessly rid themselves of the Native Americans. As a result, in 1822, the New Stockbridge Indians of New York (Oneida, New York), gradually headed west.

In turn, many surviving Native Americans in the east were uprooted, and moved to pre-designated areas in Kansas, Oklahoma and Wisconsin. Sadly, Upstate New York's Native American population bottomed-out, and all but vanished.

* * * * * * * *

I began to hear scuttle about the possibility of Native American burial grounds almost immediately after the release of my first book, *207*. Some sources stated that the grounds were within close proximity to 207, if not directly underneath the house. At that time, I had very limited knowledge of the Indians that inhabited the area, yet could understand that it was a plausible theory, given the history of the region. At the very least, it warranted deeper investigation.

Some residents of the city had sworn of the existence of a burial ground, while others quipped at the thought, chalking it up to sheer nonsense. This very subject actually became the focus of downright abusive attacks made against me, for having merely mentioned the possibility.

With time and research, it was very clear to me that there was the need for strong consideration to be given towards the claims. My quest led to a virtual tug of war with some members of the community. It was quite appalling.

To this very day, I cannot understand why some people bully and threaten others. More so, over something with such a plausible concept, especially given a history that validates the entire region to have been swarming with both Algonquian, and Iroquois.

Keeping a level head, unlike some of the more vocal protesters of the community, I plunged into my research and began to see a very definitive picture emerge. Indeed, there was some truth behind the burial grounds. The encampment at Stone Hook was a big find, but another connection added further validity to assertions of Indian burial plots.

The first beam of light that came shining my way, was in the form of an acquaintance's suggestion to contact *Doug George-Kanentiio.* My source recommended that I contact him via email. Evidently, the source had previously mentioned my book to Mr. Kanentiio, and in turn, provided me with his e-mail address.

In summary, Mr. Kanentiio is an author, lecturer and historian. Most impressively, his is a *Bear Clan* member and *Akwesasne Mohawk.* He is also the co-founder of the *Native American Journalists Association,* the *Hiawatha Institute for Indigenous Learning,* as well as a member of the Board of Trustees for the *National Museum of the American Indian.*

His work is widely recognized throughout the Native American Community. Needless to say, I wasted no time contacting him for an opinion relative to the matters at-hand.

Taking to my computer, I sent Mr. Kanentiio a summary of my experiences at 207, along with my familial history relative to the Chippewa tribe. I had advised him that I was conducting research for my upcoming book (*Saints*), and had asked if he could provide any relevant information as to the impact of the land, and the history of

Native Americans in the exact vicinity of 207 19th Street, Watervliet.

Listed below, is the first response that I received from Mr. Kanentiio, dated November 6th, 2011 at 8:16PM:

"Sekon Jill,

Thank you for your letter and the powerful story it tells. I will do what I can to help. The region in which you lived is the ancestral lands of our Mohawk people. That specific area was a great meeting place where nations gathered to discuss trade, diplomacy, to secure peace and simply come together as people and celebrate. But as is true with all peoples there were instances of conflict and people died, some unmourned, the words and rituals of release never spoken, never conducted. Restless spirits, caught between worlds, unable to go on their journeys, causing disruptions by pushing into this realty. By circumstance we are returning to the Cohoes Falls, a place we lost to land thieves over 300 years ago. The land is on the north shore of the Mohawk River across from Cohoes in the town of Waterford. We are scheduled to meet with the town officials to discuss a Native Arts Festival this coming May. Meanwhile, I would welcome additional information. My address is: (omitted).

Sincerely,

Doug-Kanentiio" (Kanentiio, 2011)

I sent Mr. Kanentiio a copy of *207*, and decided to give him an opportunity to read the book before sending him additional information. I received a response from him on November 28th, 2011 at 2:13PM:

"Greetings Ms. Morris,

I trust you are well and finding your time most creative. Our group, the Hiawatha Institute for Indigenous Knowledge, went to Cohoes two weeks ago to begin planning for a Native Arts and Culture festival in that town this coming May. We are also considering ideas for the 100 acres of land we received from the Brookfield Power Company this September 26th. We intend to have a positive and permanent presence in the region which is within the ancestral boundaries of the Mohawk people. Since Watervliet is on the west side of the Hudson River, it is within our territory-that which is the Mahicans. Ausable Chasms in the Adirondacks is also Mohawk territory but the region was a significant tourist area in the late 1800s. Many Native people went there for work either as lumberjacks or as craftspeople. The Albany region has had a powerful, tragic history. Many battles have been fought there and may Native people murdered by the European setters. I am interested as to what spirits may have shown themselves and when. We have very specific customs and places for burials so any details you can provide would help. I trust you are in a safe place now.

Onen,

Doug-Kanentiio" (Kanentiio, 2011)

My response is dated December 31st, 2011 at 1:14PM:

"Dear Mr. Kanentiio,

This email is long overdue. I have been waiting to gather more information before I answer your questions as asked in the prior correspondence.

… Relative to your prior message, you had asked what specifically, I 'saw' while living in the residence. I was aware of at least two energies: One was that of a male; a priest – and the other energy was not male or female, but a very dark and dangerous entity. It can at best only be described as what I would say as heinous and seeking souls to eat, or devour. This entity was ancient and a mixture of many things. It controlled everything else, inclusive of the other spirit energies in the home. It was without a doubt, or exaggeration; evil and I can only state that if fed off the living and spit them out. I have no idea what it is, other than I know it is ancient and cruel.

I did conduct a paranormal investigation on-site with another person. I did not step foot on the actual lot, but walked all around it. I was able to capture some very interesting video/sound and photographic evidence. The photographs in particular, were extremely unsettling and from what I, as well as what others have noted, makes me think that the lot, and surrounding area, may have been a disposal ground for those who were killed. With a history of at least three suicides connected directly to that house, it is speculation if what showed itself in the evidence, is that of trapped spirits, or a combination. My abilities have led me to believe, especially after my experience on the night of the investigation that many souls are harboring in that location, some of which may indeed, be Native American people. What I 'see' is a mixture of different time periods, being held hostage if you will, in that location. There is anger, sadness and entrapment all under the grip of whatever this evil energy is.

I prayed while I was there and asked that spirits leave and rest, letting them know that anyone taken from this earth was free to leave. I did find that the energy partially lifted, but I still sense this very powerful force. In talking with other families who have lost loved ones as a result of suicide within a close proximity of the old house, it appears each case but one, was identical to the next: all male, all developed trouble after moving to the area. Very sad. Certainly, your theory of the history of the Native American people whom were murdered on their sacred land makes tremendous sense to me, based on the research I have done through archived records, as well as what I sense as a Spiritual Medium. The question remains: What to do? Let it stay there, or perhaps, as I was questioning, want to know if a Shaman, or a Tribal Elder versed in doing so, could go and bless the land?

As for the land that you will be receiving from Brookfield Power Company: I am so happy for you, and all Native American people, especially those that called the area their own.

Thank you for your time. Happy New Year.

Jill" (Morris, 2011)

To-date, I have not received a response from Mr. Kanentiio, yet am aware that he has been extremely busy with the development of the gifted land, in addition to other projects that he has been working on. I hope to contact him for follow-up, relative to the information he has provided, as well as what I have furnished to him.

Continuing to conduct my investigation relative to the Native Americans of Watervliet, and the immediate, surrounding area, I did question if any remains had been found within city limits. Surely, there had to be some type of documentation as to archeological reports.

Not only did I find record of artifact and human remains, but also detailed reports as made available online by the *Department of The Interior, National Park Service*. These reports contain specific, and detailed information, inclusive of the location(s) of discovered items.

I have listed excerpts of two of the most recent reports as follows:

"DEPARTMENT OF THE INTERIOR
National Park Service

Notice of Inventory Completion for Native American Human Remains and Associated Funerary Objects in the Possession of the New York State Museum, Albany, NY.

Agency: National Park Service, Interior.
Action: Notice.

Notice is hereby given in accordance with provisions of the Native American Graves Protection and Repatriation Act

[[Page 50675]]

(NAGPRA), 43 CFR 10.9, of the completion of an inventory of human remains and associated funerary objects in the possession of the New York State Museum, Albany, NY.

This notice is published as part of the National Park Service's administrative responsibilities under NAGPRA, 43 CFR 10.2(c). The determinations within this notice are the sole responsibility of the museum, institution, or Federal agency that has control of these Native American human remains and associated funerary objects. The National Park Service is not responsible for the determinations within this notice.

A detailed assessment of the human remains was made by New York State Museum professional staff in consultation with representatives of the Stockbridge Munsee Band of Mohican Indians.

In 1969, human remains representing a minimum of one individual were removed from the Coffin site (NYSM Site Number 1304), Easton Township, Washington County, NY, located on the eastern floodplain of the Hudson River. Excavations were conducted by New York State Museum staff. Although the site was a habitation site, a single burial was encountered in a storage pit. No known individual was identified. No associated funerary objects are present.

Field records and descriptions of the site indicated that all excavated features originated in the Oak Hill Phase Late Woodland occupation of the site, dated to circa A.D. 1300-1400. The Oak Hill phase is part of a developmental continuum attributed to Algonkian speakers. The site is within the historically known aboriginal homeland of the Mohicans.

Between 1954 and 1974, human remains representing a minimum of 39 individuals were recovered from the Menands Bridge site (NYSM Site Number 1361), located on the alluvial flats west of the Hudson River, Menands, Colonie Township, Albany County, NY. Salvage excavations were conducted by New York State Museum staff and local avocational archaeologists R. Arthur Johnson and C.S. Sundler. No known individuals were identified. The three associated funerary objects are two rounded pebbles and a soil sample from one burial.

Field records, diagnostics artifacts, a radiocarbon date, and descriptions of the site indicate that most of the burials were interred during the Late Woodland period, circa A.D. 1275-1400. Based on the archaeological evidence and the geographic location of the Menands Bridge site within the historically known aboriginal homeland of the Mohican, human remains and associated funerary objects from the Menands Bridge site are most likely to be culturally affiliated with the Stockbridge Munsee Band of Mohican Indians.

Based on the above-mentioned information, officials of the New York State Museum have determined that, pursuant to 43 CFR 10.2(d)(1), the human remains listed above represent the physical remains of 40 individuals of Native American ancestry. Officials of the New York State Museum have also determined that, pursuant to 43 CFR 10.2(d)(2), the three objects listed above are reasonably believed to have been placed with or near individual human remains at the time of death or later as part of the death rite or ceremony. Lastly, officials of the New York State Museum have determined that, pursuant to 43 CFR 10.2(e), there is a relationship of shared group identity that can be reasonably traced between these Native American human remains and associated funerary objects and the Stockbridge Munsee Band of Mohican Indians. . .

Dated: June 14, 2001. John Robbins, Assistant Director, Cultural Resources Stewardship and Partnerships." (Robbins, 2001)

A second, and more recent report from June, 2013 reads:

"DEPARTMENT OF THE INTERIOR
National Park Service
[NPS-WASO-NAGPRA-1311f; PPWOCRADN0-
PCU00RP14.R50000]

Notice of Intent To Repatriate Cultural Items:
New York State Museum, Albany, NY
Agency: National Park Service, Interior.
Action: Notice.

SUMMARY: The New York State Museum, in consultation with the appropriate Indian tribes or Native Hawaiian organizations, has determined that the cultural items listed in this notice meet the definition of unassociated funerary objects. Lineal descendants or representatives of any Indian tribe or Native Hawaiian organization not identified in this notice that wish to claim these culture items, should submit a written request to the New York State Museum. If no additional claimants come forward, transfer of the control of the cultural items to the lineal descendants, Indian tribes, or Native Hawaiian organizations stated in this notice may proceed. . .

History and Description of the Cultural items

In the late 19th and early 20th centuries, 93 cultural items were removed from sites in Albany, Rensselaer, and Saratoga Counties, NY, by Mr. Dwinel F. Thompson of Troy, NY. Museum records indicate that the cultural items were found in association with human burials, but the human remains are not present in the collections. From the former Laureate Grounds in Troy, Rensselaer County, NY, the 90 unassociated funerary objects are 6 perforated elk teeth, 2 iron objects (possibly awls), 3 copper spiral ornaments, 74 glass beads, 1 kaolin "EB" smoking pipe, 1 copper tinkling cone, 1 bone comb, and 2 perforated triangular brass projectile points. From Green Island in Albany County, NY, the 1 unassociated funerary object is 1 iron trade adze. From the vicinity of Schaghticoke in

Saratoga County, NY, the 2 unassociated funerary objects are 2 small dicoidal shell beads.

The Lansingburgh and Troy sites are burial grounds that may have been associated with Unawat's Castle, a Mahican village recorded on a 1632 map of Rensselaerswyck. The exact location of Unawat's Castle has not been established, but deed records indicate that the area where the sites are located was in the possession of the Mahican people until 1678 when it was sold by the Mahican leader, Amenhamit, to Robert Sanders. Prior to that, Mahican Indians allowed Sanders to use the property for his cattle as early as 1668. The objects from the Lansingburgh burial sites date to circa A.D. 1650-1670. The objects from the Troy burial sites date to the early 17th century. Based on the archaeological and historical evidence, the unassociated funerary objects from the Lansingburgh and Troy sites are likely to be culturally affiliated with the Stockbridge Munsee Community, Wisconsin.

Green Island is an island in the Hudson River of eastern New York where archaeological evidence indicates recurrent Native American occupation over several thousand years. Museum records indicate the culture item was washed out of an Indian grave at the upper end of the island in 1904. The cultural item dates to the 17th century. Early deed records indicates that Green Island was in the possession of the Mahican people until 1665, when it was sold by Mahican leaders, Amanhanit, Aepjen, and Wanapet, to Jeremias Van Rensselaer. Based on the archaeological and historical evidence, the unassociated funerary object from Green Island is likely to be culturally affiliated with the Stockbridge Munsee Community, Wisconsin.

Museum records indicated two cultural items were found in an "Indian grave near Schuylerville," which is located on the west side of the upper Hudson River in Saratoga County, NY. No specific site information is available, but extensive evidence of Native American occupation has been documented in the area of Fish Creek near Schuylerville. The cultural items date to the 16th century. Archaeological evidence suggests the Schuylerville area was occupied by Mahican people in the centuries just prior to European contact. Based on the archaeological evidence, the unassociated funerary object from the vicinity of Schuylerville is likely to be culturally affiliated with the Stockbridge Munsee Community, Wisconsin.

Determination Made by the New York State Museum

Officials of the New York State Museum have determined that: Pursuant to 25 U.S.C. 3001(3)(B), the 169 cultural items described above are reasonably believed to have been placed with or near individual human remains at the time of death or later as part of the death rite or ceremony and are believed, by a preponderance of the evidence, to have been removed from a specific burial site of a Native American individual.

Pursuant to 25 U.S.C. 3001(2), there is a relationship of shared group identity that can be reasonably traced between the unassociated funerary objects and the Stockbridge Munsee Community, Wisconsin." (Hutt, 2013)

These reports bolster the well-documented presence of Iroquois, and Algonquians in both Albany and Rensselaer counties. This includes the city of Watervliet. In fact, their existence is accounted for on various, and old maps of Rensselaerswyck.

Several maps show two Mahican settlements as being located opposite of one another: one in Troy, and the other across the river, in Watervliet. Not only were the Algonquians part of the city's history, but the Iroquois (Mohawks) saturated the surrounding land, as well.

Considering raids, intertribal fighting, and the ruthless land-thieving of the settlers, evidence reveals that many Indians were left for dead in, and around Watervliet, and its immediate neighboring areas. The reports both interest and alarm me, as they bring to light a glaring question: since remains have been found in the areas *surrounding* Watervliet, why hasn't anything been reported *within city limits?* This prompted me to do a bit more research into laws of discovery relative to human remains and artifacts.

It is important to state that *The Native American Graves Protection and Repatriation Act* applies *only* to federal and tribal lands. Other regulatory commissions have jurisdiction over state, county and local municipalities. Examples of such governing bodies include: *State and Federal Cultural Preservation, New York State Department of State Division of Cemeteries, New York State Department of Public Health,* and the *New York State Archaeological Council Standards Committee.* Additionally, there may be other departments that handle applicable state and local law.

Given artifacts and remains have been reported in Menands, a city immediately to the south of Watervliet, as well as in Green Island, a town directly to its north, and in areas across the Hudson River in Troy, and Lansingburgh, it is in my opinion, somewhat suspicious that none have been found within the small city of Watervliet, bearing in mind known camps. Documentation and evidence shows the Mahicans, and Mohawks inhabited the city with many having died in the immediate area. I find it very hard to believe that *not one* Native American body, or artifact, has been found in the entire 1.5 square mile radius of Watervliet.

The explanation for this could be due in part of the fact that there is a stringent set of guidelines established for the documentation of, and investigation into remains and artifacts. Given the prime location of the city whose footpath commences at the base of the present-day *Congress Street Bridge* (or, Stone Hook, circa 1675), this area has been a central focus for development in the past, and present. This alone equates to high property valuation of the area. 207 19th Street sits square in the middle of *prime commercial property.*

In my opinion, I have strong reason to believe that for hundreds of years, city officials have looked the other way when developers stumbled upon remains. This makes sense, and could have become a routine practice, in order to avoid the issue of a viable tract of land being potentially designated as a historic site. Conceivably, the significance of any such find could trump a large (or small) scale commercial endeavor.

Quite possibly, the entire region of the Congress Street Bridge, at the intersections of 19th Street and 2nd Avenue in Watervliet, reaching west beyond the old Saint Patrick's Church, may have been too valuable of a commodity to *do the right thing*. This very issue later surfaced as my investigation continued, further strengthening my hunch.

Referring to historical data and oral histories, there were, and probably still are, multiple Potter's Fields and unofficial burial sites scattered throughout the city. Removing culture, date, or cause of death, the simple fact that bodies have been desecrated and disgraced, can attribute to strong pockets of paranormal activity within the city.

It is probable that many, if not hundreds, may be entombed on city land, more specifically, remains of Native American Indians on an established, *sacred ground*. It is also no stretch to acknowledge this to be a reasonable opinion, given documentation, and data.

Case #2: Lissie Ferrard, 1876.
Location: The Mansion House.
Broadway & 16th Street.

The Troy Daily Times, February 19th, 1876, states: "Tired of Life. A Woman Commits Suicide at the Mansion House. . . Last Wednesday a woman apparently about 60 years of age called at the Mansion House and engaged a room. She did not register her name, a fact which excited

SAINTS SINNERS & SACRED GROUND

no suspicion. During yesterday she did not make her appearances and this morning a chambermaid upon trying to gain an entrance to her room found the door locked. The door was forced open by Mr. Crowley, proprietor of the hotel, when the woman was found to be dead. She was lying on the bed with her night clothes on. Near her bedside a small bottle, which formerly contained morphine, was found, and it was evident that the deceased had COMMITTED SUICIDE.

The supposition was verified by the finding of a letter, in which she said she was tired of life. The name signed to the epistle was "Lissie Ferrard." She said she had a sister, Mrs. Wm. Fonda, residing in Cohoes; two cousins named Winslow, one a sheriff at Elmira, and the other holding the same office at Cleveland, Ohio. Previous to her disappearance her actions excited no suspicious, except that she did not appear at meals. Her letter was written in a manner that indicated she knew her friends were few and her means of support limited. She was evidently trying to STARVE HERSELF TO DEATH, but finding that process rather too protracted, resorted to poison. Coroner Flood was notified. . ." (Troy Daily Times, 1876)

3. SAINTS

"All the science of the Saints is included in these two things: To do, and to suffer. And whoever had done these two things best, has made himself most saintly." Saint Francis de Sales

The role of religion within the city of Watervliet was often a tempestuous undertaking for its founders. Initial intentions were robust, as religious leaders made countless, painstaking efforts to create a positive impact on the community. Too frequently, their quests proved frustrating and strangely competitive due to the volume of change in the course of the Industrialization era.

The New World had a tremendous impact upon religion and religious leaders, especially those that came to America in the mid-to-late 18th century. For its time, religion was widely viewed as an opportunity for experimentation. Strange things can happen when people start experimenting.

Many toyed with spiritualism. I found this rather striking, considering the era prior that involved religious persecution in the 17th Century (aka: the *Salem Witch Trials*).

With the settlement of the Dutch, the earliest wave of organized religion began to shape the region by means of the *Reformed Church*. The main church in Albany County was known as the *Reformed Dutch Church of Albany* (aka: Dutch Reformed Church).

Located near Fort Orange, the Reformed Church underwent a renovation, circa 1715. The church stood until the early 19th century. Johannes Megapolensis, Jr., served as the church's first Minister.

The *First Church in Albany*, or *North Dutch Church*, was erected in 1798, and incredibly so, still stands today. As a matter of fact, it is listed on Albany's *National Register of Historic Places*.

Also occurring during the early 18th century, the Albany Shaker community was taking shape across the pond, in Great Britain, thanks to James and Jane Wardley. The two were former Quakers.

Contrary to Protestant (and Puritanical values), the Wadley's promoted celibacy, and the scandalous aspect that God could be either male, or female. England's Ann Lees Standerdin was one of the members of the controversial movement. Ann was said to have been a woman who had great visions, relative to the gift of prophesy.

By chance, Ann managed to find out about the Wadley's. Rather quickly, she became a vocal and active member of their organization. Often boisterous, Ann was a rebel with a cause. Apparently, she was incarcerated quite a few times because of her rather loose-lipped ways.

Unscathed, she continued with the outbursts, and wound up thrown in the slammer, yet again. However, all was not lost.

Ann made the most of her 'quiet time,' and had a revelation to organize a religious society in the New World. Leaving the conservative ways of 18th century England in the wake, Ann, her husband, and a few family members set out for New York. She also changed her name to Ann *Lee*, a slight variation of Lees.

Ann found her calling, and established the region's first

Shaker community. The village was small to start, and grew over the course of time.

The Shakers were very adept at crafts, such as weaving, and were known to be impressive blacksmiths. Most of their goods were sold outside of the village as a means of income. Even today, many Shaker crafts can be seen at the Shaker Village, located near the Albany International Airport.

Not all were pleased by this rather strange group of people from England, more so due to their odd beliefs, and rather freakish ways. The group remained quite outspoken relative to their belief that men and women were equals; a true scandal, for its time.

Most outrageous for the starched and staunch reformers of the era, Ann often preached about sex, celibacy, and equality. This was considered a big no-no for the day, as men were the only ones *outside* of the Shaker community allowed to wear the family pants.

Also alarming: Shaker sermons were often characterized by uncontrolled, almost hysterical behavior. Its members frequently spoke in tongues, and claimed to have prophetic visions. Mostly all, violently shook while doing so. It was this aspect which led them to become known as the *Shakers*.

The Shakers did have a positive impact on the community by means of education. In view of their rudimentary beginnings, the Shakers were progressive with their teachings.

It was common for parents in the surrounding area, inclusive of West Troy (Watervliet), to send their children to live with, and be schooled by the Shakers. Quite interesting, bearing in mind the aforementioned details of their services. In time, the adjacent communities grew to tolerate the odd group.

Ann Lee died in 1784. Her legacy is hailed as one of the most impacting religions in the history of Albany County, and greatly influenced residents of West Troy. It wouldn't be the first, or last time persons with prophetic visions trod upon Watervliet's soil.

The *Reformed Protestant Dutch Church of Washington and Gibbonsville* was the first church built in West Troy. Several churches followed; each with the unnerving task to convert as many residents as possible before the city burst into flames. Strangely enough, and as documented in several journals and historical pieces, those flames licked nearly every church in town, at one time or another.

Between the building of the Watervliet Arsenal and the canal system, West Troy was barreling down a one-way street, straight into Hell. When one church failed, another popped-up, in hopes of kicking the devil out of West Troy.

In 1831, the *Washington Street Methodist Episcopal Church* was established in Gibbonsville. A year later, *Trinity Church* was established.

Other churches opened their doors, too. Safe to say, it seemed as if there was a church on every street corner of the city.

This also holds added significance relative to the Shaker community, and has often been referred to as the beginning of the *Era of Manifestations*. Yes, long after her death, Ann Lee seemed to be fulfilling her prophesy in spirit.

For some rather bizarre reason, Shaker children started to have visions by which Ann Lee appeared to them in spirit. When the residents of West Troy got wind of this, they were both fascinated, as well as frightened.

Many children were said to have received messages while speaking in tongues. For the Shakers, it was considered a blessing to be able to communicate with spirit, however, leery outsiders thought otherwise. Some perceived the Shakers as *witches*.

Notably, these prophetic visions appeared at the same time as the resurgence of *Christian Mysticism*. The revival gained momentum in Europe, and spread west, to America.

By 1839 the *Reformed Protestant Dutch Church of Washington and Gibbonsville*, became two entities: the *North Church*, and the *South Church*. Outbreaks of fire cropped-up all over the city. Most are noted to have been the work of an arsonist, while there are occasional, weather-related issues to blame.

Up until this point, the Catholic Church had yet to step in, and take a stab at saving the souls of West Troy. That soon changed when the Irish began to arrive in droves.

Troy's Father Shannahan came the rescue of the Irish-Catholic community of West Troy. His first task to save the sinners, was demonstrated when he supervised the construction of the *original* Saint Patrick's Church, in 1840. Rev. James Quinn presided as pastor for the church, located at 23rd Street, near 4th Avenue.

Predominantly an Irish congregation, St. Patrick's held its first mass on Christmas morning, 1840. The mere fact that the church was made from brick gave it a far greater chance of survival, compared to buildings of other faiths.

It seemed that the moment one church was built, another caught fire, and fell to the ground in ashes. Church burnings continued well into the latter part of the century, by which I find a rather fascinating piece of the city's history.

In 1849, the *Third Street Methodist Episcopal Church of Watervliet* was organized, and built. This remains *the closest church to 207*.

The church is situated a block west of the lot, and sits in a northerly, diagonal line to the rear of the house. I never sensed anything malevolent about the little church, and was actually somewhat comforted by its proximity to the dastardly house.

Matter of fact, the church buffered the ominous, black swath that loomed in the distance, in the direction of St. Colman's Home. I saw that dark cloud *every time* I looked out of my kitchen window while living in 207.

I cannot tell you how many times I shifted my eyes

back to the small church and blessed myself, almost in a gesture of gratitude for simply being there. It lessened the blow of what festered in the distance.

Considering the success of St. Patrick's, the Catholic diocese built another house of worship: *Saint Bridget's Church* (1850). The community now had two, distinct Catholic churches within blocks of the other.

By mid-century, sinners were running rampant in West Troy. Uniquely positioned between two industrialized cities, the building of the Erie Canal proved to make sex, and alcohol a lucrative industry. Pastors, priests and clergy assumed the daunting duty of saving the community quite seriously, and became quite competitive.

As of this point, West Troy had made an indelible mark in history. Several accounts mention the city was noted for its pillaging, corruption and engorgement of all things damning. For some peculiar reason, Troy had escaped the wrath of sin, leaving it a desirable location for the prominent to build on the eastern side of the Hudson.

The Catholics in particular, were devoted to the antithesis of what West Troy had come to stand for. Prayer, Rosary and the sacraments, especially among the many Irish families, gradually shifted its religious makeup for the better. Things were slowly, starting to turn around – or so some thought.

Between the spiritually-connected Shakers, and the highly symbolic Catholics, the resurgence of Christian Mysticism swept through the region. Séances, parlor games, and otherworldly means of communicating with the deceased became the fodder of many in West Troy.

Not all embraced the notion, and were both fearful, as well as enraged with the metaphysical undertakings of their neighbors. I for one, often wonder what my life would have been like back then, given my own set of abilities. Three things come to mind: tar, feathers, and fire. None of which are pleasant, in conjunction with their symbolic attributes.

One example of scorn directed at a professed 'seer' occurred in West Troy, in November of 1850, when a well-known medium named *Margaretta Fox Kane* (Maggie), was targeted by city folk, while visiting at the home of West Troy resident, Mr. Bouton.

Maggie, along with her sisters, were famous for conducting séances, and *allegedly*, speaking with the dead. When the more conservative residents of West Troy found out that the wicked woman was staying in their beloved town, they took to the streets in a good old fashioned witch hunt – although, not so good for Maggie.

For several days and nights, the villagers kept watch over their neighbor's abode, for it housed a heathen. The Bouton residence was riddled with gunfire, and took a beating from thrown stones. Some accounts mention the drama took a toll on Maggie's health: terrifying, and quite ridiculous to think that such a thing once happened in Watervliet. I will attest that with time, some people still are stuck in that antediluvian mindset.

Somehow, Bouton managed to sneak Maggie out of the house, across the Congress Street Bridge, and into Troy. She was later smuggled back across the Hudson River into Albany, where she recuperated without detection from the angry mob. Due to the ease of access to the bridge, it seems that Bouton's house was close to 207. I sense it was very close.

After several years of trickery, Maggie revealed that she, and her sisters were not real mediums, but swindlers. Their séances were nothing other than well-orchestrated schemes that duped many a believer. The gimmick was just shy of becoming a clever, celestial circus act.

Other signs from above tested the villagers. A series of storms rattled the community's spiritual bootstraps, and created catastrophic damage. Some thought it was the work of the devil, due to the widespread sin and conjuring that had taken place over previous years. Residents were truly frightened by the wild weather, and saw it as an omen of bad things to come.

It's interesting to contemplate that even by today's standards, some still consider it an epic warning when Mother Nature short-circuits. How many times have some thought that the world was coming to an end after a terrific storm, or natural disaster?

* * * * * * * *

Meanwhile, across the Atlantic in the small, French town of Lourdes, a series of mystical happenings transpired between February, and July of 1858. Those goings-on had a tremendous, and indirect impact on tiny Watervliet. However, it is important to take a brief look at *Christian Mysticism*, before delving into details, and applying it to the resurgence of the 19th century.

Christian Mysticism is based widely on all things mystical, but is a blend of Catholicism, and the Orthodox Catholic Church. Christian Mysticism consists of prayer, and the study of scripture, in conjunction with prophetic visions. The collective goal of each aspect is to create a path by which one can seeks to connect their soul with God, or a Creator.

Most religions have fundamental ties to mysticism through both prayer, and meditation. This applies to both monotheistic faiths (the belief, or worship of one God), and several polytheistic faiths (the belief, or worship of more than one God).

From ancient civilizations, to modern applications, the existence of sects, groups, and individuals who practice(d) white, or black magic, have been linked to the occult. A tad unsettling, but before getting twitchy, it is wise to consider the origin of its roots.

Perhaps the earliest glimpse at mysticism can be traced back to the *Druids*. Druids were *priest-like* pseudo-clergy folk, dating back to ancient France, Britain, and Ireland. Leaving very little evidence, and barely any written account of their structure, most Druid practices have been handed-down by storytellers.

Going back as far as 300 B.C., the Druids had multiple views; they were a potpourri of spiritual aspects. Seeing little information exists, they are considered to have been divided into one of three categories: *monotheistic, duo-theistic,* and *polytheistic.*

The monotheistic Druids believed in a single, higher power. The duo-theists believed in a set of two higher powers (God and Goddess), and lastly, the polytheistic Druids believed in numerous higher powers. It's really not as confusing as it may sound.

Earth (or nature), was the foundation to the Druid's varied belief system. They celebrated the cycle of life, death, and the seasons – or solstices. They were also big believers in the *Otherworld* (insert creepy music, and cue the fog machine).

The Druids maintained that the Otherworld was capable to send signals to, and receive mystic messages from those who practiced the doctrine. It was also a destination for the human body to travel in life, or in death.

Many believed in reincarnation, although some believed that the soul was born only once. For those that did buy into the reincarnation theory, they did not limit what life form they transformed into at death. Trees, insects, and reptiles were all fair game.

Despite the fun-loving, tree-hugging image that the Druids cast, Julius Caesar painted an entirely different picture of the sect. He repeatedly insisted they were vicious in nature, and practiced human sacrifice.

Objectively, there does remain question as to the truth of Caesar's claims. After all, he was a ruler, and was known for gobbling up most everything in his path. Instilling fear could have been a well-thought strategy to turn others against the ancient hippies.

Following the Druids, *The Iron Age Celts* surfaced. More

SAINTS SINNERS & SACRED GROUND

commonly, the Iron Age Celts were known as *Pagans*. This is where the folkloric blood, lust and guts begins.

Paganism dates back to approximately 500-600 B.C. The Roman's claimed that Pagans were foul, black magic fanatics. Some accounts trace them back to both Ireland, and Britain. Pagans were considered more dangerous, as opposed to the Druids.

Most stories and recorded histories state they were a blood-thirsty, dangerous cult, while many claim them to be an evolved, or hybrid form of the Druids. Unlike their Druid counterparts, Pagans still exist today, and conjure all sorts of reactions by the uniformed, and misinformed.

In addition to the Druids and Pagans, there were also the *Animists*. Animists believed that nature itself, was the home to a very special group of spirits.

Bodies of water such as lakes, streams and rivers, in addition to forests, and mountains, were all prime locations for what they believed to be the most sacred spirits. In turn, they made offerings to these naturally occurring formations, as a symbolic gesture of respect to the higher powers.

Strongly associated to these aforementioned, pre-Christian, mystical makings is *Celtic*, or *Irish folklore*. Fairies, leprechauns, mermaids, the Blarney Stone, the Demon Bride, banshees, and much, much more, are examples of how ancient Druidism, and Paganism, had a lasting mark on the culture. Believe it, or note, this aspect alone is something to consider relative to Watervliet, as the population was largely Irish, and led by many Irish clergy members.

Fast-forward to the 17th century, when components of mysticism were widely incorporated into many religious, and fraternal orders. Several of these organizations have origins in Europe. *The Freemasons*, as well as the *Rosicrucian Order* (aka: *The Ancient and Mystical Order Rosae Crucis*, or AMORC), are two of the more well-known groups that are still popular in today's society.

The Freemasons are the second, most popular of the groups still in existence. The Freemasons, also known as the *Mystic Order of Noble Knowledge*, have far-reaching ties to medieval stonemasonry, and craft guilds. Their lodges, *Masonic Lodge*, or *Masonic Temple*, are based worldwide. Additionally, they are said to be descendants of the *Knights Templar*.

The Knights Templar found their way to the United States of America, where they drew the attention of some of the nation's most prestigious, and well-known men. Its Grand Lodge was first established in England, circa the early 18th century.

Most do not realize that the Masonic Lodge is riddled with symbolic representation, holding significant religious, and mystical connotation. The elements that incorporate the lodge are: the seven stars, the eye, the compass, and the triangle. There are several more cyphers, aside from those listed above.

Seeming to originate as a high-end gentlemen's club of its time, the Freemasons, and their Masonic Lodge, have always been referred to as a *secret society*. A short list of America's founding fathers whom were part of the 'club,' reads quite impressively: George Washington, Benjamin Franklin, Thomas Jefferson, John Hancock, Paul Revere, Theodore Roosevelt, Franklin Roosevelt, Harry Truman, and Gerald Ford.

By the early 19th century, Christian Mysticism had crossed the big pond, and taken off in the west. In an era that underwent tremendous, and quite often extreme change, the typical paths utilized were infused with the occult.

As evidenced with Maggie Fox Kane, spirit communications via séance, tarot, the use of mediums, and psychics were commonplace in the 1800s. The same can be said for the use of entheogens, and hallucinogenic drugs such as opium, cannabis, peyote, and 'magic' mushrooms. Most drugs were used for spiritual, or medicinal purpose.

Including an obituary about the man who committed suicide by opium use (Chapter 1), seemed rather symbolic of the time.

Frequently, many of the drugs were taken to produce visions, as well as create a state of heightened spiritual awareness. Commonly used by the Native Americans and Shaman, these mind altering substances were thought to foster universal enlightenment, as well as bring one closer to their Creator, or God. Understanding how much the Indians impacted the area, it makes sense that some of their customs were passed along to the settlers, and early residents of West Troy.

Two key movements involving the resurgence in Christian Mysticism occurred in tandem, for the duration of the 19th century. The first was that of the practice of *Theosophy*, and the second, the movement called the *Golden Dawn* (also known as the *Hermetic Order of the Golden Dawn*).

Theosophy, meaning *divine wisdom*, is a belief system centered in investigating spirituality. Theosophy traces back to early Egypt and Greece, circa the 2, and 3rd century. By the late 13th century, it had made an appearance in *Jewish Mysticism*, as represented in the *Kabbalah*. The Kabbalah is known for its mystical teachings, and doctrine, and has been a noted favorite of celebrities such as Demi Moore, and Madonna.

The impact of Theosophy did not take place until the 16th century. It was during this time that the practice blossomed. It was refreshing to many, and was a welcome change from the dogma of decades prior.

The Hermetic Order of the Golden Dawn, or Golden Dawn, originated in Britain in the 19th century. It is widely considered a foundational branch of the occult. With magic and ritual a big part of the practice, the Golden Dawn gave birth to both *Thelema*, and *Wicca*.

As opposed to the Masonic Lodge, the Golden Dawn welcomed women into the organization. The similarities between the two societies consisted of initiation, and a hierarchy, heavily laden with mystery, and symbolism.

The Golden Dawn consisted of three Orders. Collectively, the orders merged under one name: the Hermetic Order of the Golden Dawn.

Dependent upon the specific order, the following skills were developed on a personal basis: tarot divination, astrology, astral travel, alchemy, magic, and the receipt, and delivery of, interpretation of apparitions, and spirit messages.

An interesting note about the Golden Dawn, relative to the Freemasons: the documents of the Golden Dawn are derived from the *Cipher Manuscripts*. They are transcribed in special code.

It was Freemason William Westcott, who finally decoded the documents. Wescott, and another fellow Freemason, worked together to develop the course outline for followers of the Golden Dawn. The Golden Dawn remained an organization well into the 20th century.

In part, or as a whole, the revival of Christian Mysticism in the 1800s had a profound impact on religion, more specifically, that of Catholicism. Its influence was later demonstrated in the building of the *second* St. Patrick's Church, of West Troy.

In the mid-1800s apparitions of Mary, the Blessed Virgin Mother, began to appear around the world. Miraculous healings caught the attention of believers, as well as non-believers.

Many Marian apparitions occurred in various countries, although only *some* were *Vatican-approved*. Among the apparitions acknowledged by the Vatican: Guadalupe, Mexico (1531), Siluva, Lithuania (1608), Laus, France (1664), Rue du Bac, Paris, France (1830), Rome, Italy (1842), La Salette, France (1846), and Lourdes, France (1858). (Miraclehunter.com, 2013)

To draw upon the influence of Christian Mysticism relative to West Troy, and the second St. Patrick's Church, one must learn about the Marian apparitions that occurred specifically, in Lourdes, France. These events indirectly impacted Watervliet, for almost two centuries via means of a new and powerful priest who came to save the city, in the mid-to-late 1800s.

As strange as it may sound, this aspect of the research into the book struck a special chord relative to my grandmother, Marie. Much as she did with Kateri Tekakwitha, my grandmother had shared the miraculous stories of the Blessed Mother with me, going back well into my early childhood.

She often spoke of one day visiting Lourdes, France, but never made the pilgrimage. How often I have contemplated the irony regarding our discussions of Bernadette Soubirous, in context of what happened during my tenancy in Watervliet, and in conjunction with St. Patrick's Church.

It all began in February, 1858, when Bernadette Soubirous, a 14-year-old, French, country-dwelling girl began to 'see' a series of apparitions. Initially, she described seeing a female dressed in a simple, white, flowing garment, with a sash.

Each one of her visions occurred at a grotto located on the *Gave de Pau* River. Mary always appeared in the same spot; a small niche above the grotto.

With each vision, Bernadette received new instruction from the Holy Mother, recited prayer, and even fell into a trance-like state. Initially, nobody believed the girl, but in time and with witness, that changed.

The series of apparitions are dated as follows:

The first apparition, February 11, 1858
The second apparition, February 14th, 1858
The third apparition, February 18th, 1858
The fourth apparition, February 19th, 1858
The fifth apparition, February 20th, 1858
The sixth apparition, February 21, 1858
The seventh apparition, February 23rd, 1858

The eight apparition, February 24th, 1858
The ninth apparition, February 25th, 1858
The tenth apparition, February 27th, 1858
The eleventh apparition, February 28th, 1858
The twelfth apparition, March 1st, 1858
The thirteenth apparition, March 2nd 1858
The fourteenth apparition, March 3rd, 1858
The fifteenth apparition, March 4th, 1858
The sixteenth apparition, March 25th, 1858
The seventeenth apparition, April 7th, 1858
The eighteenth, and final apparition, July 16th, 1858.
(Cembellin, 1997)

Following the apparitions, in addition to her overcoming personal struggles, Bernadette joined the *Sisters of Charity* convent. There, she led a life of devotion to Christ, helping others whom were ill, despite her own poor health.

The Holy Mother also appeared at the following (Vatican-approved) locations: Fillippsdorf, Czech Republic (1866), Pontmain, France (1871), Gietrzwald, Poland (1877), Knock, Ireland (1879), Fatima, Portugal (1917), Beauraing, Belgium (1932), Banneaux, Belgium (1933), and Kibeho, Rwanda (1981). (Miraclehunter.com, 2013)

For centuries, Catholic officials have walked at a slow, and steady pace relative to Christian Mysticism, long scrutinizing claims of prophetic visions, and the manifestation of holy apparitions, inclusive of Mary. A uniquely dynamic part of mysticism's influence on Catholicism is keenly identified in the course of the first half of the 19th century, when between 1800, and 1858, the Blessed Mother appeared at four, *separate* locations around the world, with Lourdes being the latter of the grouping.

News certainly reached Europe, and particularly caught the attention of a young man named William F. Sheehan. Sheehan was born and raised in County Cork, Ireland. History will show that Sheehan entered the priesthood and came to America, bringing his enraptured feelings of Lourdes, straight into Watervliet.

The inspiration and excitement of these happenings spurred both interest, as well as restored a sense of hope to people of an era who were laden with hardship and iniquity. A renewed spiritual movement born from miracles and visions, took front and center. Catholics, many of whom had immigrated to the United States from countries such as Ireland, found great comfort in knowing that God was by their side, as they left a land hit hard with famine and disease.

Word of the Marian apparitions, in conjunction with the resurgence of Christian Mysticism, chiefly in respect to the Catholic Church, soon came to play an even larger role Watervliet's history. In a matter of one decade, the entire physical, and spiritual landscape of the community forever changed.

The 1860s also marked a time of rapid development in Lourdes, France, concurrent to Bernadette's visions. In 1861, a French priest purchased the grotto and surrounding land at Lourdes. This venture initiated the building of the Lourdes church complex. By 1876, the *Basilica of the Immaculate Conception* (Upper Basilica), Lourdes, France, was completed. It was grand, in every sense of the word.

* * * * * * * *

By the last quarter of the 19th century, religious conversion was peaking, amidst a continued ebb and flow of church construction, and demolition. Fires, whether intentionally or otherwise set, continued to erupt in West Troy. Every pastor and priest was trying to keep the small city from falling into the devil's hands.

On April 16, 1879, Bernadette Soubirous died at the young age of 34. She was buried in Nevers, France. At the time of death, her complexion was said to have had a special glow about it, almost transforming much like Kateri Tekakwitha's. To my grandmother, this was miraculous, no matter what anyone else may have thought, or said.

Meanwhile, far from the plush countryside of France, West Troy's Irish population was growing by leaps and bounds. Back in his native Ireland, William F. Sheehan was in seminary school, fully aware of the miracles at Lourdes.

In the early summer of 1884, Rev. Loyzance, purchased land near Kateri Tekakwitha's original village in Auriesville. The priest named it *"Our Lady of Martyrs,"* after Kateri. Two months later, the community commemorated Father Isaac Jogues' captivity at the newly erected shrine.

Independence Day, 1889, a date of rather unique coincidence that will be addressed later in this book, was marked by the laying of the cornerstone at the *new* St. Patrick's Church on Genesee Street (19th Street), just 300 feet west of 207. The new church was built to accommodate the influx of parishioners.

The recently built St. Patrick's Church celebrated its first mass on Christmas morning, 1891. Not quite 124 years later, the present community of St. Patrick's Church, rallied against having the landmark destroyed for a city redevelopment project.

The *Panic of 1893* created added turmoil to the area, inclusive of within the religious communities. A result of financial anxiety, many different faiths began renting out church pews as a means to make money.

Families were given named markers to grace the pews, in honor of their generous, church donations. As an added perk, they were given permission to leave their bibles in the pews. The more money they donated to the church, the better seat they acquired. This became a hotly contested issue in West Troy, and resulted in significant rivalry amongst members of the congregation – even amongst many parish families.

A crafty way of collecting funds in a spiraling economy,

participating churches found it fairly lucrative to permit this unusual type of funding. Just how much of that money did any real good may never be known, but it sure did create problems in an already economically challenged time.

Seat money methods lasted well into the early part of the 20th century and gradually phased out, leaving a bitter taste in the mouths of many city residents. Some of my senior sources have mentioned seat money as being the wedge that drove some congregation members from one church, to another; an interesting annotation for future reference.

The 19th century came to a close with the completion of *The Rosary Basilica*, Lourdes, Frances (1899). The original basilica in Lourdes had become the muse of the now *Reverend* William F. Sheehan, leading him to model the new St. Patrick's Church after the Byzantine-styled *church of miracles* in France. Comparison between the two churches remains a topic of discussion, locally, nationally, as well as internationally.

September of 1909, marked the first exhumation of Bernadette Soubirous. Several religious and medical officials witnessed the state of her body after it was unearthed, only to find it had been unaffected by its interment. Yet another grand sign that the Blessed Mother had played a part in the wonder at-hand.

Ten years later, in April, 1919, Bernadette Soubirous was re-exhumed. Again; no routine changes to the condition of her body. She looked absolutely incredible. Given her remarkable condition, Bernadette was a step closer to becoming Saint Bernadette.

In turn, her face was coated with wax to further preserve her already astonishing postmortem appearance. Following the procedure, Bernadette was placed in a glass coffin. Today, her body may be viewed at the *Chapel of Saint Bernadette*, in Nevers, France. It is truly a extraordinary sight to behold.

And the Saints went marching . . .

After living the life of a missionary, and dying a terribly tragic death, Isaac Jogues was canonized in 1930. Shortly after his canonization, the land in Auriesville was turned into the *National Shrine of the North American Martyrs*.

In December of 1933, Bernadette Soubirous was canonized. A young girl once touched by the Holy Mother, was now recognized as *Saint Bernadette Soubirous*.

In October of 2012, Kateri Tekakwitha was canonized as a Saint. My grandmother often prayed to both Saint Bernadette and Saint Kateri, and often encouraged me to do the same; especially when people less fortunate were in need.

Three Saints with unique ties to the community of Watervliet had emerged as part of the region's history. Two of them, Saint Bernadette and Saint Kateri, also had significant meaning in my personal life. How oddly beautiful I have found it, to run into them at this juncture in my life. More strange was the fact the reason was the result of such personal tragedy that took place at 207 19th Street.

As I have stated so many times before, there were times when the research for this book left me jaded. No sooner had I developed a bad taste in my mouth from the crime and corruption, when a unique, and touching anecdote surfaced – and gave me an added lift.

It was refreshing to hear positive stories, and it always has amazed me when they presented themselves. One such story relates to the little church behind 207.

From 1965, until 2005, the *Third Street Methodist-Episcopal Church* remained boarded-up. It had been bought by Philip DeLollo – *my landlord from 207 19th Street.*

A conversation with Watervliet Retired Judge Warren C. DeLollo, and his daughter Nancie, resulted in contact information for Phil's niece, Ann Riley. Ann shared the following details with me during a conversation that took place in the early summer, 2013.

The long, and ever-winding grapevine in Watervliet had

frequently mentioned that my former landlord had purchased the church, years prior to my residency at 207. It wasn't until this conversation for sake of research, that she told me about the family story behind the lonely building.

Phil DeLollo was Ann's Godfather. Together, they shared the same birthday. Very close to her uncle, Ann explained that in approximately 1965, Phil DeLollo purchased the church for an *unknown reason*; he simply felt compelled to care for it, without ever knowing the purpose behind the acquisition.

Upon death, Phil willed the church to his sister Margaret. Due to her age, and the cost of property upkeep, Margaret listed the church for sale. Ann's husband, a real-estate agent, began to advertise the church.

Whether a case of coincidence or fate, Ann's son, a priest in the Boston area, heard that the little church was available for purchase. He then advised a friend, and fellow priest at *Saint Ann's Troy*, of the vacant church's status.

Saint Ann's purchased the Third Street Methodist-Episcopal Church in December, 2005, and made plans to restore the structure to its original purpose as a *Maronite Catholic Church*. Saint Ann's (Troy) then started the application process to have the Watervliet church listed as a historic site.

In May, 2013, the church received its dedication. As of the publishing of this book, *St. Ann's Maronite Church*, is open to the public. Note: St. Ann's is not part of the Albany Catholic Diocese.

Astounded by the chain of events that occurred with St. Ann's, I could not help but feel badly for St. Patrick's. A tiny, abandoned church for years, the Third Street Methodist-Episcopal Church was all but forgotten, yet saved by a single man who felt the need to care for it. How cruel it was to know of a fate far less fortunate, for the one church *so many* nurtured, and fought to save.

They say that some cities have a lasting legacy, be it

commerce, corruption, or geographical juxtaposition, but Watervliet's has been heavily imprinted with religious undertones. An eclectic, spiritual journey that connects itself to three saints, and yet still cannot escape the dark cloud that seems to hang in the air.

Case #3: Joseph H. Peters, 1933.
Location: 1427 Eighth Avenue.

The Troy Times, Troy, N.Y. Wednesday Evening, July 19th, 1933, states: "Painter, Despondent Because of Ill Health, Ends Life With Shotgun…Joseph H. Peters Takes Life by Shooting Self in Abdomen With Shotgun – Had Been in Poor Health. Joseph H. Peters, 68 years old, a painter, committed suicide this morning shortly after 4 o'clock at his home, 1427 Eighth Avenue, by shooting himself in the abdomen with a single barrel shotgun. Members of the family, hearing the report, rushed to the bathroom, where they found Mr. Peters on the floor unconscious. He was carried to his bedroom and Dr. William Kirk of Troy summoned. Mr. Peters was past all medical aid when he arrived.

Coroner Edward W. Spillane rendered a verdict of suicide. Mr. Peters, who was born in the old village of West Troy had resided in Watervliet and Colonie all his life. For the last few years he had been suffering with an incurable disease and of late had been despondent. He was affiliated with the Painters' Union. He was a member of the Third Avenue Methodist Church and, besides his widow, who was formerly Miss Jennie Fitzpatrick, is survived by a daughter, Mrs. Schuyler Yearsley, and three sons, William, Joseph, Jr., and Frank Peters, and 11 grandchildren." (Troy Times, 1933)

Case #4: Name Withheld Per Family's Request, 1952.
Location: North of St. Patrick's Church.

The family had moved from Cohoes, into Watervliet in 1951. New members of St. Patrick's Church, the family patriarch went through what the family described as "an unusual depression." The male, aged in his mid-50s at the time, began to pull away from family, and friends. He refused to go to church, which caused a tremendous amount of conflict in the family.

The grandson, who contacted me about this tragedy, describes how his grandfather apparently began to "act like an animal" causing the family to contact the police. The officers were unsuccessful at handling the situation, yet the family did not want the male jailed. The family member remained in the house, under guard of several, male relatives.

Less than a week later, after making what was described as "a positive turn-around," he told his family that he was feeling much better. With less concern about his welfare, the male returned to going about his normal business.

Unexpectedly, just days after making what appeared to be progress, he took his hunting rifle, and committed suicide by shooting himself in the head. The family has long speculated the house as the culprit for the behavior, and actions of this male.

Reports of paranormal activity, along with feelings of "extreme heaviness" in one of the bedrooms in particular, have been described. The family moved from the house several months after the suicide, and resides blocks away, in the southern section of the city.

4. OUR FATHER

"And he shall wash his flesh with water in the holy place, and put on his garments, and come forth, and offer his burnt offering, and the burnt offering of the people, and make an atonement for himself, and for the people." Leviticus 16:24

Catholicism first came to America during the Colonial era, in the early 16th century, when Spanish explorers and settlers made their way into Florida. Several reference materials list the first Catholic Mass to be held in the United States, as having occurred in this timeframe. By mid-century, St. Augustine, Florida had become the country's first European colony.

In Florida, the Franciscan missions flocked to the area. Many of the communicants were Native Americans that lived along the Florida, and Georgia coasts. Oddly enough, within three hundred years, hardly any Catholics remained in the state.

In the course of the settlement of English colonies along the eastern half of the country, *anti-Catholicism* had taken shape. Many considered the faith to be over-the-top. A doctrine steeped in ceremony and ritual, it presented as more of an oddity to the non-Catholics.

This was later exampled in Upstate New York. Not a single church among the English, was of Catholic denomination. This includes Albany County in its entirety.

Lord Baltimore, the founding father of Maryland, was the first Englishman to bravely establish a *non-denominational* colony. This was an attractive concept to Catholics in the region.

By the early 1600s, the *Maryland Toleration Act* completely enraged early, puritanical settlers. They did not want a trace of any outside doctrine to interfere with their religious, and moral code of ethics.

Rescinding the *Toleration Act*, the Puritans outlawed Catholicism, causing the priests to bolt for safety. The Catholics were considered statue worshippers, which was inappropriate in the opinion of the Protestants. Within one century from a humble, and humid beginning, the tables had turned on America's earliest missionaries, leaving them to flee, or fight.

Eight years later, the Act was reinstated, but not without criticism and widespread angst. The Protestants maintained a foothold for decades.

It was a rarity that Irish Catholics immigrated to America. New York, along with a few other New England and Mid-Atlantic States, excluded them from approval. Only in the 19th century did that begin to change, more so when the Irish made exodus to the States.

By the end of the American Revolution only a tiny portion of settlers within the 13 colonies on the eastern seaboard of the U.S., were of Catholic faith. Most of them lived in Maryland; a safe, and progressive place to be at the time.

With a less than desirable start, the Catholic Church continued to organize more heartily. The *General Chapters* were held in Maryland. Associated meetings led to the Vatican's appointment of the first 'head priest,' aka: *Prefect Apostolic.* Granted this esteemed title, Rev. John Carroll marched the Catholic Church into more than a dozen states. Noteworthy, is the fact that Carroll was later elected the country's first bishop.

This change ushered in a new era for the Irish. Catholics Thomas Fitzsimons, and Daniel Carroll, later traveled to Pennsylvania, in order to work on the *U.S. Constitution.* By the end of the 1700s, endorsement of the First Amendment overturned intolerant, anti-Catholic law. Choice of faith, or religious freedom, was granted to all American citizens.

At the turn of the 19th century, a potpourri of nationalities and religions made their home in West Troy (Watervliet), carving the tiny city into one of the most tight-knit communities that I have yet to see. The Catholic population in the United States continued to explode. With the tremendous flood of Irish, along with a smattering of German, French and Italians, Catholics quickly became America's largest religious population – a far cry from a century prior.

Between 1850, and early 1890, the number of Catholics almost tripled. Religious reform was abound, and with America bursting with attractive employment opportunities for many Europeans, Upstate New York was a striking location to settle, and start life anew.

Many European families, more so the Catholic, produced one, or more children that answered a calling to serve the Lord. Some stayed-put in their motherland, tending to their native flocks, while others daringly crossed the ocean to fulfill their mission, and establish religious communities in the States.

In the early 1800s, Ireland passed the *Catholic Emancipation Act.* As a result, Ireland became part of the *United Kingdom of Great Britain and Ireland.*

A portion of the Emancipation Act is based upon the *Catholic Association.* Catholics were *expected* to offer a hefty penny per month, to assist the priests, nuns, and other religious officials. This idea caught-on like wildfire, and years later, was carried to the U.S., as well as to other countries.

Charities and other organizations were established as a means of helping the poor. Many Irish-based religious communities formed, including: *The Ancient Order of Hibernians*, and the *Knights of Columbus*. Both organizations have remained a very large part of present-day Watervliet.

Despite its rocky start, Ireland's religious freedom movement brought great opportunity to the homeland, as well as to the United States. The stars had aligned for one Irish-Catholic in particular: William F. Sheehan.

* * * * * * * *

Situated on the Blackwater River, County Cork, Ireland, lies a sleepy town called Fermoy. County Cork is the most southerly of Ireland's counties, bordering the Celtic Sea.

A curious village, it once was home to a monastery. By the late 18th century, the abbey and its surrounding land had been deserted, boasting less than a handful of meager dwellings. The town later became the home of a British Army garrison, and by the mid-1800s, was one of Ireland's largest installations.

William F. Sheehan was born in 1833, during the height of the local military base's existence. Born in Fermoy, William had seven older brothers, and sisters.

In his childhood, Sheehan attended the *National School* in Fermoy, Ireland. Having tried to locate the exact school with the same namesake throughout my research, proved a bit frustrating. Without confirmation, it is suspect that he may have attended the *Adair National School*, in Fermoy. Most references to existing national schools, reveal construction taking place long *after* William left his native Ireland.

From the National School, Sheehan furthered his education, and attended the *Trappist Monastery of Mount*

Mellary. Most documentation relative to Sheehan lists the *Trappist Monastery of Mount Mellary, County Kerry, Ireland,* however, the only school that I found is the *Trappist Monastery of Mount Mellary, Cappoquin, County Waterford, Ireland.* Taking into consideration that there are only five of these schools in the country, it appears that some documentation relative to Sheehan, may be inaccurate.

Founded the same year as his birth, the monastery was well-known for their homemade goods, such as cheese, bread, and other food items, as well . . . coffins. Yes, *coffins:* another befitting twist to an already unusual history lesson.

More central to this story, I found that the Trappists were known for *beer-making.* Allegedly, they *did not* require attendees to practice self-restraint around the brew. Every time I consider this, the term drunk monk comes to mind, along with a rather popular statuette of an unnamed, broadly smiling monk, holding a jug of spirits.

In all seriousness, this is a very important aspect to ponder as to whether or not Rev. Sheehan may have had a fractured psyche, of sorts (i.e. drinking problem). I am not stating that he did have a substance, or alcohol abuse issue, but as a matter of opinion, it is possible he may have been a drinker, which could have lowered his spiritual threshold.

A lowered spiritual threshold (via a fracture), could have allowed something dark to enter. Although Sheehan was ordained a priest, it is wise to contemplate that *nobody* is immune to the unholy – *not even a priest.*

Another interesting piece of information that is noted relative to William F. Sheehan's stint at the monastery, has to do with the fact that the order allowed the monks to sell their wares, however, they were not allowed to pocket the money. All revenue from the sale of produced goods was required to go the monastery.

I find this element intriguing, as some documentation states that Sheehan was wealthy upon his arrival in America. This directly conflicts with other documentation that states he came from a family so destitute, that an order of nuns petitioned for the bishop to pay for his education, in exchange for his working in the United States. A section of his necrology states: ". . . he was a most zealous priest, a competent business man, and had sprung from a family of church architects and builders. (United States Catholic Historical Society & Cahalan, 1911)

Other information presented in his necrology also challenges additional resources. Somehow, the motivated priest managed to show up in Watervliet with a large enough stash to build an enormous church, several schools, and an Orphan Asylum. Either way, humble beginnings, combined with rigorous, yet entrepreneurial values became part of Sheehan's ambitious crusade in Watervliet.

Back in the States, the original St. Patrick's Roman Catholic Church, West Troy, celebrated its opening on Christmas Day, 1840. Initially founded by Father Shannahan of *Saint Peter's* (Troy, NY), the location of the church was considered to be in the heart of the Irish Ghetto; a focal point for Irish immigrants to congregate, and establish residency after a long trip across the Atlantic.

Between 1845, and 1852, both the United States and Ireland were overwhelmingly impacted by the *Great Famine.* Ireland heavily relied on its potato crop, and was tragically crippled by the events.

For the duration of the famine, hundreds of thousands died from starvation, and disease. An equal number of natives migrated to America.

After leaving the Trappist monastery, Sheehan attended seminary school in Dublin, Ireland. There, he received the remainder of his official education, relative to the priesthood.

On June 27, 1858, William Sheehan was ordained as a priest in Dublin, Ireland. A few months later, in October Rev. Sheehan, was summoned to the United States by Bishop McCloskey, of Albany, New York. (United States

Catholic Historical Society., & Cahalan, J. E., 1911)

Sheehan served the Catholic community of Albany for approximately two years, until relocating to *St. John's Church*, Utica, New York, followed by another church (St. Patrick's), in Oneida, New York. Within ten years, Sheehan returned to Albany.

Before continuing with Sheehan's journey back to Albany County, I will share a series of events that took place in the Utica area, where my family had relocated in the spring of 1991. It took approximately 23 years for me to make any sense of the extremely frightening occurrences that transpired almost immediately, upon moving into our new home.

* * * * * * * *

Remarrying far too soon after becoming a widow, it was late spring of 1991 when my second husband, along with three-year-old Jimmy, and newborn son Kyle, headed to western New York State. The Utica area had been my new husband's hometown, and seemed a wise choice.

Fortunately for us, one of my husband's cousins had a rental property located on the border of New Hartford, and Utica. Tucked-away in a nice neighborhood, and close to the in-laws, it was a perfect place for us to establish roots.

Taking to the daily tasks of working a full time job and raising two, small children, my husband and I juggled our schedules which allowed us the privilege to care for the children without having to bring them to daycare. With summer just around the corner, our large backyard provided ample space to set up a small pool, plant a garden, and relax when we weren't working.

My days off were very much routine: laundry, tending to the boys' needs and of course, and putting them down for naptime. Once the boys laid down for their siesta, I caught-up on dishes, and housework.

More times than not, I was anchored to the sink, up to my elbows in suds, while I tried to enjoy a lukewarm cup of coffee. The quiet of the house was relished before the next wave of activities resumed post-nap.

It was the afternoon of June 22th, 1991, when all hell broke loose. The quiet of the day was shattered when Jimmy's screams pierced the peaceful, summer afternoon air.

I jumped out of my skin while standing at the kitchen sink, as he ran into the room, hysterical. He was nearly inconsolable. It could not have been more than a flash, from the moment I heard his first scream, until he had reached my side.

Attempting to dry my hands, he literally attached himself to my hip and leg, and clamored at my clothes. He shook.

His platinum blond hair was matted from sweat; his eyes round with fear. I picked him up in an attempt to console him, and could not imagine what had happened. He was *not* prone to nightmares.

Tears poured out of his big, green eyes and down his little, red cheeks. Stuttering, and hyperventilating, he spit out bits and pieces about what had transpired. I can assure you that even as I wrote this, I shuddered, knowing that nothing could have prepared me for what he said.

Clinging to me, he sputtered that *a man came to get him* while he was sleeping in his room. Initially, I thought someone had gotten into the house, and immediately jumped up to make sure the doors and windows were shut, and locked. I made my way to each room, all the while dangling Jimmy from my chest, and hip.

Having established an 'all clear' in the house, I told Jimmy that he had a nightmare. Although, prior to, he had not once had a single fright.

He insisted that he was awake. He then continued to tell me that he was playing with *Wee Wee Raboo*, his favorite, stuffed rabbit buddy, when the man appeared.

Asking what the man looked like, Jimmy cried, telling me that the man was, "really big . . . and all black." In effort to decipher further, I had asked him if it was a *black man* or, if he was wearing black. Jimmy replied, "He has all black clothes on, Mommy!"

Knowing that Jimmy was not the type of child to have such a vivid imagination, I thought that he had fallen asleep, and interpreted his dream as reality. Fetching him a cup of water, along with a cold washcloth, we sat together on the sofa.

Gradually, he calmed down. The only other thing he mentioned about the afternoon's ordeal, was that he was glad *the man was gone.* I was too.

Accustomed to 'blocking' since the events of two years prior at 207, I had not even considered 'reading' our new abode; I wasn't ready to open myself up to that. Having considered that Jimmy's terror was the result of a bad dream, I remained bothered by the fact that he had no type of nightmares in the past. Additionally, we had lived across the river from Watervliet for almost two years prior, and never had any trouble. *Why all of a sudden?*

Later that evening, while Jimmy played in his room, I considered mentioning the incident to my husband, but felt that it was best not to bring it up. After all, it was more than likely a bad dream. My only concern at that point had to do with Jimmy going to sleep; I wasn't quite sure how he was going to react once it came time to say prayers, and crawl into his bed.

Surprisingly so, and without further episode, Jimmy jumped right into bed; he seemed to forget about the earlier fiasco. He, unlike me, slept through the night. Off to work I went the following morning, exhausted from a night of tossing and turning.

Two days had passed, and all was quiet on the western frontier until Jimmy requested that I lay down with him at naptime. This too, was not of the norm for him.

Climbing onto his twin bed, Jimmy scooted to the far

left side, closest to the wall, while I stretched out on the right. I turned onto my left side, and faced him.

Tired from a busy day's play, Jimmy drifted to sleep with my arm draped over his chest. It didn't take long until I had nodded-off, too.

I do not have any memory of a dream, but recall momentarily waking to the sensation that someone had walked into the room. No sooner had I briefly opened my eyes, did I pass right back out.

There is no way of telling just how long I had fallen back to sleep for, when out of the blue, someone – or something – violently jabbed my exposed, right shoulder. The jolt shoved me towards Jimmy.

Terrified, I jerked my head to the right to see who it was, and for approximately two-to-three seconds, saw the silhouette of *a man dressed in black*. I heard a low laugh, and then he vanished.

The shock of the encounter sent me onto the floor, shaking. Jimmy stirred, but did not wake. It was at that point I remembered my last encounter with a man dressed in all black – and began to quiver. I did not see a face, or any other type of indication it was identical to the figure that had appeared in front of the Christmas tree in 207, but it *felt the same*.

It was surreal; sitting on the floor of my son's bedroom surrounded by all things Mickey Mouse, I blessed myself and prayed. *Why here, and why now? What did it want?* Better yet, *who did it want?* I refused to let it harm my son, and demanded it leave, in the name of Jesus Christ.

Praying for several minutes, I got up off of the floor, and fetched a small bottle of holy water. Finding only a miniscule amount remaining, I softly blessed my slumbering son, and then myself. A little bit was better than nothing at all. So many memories came flooding back: I had blessed the two of us in 207, just a few years before.

Not wanting to leave Jimmy alone, I climbed back into

bed, took my son's warm hand, and silently prayed. I could not sleep.

I analyzed everything. The only change that had been made to-date, was the move approximately two months prior, which was in my opinion, benign.

If anything, I had felt relief to move over 90 miles west of Watervliet; no more daily reminders of that horrid place. Despite consideration of every angle that I thought to be a possible cause, I could not make rhyme or reason out of the situation – and it scared me.

I did not tell my husband about the two incidents. I did however, continue to pray and considered calling our priest for advice. So reminiscent of the past, I admit to being rather reluctant.

Time would tell. Perhaps the blessing worked?

As usual, bedtime was uneventful that evening. Never did any of the events occur at night; only in the afternoon, which seemed rather odd to me. With my husband home the following day, I wondered if Jimmy was going to be okay.

That very next afternoon, I received a frantic call from my husband. "Jimmy is freaking out, Jill! He totally scared the crap out of me! He said there is some black guy in his room!"

Stunned, I scrambled to find some privacy in the confines of my cubicle, as he himself, was on the verge of hysteria. Not wanting to draw attention, I attempted to calm my husband, while I heard the sound of poor Jimmy crying in the background.

Frustrated that I could not leave work to assist him, my husband told me that he was going to *deal with it*, and hung up the telephone. Trying to process what had just happened, I had a sinking feeling that something was *very wrong*.

Come five o'clock, I could not seem to get home fast enough. Once there, everything appeared to be normal, but my husband was still quite upset.

Dinner conversation was kept low-key, in effort not to create additional drama. My husband and I remained in the dining room discussing the events, while Jimmy ran to play. We were equally disturbed by what happened.

After telling my husband about the prior experiences, we agreed that we needed to speak with Jimmy. Calling him into the room, Jimmy nonchalantly climbed into my lap, as my husband asked him about the man that he had seen in his room, earlier that afternoon. His words scared the ever-loving daylights out of the two of us.

"He was all black, Mommy. He doesn't have a head. He said he wants to take me to see his mother. Mommy, why doesn't he have a head?"

I do not know whose blood left their body the fastest, but both my husband and I knew only one thing: whatever this was, had come from Watervliet. Having never, ever discussed what happened to Jimmy's father in front of him, or around him, there was no way possible Jimmy could have known that his father had literally blown his head off with a shotgun. Also factoring into the equation, was the fact that Jimmy had very little contact with his paternal grandparents after his father's death.

Almost three years had passed, and he could not possibly have remembered his grandmother. And why would he even say that this man wanted to take him to see *his mother*, instead of his grandmother, if it was Jim?

My husband's reaction was definitely more theatrical than mine. He jumped out of his chair, and frantically paced back and forth. Jimmy needed comfort in knowing that he did nothing wrong, so I held him and told him that we loved him. I also knew my son needed to tell 'it,' to leave him alone. I stated, "Jimmy, if you ever see that man again, you tell him to leave you alone, and that God, mommy and daddy are protecting you. You tell him that you will NOT go with him. You also tell him you're not afraid of him, okay?"

Responding with a nod, Jimmy slid off of my lap, and

ran back into his room to play. We were dumbfounded.

My husband and I tried to figure out why all of a sudden we were experiencing strange activity. I had been blocking, and had no residual issues since just after Jim's death. Even back then, the activity stopped after blessing my mother's apartment.

Here it was, June 25th, 1991, almost two years to the date of Jim's death at 207, and whatever, or whoever this was, had come back with a vengeance. One thing was clear, and my husband agreed: we had to call our priest.

I look back, and remember the conversation with our priest. After explaining the death of Jimmy's father, and the possible oppression and possession, our priest advised us to *immediately* bless the entire house, inclusive of the whole family. Informing him that I had used the last bit of holy water available, he instructed me to use salt water for the blessing. He inquired if we had any kosher salt, or distilled water in the house.

As my husband continued to get even more disturbed, I kept one hand on the telephone, as the other fumbled through the cupboards for kosher salt. No such luck; we only had the regular stuff.

Father instructed me to get a clean dish, and pour the salt in to it. Next, he had me add water as he said a short prayer. I was later told that he saying the prayer to purify the tap water. He then instructed me to mix the two together as he said another brief blessing.

With permission to use the make-shift holy water, our priest had me bless myself, followed by the family. He advised me to bless each room, and sprinkle the water with my fingers.

My husband and I proceeded to follow his instructions. Jimmy tagged-along, as we blessed every room. We told Jimmy that we were doing it to "get rid of the big, bad man." We even blessed Wee Wee Raboo.

Thankfully, we never had another issue. To me, that was almost miraculous, seeing what had happened in 207.

With the problem resolved, I did not want to open myself up to do a house reading. Although a sense of peace had been restored, nothing about what happened, the events remained a mystery until fall, *2012*.

Book research was often tedious. Painstaking hours have been spent hunting down information, interviewing witnesses, collecting data, and weeding out hundreds, if not thousands of articles, and emails. It was through a conversation with my dear friend Sarah, in the fall of 2012, when it clicked.

Sarah is one of those people who I refer to as a *forever friend*. Bound together with memories of the best of times, we are also joined by the worst. As stated before: I simply do not know what I would have done with her support when Jim died.

Making it a point to stop and see Sarah whenever I am home in New York, last fall was no exception. Gathering with the incredible Ms. Kathleen, as well as Sarah, we ate pizza, had a drink, and did a lot of laughing. Calling it an early night, Kathleen left, while Sarah and me chit-chatted a bit more. I can still hear the following words she spoke, as if they were mere moments ago.

"I have never told anyone this, but I had the same, exact dream that you did – the one with the fire, and the thing that chased you. I had it when I lived next door to 207."

You could have heard a pin drop. It took moments for her words to register. It seemed like an eternity, as I tried to overcome the shock.

"You know that I always felt something was upstairs - in the back bedroom. That's why I hated sleeping up there. Then I had that dream. I was too afraid to tell anyone about it because I was already getting made fun of over the other, crazy stuff. That dream was scarier than shit."

My heart skipped a beat. I could tell by the look on her face that she was still traumatized by it, and understandably so. It was by far, one of the most horrifying dreams that I have ever had. Detailing the dream in my first book brought back a tremendous amount of anxiety, just from recall.

Sarah then asked me a question which led to the revelation about the strange series of events that had occurred in Utica, so many years before. She asked, "Have you had any more spirit trouble, aside from just after Jim's death?"

I explained that we had, sharing particulars as to the man in black, at our house out in Utica. That's when it hit me.

I had known that Sheehan had been sent to St. John's in Utica, yet for some reason, it hadn't clicked until the night I was standing in Sarah's house, in Watervliet. It hit me like a ton of bricks, causing me to gasp, and cover my mouth with both of my hands. I was frozen in place facing Sarah, as if I had seen a ghost.

"It's him! It's him! It *has* to be him!" I blurted.

Sarah, not quite understanding what I was talking about, asked me to explain. Relinquishing the history of Sheehan, she then agreed that it was just "too damn weird" that I was living within a short distance from St. John's in Utica, when everything unfolded.

I then came to the realization that although I had been blocking at the time, I may have subconsciously lowered my shield. This made tremendous sense to me, as I have always exercised more caution and use a higher level of spiritual protection, any time that I go back home to the Capital District.

By the simple fact that I happened to move to an area that Sheehan had lived for close to ten years prior to heading to St. Patrick's in Watervliet, created a unique set of circumstances. He, or whatever had taken control of him, had found a way to come through.

Sarah and I shivered. Nothing is a coincidence. *Nothing.*

Just prior to my writing this chapter, I had to make a quick phone call to my ex-husband. I wanted to make sure that I had the sequence of events that occurred in Utica, in the correct order. Very seldom have we spoken since our divorce. Matter of fact, I didn't even have his telephone number.

Calling my son Kyle, I asked if he could give me his father's number. He wasn't even a year-old when we had lived in that house, and now, as an adult, was quite intrigued to hear about the story. Wishing me luck, we ended our chat. I dialed my ex, thinking: this will either go well, or nowhere at all.

I chuckle, reflecting back to my first words, "Hi, it's Jill. I'm calling to see if you remember the time when Jimmy kept seeing the man in black in Utica?"

Perhaps a bit rude of me for not asking how he was, I went straight to the point of the call. His response caught me off-guard when he replied, "how could I ever forget that?! That is something I will *never* forget!"

We both managed an uneasy laugh; after all, how *can* someone forget that? I surely hadn't, nor had he. I then explained that I needed to make sure I had all of the information for my book.

We talked about the events as if they were yesterday. It was both sad and creepy, to think that it had been over 22 years.

Quite unexpectedly, he then shared, "Jill, what happened in Utica with Jimmy was what made me a believer. There was absolutely no question, after that." More nervous laughter. He made a whole-hearted confession.

We then exchanged a few pleasantries, and that was it. He wished me his best with the book, and the call ended.

Talk about memories. Yikes. For better, for worse, for richer, for poorer, for demonic spirits that invade the home and create havoc, years after your ex-wife's first husband commits suicide. It is amazing what brings people together, and tears them apart.

Even today, neither my ex-husband nor I, think that it

was a coincidence. Not a twist of fate, at all.

* * * * * * * *

In the fall of 1868, Rev. William F. Sheehan replaced Rev. Quinn, and became the pastor of St. Patrick's Church. Taking the bull by its horns, Sheehan used his business sense, and straightforward attitude to whip West Troy into shape.

Approximately 11 years after taking over St. Patrick's Church, Sheehan unquestionably learned of the glorious miracles occurring at Lourdes, and embarked on a transatlantic trip to France.

Smitten by the holy events and structure, he returned with an emblazoned vision. It is said that he was *"entranced"* by the *Basilica of the Immaculate Conception,* also known as the Upper Basilica, at Lourdes. (Broderick, 2013)

The basilica had been designed and constructed between 1866, and 1872. Its stature, and miraculous history stuck the priest in a most unusual way. Having resided in West Troy for over a decade, he returned to the wayward town, with an obsessively grand plan.

Obtaining a large section of land that encompassed close to two city blocks along the northerly side of 19th Street, Sheehan made the decision to build his congregation a pretentious, new church. The plans were not simple in nature.

Managing to fund another costly trip, Sheehan asked Troy architect Edward W. Loth, to design the new church. The priest demanded that his church be built as a *replica* of the Upper Basilica in Lourdes; no holds barred. He sent Loth on his way to France, in order to draw plans.

The new St. Patrick's church cornerstone was laid on July 4th, 1889. Contradictory information was found in research which states the cornerstone was laid on July 4th, 1888, however, most records reflect 1889.

Rev. Sheehan celebrated his first mass in the new St.

Patrick's Church on Christmas Day, 1891. The original church closed, and became *Our Lady of Mount Carmel Roman Catholic Church*. Some Watervliet residents preferred to attend Mount Carmel, and St. Brigid's, over St. Patrick's, for varying reasons; old *seat money* has been mentioned as one.

According to approximately one dozen of my sources that live in the city, there existed a division within the community. Some residents attest that the division began generations back, when their family members refused to attend St. Patrick's Church due to the corruption of pew financing, while others refused to elaborate: more mystery. Worth mentioning is the fact that several of those providing this information became very quiet; almost nervous, when discussing the topic.

Respective to the new church, both the date of the cornerstone's placement, and the first church service serve as an eerie coincidence, relative to 207. All of the oddly correlating dates will be addressed, in order to shed light on how the church, and some of the tragedy at 207, fit together like a film noir.

The new church structure was massive. Just as its exterior, the interior of the church was impressive - and equally breathtaking. It was a masterpiece, and source of pride for the tiny, unassuming community.

The bell tower soared into the sky, and topped off at just under 140 feet. It housed a remarkably large church bell that weighed close to 7,500 pounds. The bell was cast, and installed by West Troy's very own *Meneely & Company Bell Foundry*. (Broderick, 2013)

The bell seems to have had a life of its own, and in more ways than one. Relative to it, there is a need to address its inscription.

Personally, I, as well as many others find the bell engraving to be rather cryptic, perhaps offering a glimpse into what may have been going on inside Sheehan's head at the time. Of course, it is speculation, but something that must be evaluated.

Before exploring the contents of the actual verse, please note that the church bell, and its associated epitaph, are extremely symbolic. Relative to most faiths, the main church bell *sets the tone for the community*.

At times, a church bell is rung to signify community events such as service, weddings, or funerals. The roots for this practice have ties dating back to the Old Testament.

Due to lack of available documentation, it is unclear if a *Baptism of the Bells*, a Roman Catholic tradition, took place with the new St. Patrick's bell. By blessing the church bell, the parish and surrounding community, were to receive protection from a host of evils, inclusive of inclement weather, and *demons*.

For starters, the new St. Patrick's Church bell was a gift of the *Holy Name Society*, and cost a pretty penny for the day. The iron giant was first rung on Easter Sunday, 1907 – yet another date that sends shivers up my spine, as it correlates with Sheehan's death.

At the time the bell money was donated, the Holy Name Society included members George Hipwood, Joseph Cavanaugh, Francis Powers, Thomas McLoughlin, and Rev. W. F. Sheehan. Together, the group chose the following inscription and had it engraved on the bell:

"In Nomine Jesu Genu Flectatur Coelestium Terrestrium et Infernorum." The Latin to English translation being: *In the name of Jesus the Knee Should Bow, of Things in Heaven, Earth and of Hell* (Underworld).

A rather odd verse, I have spoken with three, active, Roman Catholic priests about the inscription. The consensus: it is quite *unusual*. I completely agree with their sentiments.

In early August of 2013, I was contacted by Peter Reilly, who helped to shed some light on the mysterious verse. Peter holds a Master's Degree in *Biblical Studies* from Notre Dame University, and undergraduate degrees in both *Theology* and *Philosophy*, from the University of

Scranton. Additionally, he has been an Education Director for his church, and an Adjunct Professor at Elmira College, having taught World Religions.

Peter advised that the Latin verse on St. Patrick's bell, comes from Philip 2:10, 11. Below, I have included some of Peter's correspondence to me, relative to the bell inscription.

Reilly states, "The entire Latin prayer for the *Feast of the Holy Name of Jesus* reads: *In nomine Jesu omne genu flectatur, coelestrium, terrestrium, et infernorum: et omnis lingua confiteator, quia Dominus Jesus Chirstus in floria est Dei Patris. – Domine Dominus noster: quam admirabile est nomen tuum in universa terra! V.: Goria Patria ... -- In nomine Jesu omne genu Flectatur . . .*

The Vulgate translation reads: *In the name of Jesus let every knee bow, of those that are in heaven, on earth and under the earth: and let every tongue confess that the Lord Jesus Christ is in the glory of God the Father.*" (Reilly, 2013)

Peter then explained the following, relative to the prayer and inscription:

"Jesus is Lord of the whole Universe, including the Underworld (which in the 1st century was seen as a holding place for the dead until the Messiah came). The Creed at mass mentions Jesus descended into hell, which early Christians took to mean that he arrived to also save those in Sheol (The Underworld) as well as the living. It also implies that Jesus is Lord over all Angels, including the Fallen Angels (i.e. Satin and Lucifer). This prayer is "used often as an Intruit (or Introductory Call to Prayer often replaced by and Introductory Song at mass) for certain feasts. Most significantly the feast of the Holy Name, on January 2nd. Since the bell was donated by the Holy Name Society, it's a very appropriate phase for the bell." (Reilly, 2013)

While Peter's explanation certainly helped shed light on the basis of the inscription, the partial choice of verse on behalf of the Holy Name Society, by which Sheehan sat as Secretary, still bothers me, as well as the priests I have spoken with. It also has had a less than favorable reaction by many others.

The oddness centers on the words chosen, inscribed, and thus translated. In a literal sense, it advises one to *bow our knees, in Jesus' name, to Heaven, Earth and Hell* (the Underworld). Frankly, it is a matter of personal opinion by which I find it rather profane for anyone to be directed to bow in any way, or part, to Hell, or to the Underworld.

I did not find any documentation relative to whom exactly chose the phrase, but in all objectivity, Sheehan had to play some part in the decision. Specifically, out of the five men who ran the Holy Name Society, Sheehan was more than likely the individual most familiar with the prayer, and Latin translation. Choosing those exact words to have engraved on the bell screams duplicity, and utter creepiness.

Examining Peter Riley's connection that the inscription was part of the prayer used for the *Feast of the Holy Name*, and in turn donated by the Holy Name Society, brings light to the reasoning behind the verse, yet does little to convey a positive message. Knowing that the church bell sets the tone for the community, coupled with the chosen inscription, lends connotation to the fact we must bow to not only Heaven and Earth, but to Hell.

Conducting a survey amidst populations of multiple denominations (inclusive of Catholic), in addition to speaking with the priests in different states (New York, California, and Florida), the consensus is that despite the knowledge of the actual prayer, feast and society, it was both in poor taste, and a poor choice, to place the verse on the church bell.

Those surveyed about the bell verse used the words: *Awful, wrong, diabolical, creepy, ungodly, unholy, hypocritical, scary, bizarre, profane, concerning, confusing* and *offensive*. I might add that not one, single person thought it appropriate, or acceptable, including the Catholics.

Another pressing question surfaced as a result of the bell verse: *what was Sheehan thinking?* As a matter of opinion, I find it extremely difficult to understand that he knew nothing about its meaning, and the possible ramifications.

There is little to convince me that it was an innocent oversight, as the message is quite direct, and nonetheless equally obvious. I have often wondered what must have gone through the minds of the community members when it was finally placed in the bell tower. If current members of society have grappled with the verse, it is reasonable to consider the same applied for the community when the bell was inscribed.

Nevertheless, bell inscription controversy or not, the congregation of the new St. Patrick's Church continued to grow. The physical appearance of the church continued to change, improving upon itself with time.

The church's size alone, caught the attention of many. As originally written by the Troy Record, and published on the St. Patrick's Church Memorial website, "No other church in the United States is like it. Saint Patrick's church can be seen for many miles about and the attention of most strangers is attracted to its height." (Broderick, 2013)

Even from Troy's Prospect Park, which is located on the opposite side of the Hudson River, the church was a breathtaking sight to behold. It exuded a quiet, comforting respect.

And respect was exactly what Sheehan commanded. He is described as having been a tall, quiet, lanky Irishman, who always wore a white flower, signifying a *"blameless life."* (United States Catholic Historical Society., & Cahalan, J. E., 1911).

With a community that was imploding upon itself, and also known to be one of the most dangerous places on the eastern seaboard in the 1800s, Sheehan took charge of his flock, in more ways than one. He was their caregiver, confidante, governing official – and police force.

Worth mentioning is the fact that throughout my investigation, and conversations with various sources in the city, I was told that the IRA (Irish Republic Army), had a hold in the region during the canal period, through the early 1900s. The region was said to be a hot spot for transport of munitions, and organized crime, with origins tied directly to some of Watervliet's early, Irish residents. That was quite a revelation. I actually stated to the first informant, "you're kidding me?! Little Watervliet?"

Several sources have stated that they were made aware of this information through family stories. Three unrelated sources actually described a route that ran from Watervliet, through the canal, to *Derby*, a village located in western New York State. Two sources suspect religious, and other Watervliet officials were involved.

With my focus being on the spiritual, rather than criminal aspects of the city, I chose not to look into such matters. It is an eyebrow-raising notion though, and makes sense, given the city's history. So many of my discoveries warrant an appropriately titled television series: *Watervliet: City Confidential.*

Perhaps the most ironic, and startling date of coincidence that transpired in the course of my investigation and research, has to do with Sheehan's fiftieth anniversary as pastor to St. Patrick's Church. His *Golden Jubilee* took place on Sunday, *June 28th*, 1908. It was an extravagant affair.

A very large parade comprised marched along 19th Street, to the steps of St. Patrick's. The church and its grounds were adorned with hundreds, upon hundreds of lights for the event.

The celebration was followed by a dinner (in the basement of Saint Patrick's). The day's festivities were drawn to a close with music, followed by a loud, and impressive fireworks display. In an over-the-top, and flamboyant manner, Sheehan received praise and accolades, fit for a king.

As for the basement of the church: I have had a handful of sources tell me that they were never comfortable in the basement. Two individuals remarked that they were outright terrified of it. Only one of the

SAINTS SINNERS & SACRED GROUND

sources is under the age of 50.

The elephant in the room, has to do with the actual date of Sheehan's jubilee. Exactly 81 years later – to the exact date of his celebration – a loud explosion once more rang out in Watervliet. This time the racket was not caused by merriment, parade, or fireworks, but was the sound of a single gunshot being fired from my husband's .12 gauge shotgun, as he committed suicide inside 207. Indeed, the house was standing at the time of Sheehan's celebration, and located just 300 feet west of the church.

Sheehan remained the head St. Patrick's Church until his death at the rectory in Watervliet, on Easter Sunday, April 11th, 1909 – two years to the day, after the Meneely bell first rang in the city. It has been said that local flags were ordered to be flown half-mast, and businesses went black for the day. Thousands were noted as having attended his funeral.

In a strange twist of fate, in an equally strange story, Sheehan's sister, Sister Mary Teresa (Sheehan) suddenly died in Killarney, Ireland, on April 12th, 1909, the same day (time difference is the accounted for as the variance in date). The New Zealand Tablet states: "A Remarkable Coincidence . . . The painfully sad coincidence of the deaths on the same day, in places so far apart as New York and Killarney, of a brother and sister – the one a priest, the other a religious of the Order of Mercy – was chronicled in the following announcement in the obituary columns of the Cork Examiner of April 13: - Sheehan – On April 12th, 1909, at his residence, Watervliet, New York, Rev. William F. Sheehan (late of Fermoy, County Cork), pastor St. Patrick's Church, Watervliet. Sheehan. – On April 12th, at the mercy Convent, Killarney, Sister Mary Teresa (Sheehan), sister of the late Rev. William F. Sheehan, P.P., Watervliet." (National Library of New Zealand, 1909)

A man who was alleged to have led a virtuous life, banishing excess, and upholding Canon Law, left his entire estate to Saint Colman's Home, with a rather large sum of money to be equally divided between two, Albany hospitals.

His reserved demeanor was not to be underestimated. He exerted authority when necessary, and brought about a long-needed change within the *entire* community, not just among the Irish-Catholics. Transforming the town, his actions created a new era, as he gave the people a magnificent church, two schools and an asylum. Sheehan was a man with great influence, enveloped in mystery.

As previously mentioned, some documentation revealed that Sheehan came from a wealthy family of architects and church builders, however, others state that his mother was widowed, with eight children to raise. *The Sisters of the Presentation* were also noted as having requested his seminary schooling be paid for, due to the family's financial issues; a direct contradiction to the alleged 'wealthy family' he had been born into.

Despite his service as a priest, he was obviously spellbound with the events of Bernadette Soubirous, of Lourdes, France. Detailing a brief timeline of events relative to Sheehan and Soubirous, shows the connection.

Given that Sheehan was born in 1833, means that he was approximately 25-years-old at the time that the Holy Mother began to appear to Bernadette, in 1858. This timeframe puts Sheehan square, in the middle of the resurgence of Christian Mysticism, pertaining to the Catholic Church.

Between 1858, and 1879, he managed to both go to Lourdes, as well as pay for his architect to travel to the location in order to build a replica of the Upper Basilica. As noted, construction of the Upper Basilica was completed in 1872. I find this extremely fascinating for a few reasons.

Where did he get the money to build the church, schools and asylum? Although only some orders make their priests take vows of poverty, Sheehan acquired an impressive amount money to purchase land, and build many properties.

Without knowledge of the exact vows Rev. Sheehan did, or did not take, the question still applies. Where did he get this money? Did he inherit it? If so, why did the sisters write to have his seminary school paid for, and why did his own mother need so much help with her eight children?

For purpose of reference, it is important to mention that regardless of vows, Code of Canon Law 281.1 states: "Since clerics dedicate themselves to ecclesiastical ministry, they deserve remuneration which is consistent with their condition, taking into account the nature of their function and the conditions of places and times, and by which they can provide for the necessities of their life as well as for the equitable payment of those whose services they need." (The Vatican, 1983)

In translation, priests can receive a (usually small) stipend, or salary, for their work, but more so for necessities, and certainly not for anything lavish, i.e. fancy automobiles, trips, clothing, etc. This can be pointed out by reading Code of Canon Law 282.1: "Clerics are to foster simplicity of life and are to refrain from all things that have a semblance of vanity." (The Vatican, 1983)

In essence, clergy members of the Catholic Church are to follow a simple means of living, and are to avoid anything suggesting worldliness. By the time of his death, Sheehan emanated materialism.

Continuing with Canon Law, it is interesting to read 286: "Clerics are prohibited from conducting business or trade personally or through others, for their own advantage or that of others, except with the permission of legitimate ecclesiastical authority." (The Vatican, 1983)

Basically, a priest may work for the church, or its endeavors, but cannot make any personal monies from those ventures, nor as the result of any *outside* work. Sheehan, along with his fellow monks and nuns at the Trappist Monastery, were allowed to make money *for the monastery,* but not for personal gain, therefore excluding this as a possibility.

Regardless, Canon Law explains that priests and nuns are required to live a simple life, *even if they did not take a vow of poverty.* Therefore, removing the entire vow issue from the overall picture, the question of his financial affluence still exists.

Anything donated to him should have gone towards church expenses, or church businesses. In particular, he erected a massive church, schools and a large asylum. He purchased the land and materials, on his own. Documentation shows that he gave these things to the community, but yet upon death, willed quite a bit of money for its time, to two hospitals.

Discussion of corruption cannot be ignored, and considering his authority in the community as a whole, is plausible, especially when later discussion reveals his interests and authority over St. Colman's Orphanage. This is not the first time church corruption has made the front pages of the paper.

Readdressing one possibility, is reasonable belief that Sheehan may have been involved in the IRA movement, upon coming to America. The timing of his arrival, in conjunction with the priest's movement from Albany to Utica, onto Oneida, and then to Watervliet, certainly follows the path of the canal, which was utilized to run guns, and carryout other mob-related activities.

In my opinion, it is quite possible that if Sheehan did not have direct contact with the IRA, he may have received kick-backs prior to, and after, being sent to St. Patrick's in Watervliet. He was in a position of authority, and was both feared, loved and respected by thousands. That is pretty heavy weight to carry for a man who was said to be so unassuming.

The other issue pertains to Sheehan's so-called life of simplicity; shunning anything ostentatious, or unbecoming to his Godly character. Ambition is one thing, but taking a trip, as well as sending a local architect to France to design the new church, in addition to the actual building of the church and orphanage, is not exactly a life of simplicity. Sheehan went well beyond minimalism.

A grandiose undertaking, the new church can be argued as both a generous gift to the parish, and an impractical decision by a man that was said to be business savvy. At the very least, Sheehan's obsession with Lourdes, and erecting St. Patrick's in its likeness, demonstrates that not only did Christian Mysticism affect the priest, but indicates that it truly was not a well-thought-out plan, for the simple fact of future upkeep.

Even in an area that was growing, West Troy was not in any way affluent. The care of the magnificent structure became the burden of future generations, and ultimately contributed to its demise. As John E. Cahalan stated in Sheehan's necrology, "West Troy at that time was rather a small and unpromising town…and the (Saint Patrick's) congregation was neither numerous nor affluent." (United States Catholic Historical Society., & Cahalan, J. E., 1911).

Factoring into the equation is the very real possibility that Sheehan was besotted by the miracles at Lourdes. I cannot help but wonder if he was trying to – or wanting to – force Mary to come to West Troy, where he could have a claim to miraculous fame. It's almost an '*if I build it, she will come,*' way of thinking. Given the impact of the resurgence, inclusive of séances, and other means of attaining spirit communication, it is a plausible consideration.

There was nothing half-assed about the building of St. Patrick's; it had to be a replication of the Upper Basilica. In all honesty, I see it as more delusional for him to have built such a large, dominating church, especially after he went to Lourdes years before. I question if any of his good intentions were shattered, after he succumbed to whatever exists on the land. Again, for him to wear the symbolic, white flower, is quite hypocritical in view of his actions, and strong hand in the community.

Regarding the orphanage: you will find that Sheehan

was the deciding force of whose children were to stay with their respective families, or be ripped from them, only to become cash cows to the church through indentured servitude.

Throughout his tenure, he also functioned as the unofficial police force. Only God knows what transpired for the period of time that was saturated with sin and corruption, but something was, and still is, very wrong. His quiet authority, wealth and habit of building properties that could not sustain themselves due to scale, scope, and later scandal, do not add up to a so-called "blameless life." (United States Catholic Historical Society & Cahalan, 1911)

Perhaps tainted by the occurrence at 207 19th Street, I have truly tried to remain objective. I will not argue against the fact that Sheehan *tried* to do the right thing, but with investigation and research, most of those situations had a dark reoccurring theme, which always brings me full circle, to the night I saw him appear in front of my Christmas tree.

Sometime between Christmas Eve, and early Christmas morning of 1988, I came to face-to-face with one of the most frightening apparitions of my life. Detailed in *207*, I think its best to briefly describe the encounter for those readers whom have not had the opportunity to read my first book.

Having finished decorating our tree just minutes before, I came back into the living room of our flat at 207, and saw him: tall, thin, wiry hair, steely eyes, and dressed in black, from head-to-toe. The garb was consistent with clothing from the 1800s. I did not notice any type of priestly collar, but knew he was affiliated with the church, and was possibly be a priest.

Not wanting to upset my husband, I quietly observed the apparition. He was making a stand, and was letting me know that he was in-charge. It was a sickening, horrifying feeling.

His smirk was sadistic; he enjoyed trying to scare me. It was as though the main energy in the house had sent him to do its business. He stood in front of the tree as an omen, and ushered in the most unimaginable, and horrific chain of events to transpire.

There was nothing kind about the look on his face. On the outside he was one thing, while on the inside, a messenger of the devil. He quickly disappeared.

Within six months and three days, my husband would shoot and kill himself in the very spot the man in black stood; right in front of our tree. I always knew that I was going to recognize his face, should I see it. I certainly did not go looking for it though, and at the time, had no clue who he was. I blocked him, and prayed to God to keep my family safe.

I did not identify the source of the apparition until the summer of 2011, just after *207* was published. The revelation came while having an online conversation about the specter, with my friend, and fellow researcher, Justin Sanders. I had told him that I *just knew* the apparition was a priest – I felt it. It was almost a no-brainer, with two churches standing yards away from 207.

I also advised Justin that there was something very wrong with this priest. I had no idea that throughout our conversation, Justin was multi-tasking on his computer, in search of photos pertaining to clergy members of the area.

The first two photos that he sent to me were of former priests that served in the Watervliet community. Neither one of them looked anything like the apparition. However, the third one (sent quite a bit later), just about knocked me out of my chair.

It took but not a moment for the photo to load when I knew that it was most definitely, *without an ounce of doubt*, the apparition. Staring me in the face was that same man who appeared in front of our Christmas tree in 1988! I began to shake, and then cry – completely forgetting to respond to Justin.

Justin remembers that I became very quiet. All that I can tell you, as I did him, was that I was so shocked to see his face again, that I lost track of time. The reason for the delay was due to the fact that I was praying, crying and yelling at the photo. I was traumatized.

After collecting my composure, I asked Justin who it was. He informed me that it was *Reverend William F. Sheehan, a former priest at St. Patrick's Church.* I was floored. The entire ordeal upset me so much that I had to get the photo off of my computer. I did not go back to research the picture until I prepared myself. It was too much to process.

Trying to consider every angle, I did question if the demon(s) in the house had manipulated the environment, and showed itself as the priest that night in '88. I was truly hoping that it was not the priest, but upon investigation, conclude it was – *with a caveat.*

As both a medium-psychic, as well as a human being, I do not think that Sheehan was a bad seed, or a bad man. I do think that there is enough credible information to consider that he had a fracture in his psyche, be it from drinking, or otherwise, which lent to him become a puppet to the demonic force(s). He was in the 'perfect' position to do so.

There is a tremendous amount of duality to his life. Although he did not outwardly destroy anyone (at least, not that I'm aware of), you will find that he did use his power and authority to do some things that were not exactly wise, or deemed in the best interest of the community, inclusive of innocent children.

If anything was to have a lasting impression on the city of Watervliet, it has to be the wondrous church that he left behind. With the reputation of St. Colman's home forever tainted, and Sheehan's schools closed, the church was literally left to beg for salvation, as the congregation sought status to preserve it as a historical landmark.

A symbol of hope for a tiny city, the new church

ushered the community from days of uncivilized mayhem, to one of dignity, and *control*. Despite any perceived good, Sheehan's church legacy fell to the way-side, memorialized as a material token of greed. It became a travesty for the community that tried so hard to stabilize, even in modern times.

Torn, I have told many, inclusive of the citizens of Watervliet, that from a historical perspective, the church should have been saved, but from a spiritual perspective, think otherwise. Historical findings provide detail of its role in the reshaping of the community, in addition to its beauty, and unrivaled stature.

Spiritually, although the church itself should not be considered malevolent, the thoughts, plans and even bell inscription rendered by its founding father, Rev. William F. Sheehan, show a deep-rooted, unsettling history examined long after his death.

Wholeheartedly believing that when Sheehan was 'clear' when he first came to the U.S., it is with great supposition, coupled with fact, and an unusual string of coincidence, that something dark took hold of him in Watervliet.

I survived living it its domain. I witnessed its pure malevolence looking at me through Sheehan's eyes that night in front of the Christmas tree. It used the body of a hardworking holy man, to stealthily fulfill a long legacy of terror.

Case #5: Charles Watson, 1954.
Location: 1545 Seventh Avenue.

The Knickerbocker News, Albany, N.Y., Monday, April 24th, 1954, states: "Watervliet Man Found Hanged . . . A Watervliet man was found hanged this morning in a garage at the rear of his home. Coroner Nealon, who issued a verdict of suicide, said Charles H. Watson, of 1545 Seventh Avenue, an unemployed crane operator, died of asphyxiation due to strangulation.

The body was discovered by Harold Garrett, a tenant in Watson's home. Coroner Nealon said Watson formerly was employed by the Delaware & Hudson Railroad, but had been out of work two years. Watervliet Patrolmen Joseph Stearns and William Brothers investigated." (Knickerbocker News, 1954)

Case #6: Name Withheld, 1956.
Location: Third Avenue, north of 207 19th Street.

Several sources, inclusive of a retired Watervliet cop, verified the name, date and location of this suicide. In the summer of 1956, a male, approximately 30-years-old, shot and killed himself in his apartment. The man lived alone, however, neighbors reported that he began to drink heavily, and stopped going to work. This was described as "uncharacteristic" of an otherwise responsible, young man. I was unable to obtain an interview with his surviving family members. The retired police officer, nor the sources recall any additional pertinent information.

5. SINNERS

"Sin hath the devil for its father, shame for its companion and death for its wages." Thomas Watson

The 19th century presented with rapid change, and exorbitant growth for Watervliet. Development due to a large manufacturing boom, along with the building of the Watervliet Arsenal, made the small city an attractive location for entrepreneurs, and business-minded folk. The population of the small city continued to explode over the next ten decades.

To understand the layout of the city, as well as the name changes of the small municipalities in the 1800s, a brief geography lesson is at-hand. I sure as hell would have liked one, prior to starting my research, and cannot believe how much change the borough encountered.

The modern city of Watervliet was once part of a farm owned by John Bleecker. Bleecker's property was located between Broadway and 15th Streets, and stretched northward, across the Troy-Schenectady Turnpike (19th Street), to the Oothout family farm (near 25th Street).

In 1823, several hundred acres of land owned by John and Elizabeth Bleecker, was purchased by the West Troy

Company. A few members of the West Troy Company included: Philip Schuyler, George Tibbitts, Isais Warren, and Ebenezer Wiswall.

Shortly after the purchase, the West Troy Company befittingly named the land *West Troy*. The Upper Side-cut of the Erie Canal, located on 23rd Street, was also finished the same year.

The West Troy Company divided the land into segments labeled: East and West. Land that existed on the east side (east of West Street), was laid out into lots consisting of streets, and alleyways. The section of land on the west side (west of West Street), was distributed into large farm lots, each boasting up to 20 acres per parcel. 207 19th Street was considered within the land on the *east side*.

Since the villages of West Troy and Gibbonsville were neighbors (Gibbonsville was located south of West Troy), they named their streets differently. No consideration was given, to make sure the streets connected, or made sense to the other municipality. Not only did this lead to confusion among residents and travelers of the day, but also in the course of initial research for the book.

For example, the Troy-Schenectady Turnpike, was renamed Genesee Street. In 1888, it changed once more, and remained as present-day 19th Street.

The inventory pertaining to lots and correlating numbers, also complicated the situation. Information contained within *Last Will and Testaments* proved to be quite valuable when locating former owners and tenants of 207 19th Street.

Aside from manufacturing, the Watervliet Arsenal put the city on the map. In 1813 the Federal Government purchased 12 acres of land in Gibbonsville, from James Gibbons. This transpired one year after the commencement of the War of 1812. Occurring at the same time as the construction of the Arsenal, work commenced on the Erie Canal, only after New York State authorized the allocation of several million dollars to build the extensive waterway.

Many canal workers were Irish immigrants, and held hardworking positions as laborers, and stone cutters. Factoid: the canal was originally known as *Clinton's Ditch*, named after founding developer Clinton DeWitt, and totaled an impressive 363 miles in length.

The Erie Canal opened in 1824. Its origins began north of Albany, parallel with the river, and north, into Watervliet. The extensive canal also passed through the Arsenal, towards Erie Street, West Troy (2nd Ave.)

Water travel was cheap, and helped with the movement of materials used to create infrastructure near the towns and cities located along its path. To the north of Albany, the lumber industry started to utilize the canal ways as a means to transport timber into Cohoes, Watervliet, Troy and Albany.

Canal hands made less than a dollar. Skilled laborers made much more. I was not surprised to find that a bottle of booze was given to the workers on pay day: a welcome form of payment for their hard work, and sacrifice.

Alcoholism was a very large problem within the community, and most workers squandered their pay checks in a matter of hours. As discussed in Chapter 3, pastors and priests were left to wrangle and rally the sinful, into a life of redemption, and abstinence.

Documented splurging of pay within the Village of West Troy included: bar-hopping, gambling (cockfighting), and the patronization of prostitutes. The city had an abundance of bars, and brothels.

Between the insurgence of canal workers, building of the Arsenal, industrialization of the region, and the constant flow of large merchant ships in and out of the area, violence and crime occurred relentlessly. The most dangerous places in the city were Watervliet's Upper, and Lower side cuts.

The Lower side cut was located just south of the

Arsenal. The Upper side cut was to its north, on 23rd Street, just a few blocks north of 207 19th Street.

One village resident had a peculiar job that resulted from the viciousness of the times. William Ryan, also known as "*Spot*," reclaimed the dead, most of which those whom were murdered. (Cerri, 1989)

Bestowed a rather suitable nickname, he made use of his stature to fetch floating, bloated bodies from the canal, and hauled the decaying corpses from city streets. He was compensated "$5" per body. (Cerri, 1989)

Just two decades into the 19th century, and the Upper side cut had close to 30 bars, and a half-dozen brothels, located within a 2 block radius – situated in 207's backyard. Disease was rampant, and the city suffered a tremendous blow after a cholera epidemic swept through the village, in 1832. Violent deaths were a known trait of the village, earning the little town the nickname of the "Barbary Coast of the East." (Cerri, 1989)

As a result, the busiest, and most profitable businessmen in the city, were Morticians. That is a bit unsettling for a city that was encapsulated in an area no larger than 1.5 square miles.

Several documents make mention of many *Potter's Fields* in the city. Potter's Fields are random holes dug by ordinary citizens, or workers, and filled with unknown corpses. The dead included: canal workers, merchants, prostitutes, the city's homeless, travelers, and wandering vagrants. In fact, the older fields are said to have contained remains of the Native Americans that were murdered in the course of the city's settlement.

The police quickly learned to ignore most crime, as it was far too dangerous for them to get involved with routine pillage, and plunder. Early efforts to keep a police force in the area were maligned by the ferocity of the era, resulting in the inability to police the town.

Not a single policeman covered the Upper side cut beat. Constables fled the area, as they were frequently jumped, and beaten. A premature attempt to establish the *Capital Police Force* had failed miserably, midway through the century.

Much of the same can be said relative to the establishment of many churches in the area. As illustrated in Chapter 3, no souls were saved for many years to come.

From 1840, until just after the beginning of the 20th century, undertaking continued to be the most lucrative business. Morticians counted on corpses for their payday.

One of the earliest, and most prominent funeral homes remains in business today: *Parker Brothers Memorial*. Mike Reinfurt, a native of Watervliet, and owner of present day Parker Bros., sent me the following historical information to be included in this book:

"Parker Brothers Memorial was founded in Watervliet on March 10th, 1881 by brothers William F. and Joseph Parker. Originally established to serve a hard-working community of diverse immigrants, who came to this area seeking work along the banks of the Erie Canal, the funeral home quickly earned a reputation for caring service. The original funeral home was housed in a former, Town of Watervliet courthouse at 2107 Broadway. In an era when most wakes and funerals were held from private homes, the funeral home building served as the Parker's offices and as a place for families to select a casket. The building was also known as a place for the Parkers, and other gentlemen of the day to congregate, smoke cigars and discuss politics and other issues.

Following the death of Joseph Parker in 1891, William F. Parker solely, operated the funeral home until his four sons entered the family business. Charles E., John E., William F. and Joseph J. Parker were all, at one time or another, involved in the operation of the funeral home with their father.

On March 9, 1934, our founder, William F. Parker died following a one-month illness and in that same year cancer claimed the life of his son John. In the years prior to his death, William and his youngest son Joseph realized the need for a larger and more modern facility and plans were made to construct a new humeral home at 2013 Broadway. The new building, completed in 1934, was truly a state-of-the-art facility. Saddened that his father did not live to see its completion, Joseph renamed the business Parker Bros. Memorial Funeral Home, in tribute to his father and uncle.

The occurrence of funerals taking place from private homes and apartments began to wane in the years following World War II . . .

Joseph J. Parker obtained sole ownership of the funeral home from his brothers and in 1950, Edward J. Reinfurt joined him to assist with the operation of the funeral home. Over the years, as the numbers of families served continued to grow, additional help was needed and Daniel R. Reinfurt and John F. Tallman joined the funeral home as funeral directors.

In 1974, Mr. Reinfurt assumed ownership of the funeral home and Mr. Parker remained as a consultant, residing in his apartment in the funeral home, until his death in 1990. Mr. Reinfurt died in 1982 and his daughter and son, Kathryn M. and Michael P. Reinfurt assumed the operation of the funeral home.

In 1992, Mr. Cummings purchased the present funeral home at 643 Third Avenue in Port Schuyler. It was formerly the office and home of Doctor John Deveny and his family. Mr. Cummings died tragically in a car accident on December 23, 1946 in Oakwood Cemetery in Troy while conducting a funeral. His son Edward J. Cummings, Jr., who was, at the time, attending Simmons School of Embalming in Syracuse, returned home to operate the funeral home.

Ed Cummings was licensed as an undertaker in 1947 and remained active in the funeral business until his death on March 26, 2003. . . Today, the funeral homes are owned and operated by Kathy's brother Michael Reinfurt and her husband Vincent Fronczek. Assisting them in the operation of the funeral homes are funeral directors Samuel F. Catalano, Jr., Mark S. Fiet and Lori Q. Purcell and group of dedicated part-time associates. Arthur E. Bowen serves as our senior director and is always available to assist as needed.

With over 130 years of continuous service, all of our funeral homes maintain the same high standards today as we did back in 1881 and those same basic beliefs, upon which we were founded, are maintained as our guide today." (Reinfurt, 2013)

West Troy was incorporated in the spring of 1836. Within one year, the great *Panic of 1837* crippled the town. When referencing information for suicides within the area, I noted an increase in occurrences between 1835, and 1845. This surge reflects the hardships that many, undoubtedly faced.

Once famous for its large, and widely anticipated parades, West Troy held its first fire parade in 1840. Not quite mid-century, the village had issued just close to 80 tavern licenses. Again, this is incredible, considering the size of the town.

In 1845, Ireland's potato crop was hit hard by fungus, resulting in the *Potato Famine*. The same catastrophe occurred the following two years. The famine of 1847, was labeled as the worst.

The famine appeared once more, in 1850. The largest immigration into the United States occurred when the Irish left the motherland between 1845, and 1920. It is during this stretch of time, that West Troy became the home of many Irish immigrants.

An exceptionally ferocious round of fires struck in the 1850s, and instilled more fear in town folk. A few years later, another cholera outbreak left many men, women and children dead, most dying in their homes throughout the village.

A second canal weigh lock was built at the northern end of the village. It is widely presumed that the lock was very close to 207. Oral histories of some of the city's elderly, as well as novice historians, state that the lock was a smidge south of the Congress Street Bridge.

Unconfirmed rumor has it that 207 was built by someone in the West Troy Company, to keep watch over the lock. This does make sense, since older maps show the lock to be diagonal to the house. As documented in *207,* the house itself, was constructed at an odd angle, and did not align with the 19th Street, as its neighbors did. The slant of the home did correlate to the direction of the lock. I, as well as Justin, went in search of this information to verify the theory, but experienced deliberate interference. This issue will be explained later in this book.

Various maps show a large lumber yard directly across the street from 207 19th Street. Behind the house: a large coal yard. Oh, the irony, for a house that could not escape its fated metaphor as *Hell on Earth.* Equally strange, I am inclined to question if Mr. Bouton's home, as described in the Maggie Fox incident, was close to 207, given the lumber yard.

Repeated property searches became a laborious issue, for not only myself and Justin, but others who helped research 207's deeds. Justin and I were able to pinpoint 207 as being Lot #20, Genesee Street, West Troy. Early enumeration of the homes (once verified), listed the house numbers in correlation with the lots, hence one of the original address for 207 was: 20 Genesee Street, West Troy.

1854 is the earliest transaction that I was given, related to the property of 207 19th Street. In March of '54, James Smith sold the property (Lot 20), to William Benjamin. The deed does not show any mention of a dwelling. This information comes via Patrick Riley, at the Albany County Clerk's Office.

Digging around a bit, additional information shows that James Smith was a foreman for John McCoughin. McCoughin was a contractor who constructed the Upper side cut of the canal on 23rd Street. Other snippets infer that Smith later become one of the first patrolmen of the West Troy Precinct, when the city reestablished their police force in 1865.

Within the *same month*, William Benjamin sold 207's lot to Everet Hawly (spelling verified by Patrick Riley). One year later, in April of 1854, Benjamin sold the property to Peter Arnold. Despite any attempt to locate records on Mr. Arnold, none were found. It is quite possible that he resided elsewhere, and prospected the area for investment purposes.

A strange, yet appropriate story caught my attention while I was combing through old articles. Late one night, in May of 1858, a West Troy village resident by the name of Brien (Brian) Rooney, set two homes ablaze, after a night of heavy drinking. (Troy Daily Times, 1858)

Based upon information, these homes are believed to be 18, and 20 Genesee Street. Keep in mind that No. 20 Genesee Street, was changed to present-day 207 19th Street.

One of the homes was described as a *three story house*, along the north side of Genesee Street, situated near Erie. The tall home is thought to be 207, given the fact it was the only three-story building on the block. Occupying the two homes were widows Bridget Burns, Mary Carr, and their respective children. Fortunately, they all escaped to safety.

The Troy Daily Times stated that Rooney had intentions of setting fire to 16 Genesee Street, but his inability to think clearly, resulted in setting the wrong home(s) ablaze. The article also references 16 Genesee was location of one of Rooney's family members, whom he had been quarreling with prior to imbibing copious amounts of alcohol. More than likely, that family member was the target of Rooney's aggressions.

Conceivably to damage, Burns and Carr moved from their corresponding homes. Governor King commuted

Rooney's death sentence by hanging, to that of life in prison. Again; more irony knowing that 207 almost burnt to the ground, more so at the hands of a man gone temporarily mad.

July, 1863, Mr. Arnold sold the property to a woman named Emily Mc--. Patrick Riley, of the Albany County Clerk's Office, advised me the handwriting on the original deed document is almost illegible. An attempt was made to decipher the records, but nothing came to surface as to who this "Emily Mc" person was.

By 1860, Charles Sheehan (unknown to be a relative of Rev. Sheehan), opened the *West Troy Bottling Works*, on 24th Street. Due to prolific consumption of alcohol, and the ridiculous number of taverns in town, his business boomed. Sheehan became a major vendor in the city.

Another interesting piece of information comes into play relative to the West Troy Bottling Works. In 1987, it became the home of the *Crestline Window Company*. Crestline Windows was both my husband Jim's, as well as his best friend Jerry's employer, at the time of their deaths in 1989. Yes: more irony.

1865 gave birth to the Watervliet Police Department. Frances Becker, the Village President declared: "We now have the means to rid the village of the scum that blackened our good name." (Cerri, 1989)

Of the same year, the Civil War drew to a close. The village had lost several hundred men in the course of the war.

It is extremely important to note that *prior* to 1868, there are no listings in city directories for house No. 18, or 20, Genesee Street. This led to quite a bit of delay on finding alternative means to investigate tenants of the building. This may be due to the prior fires.

I took note of the fact that many property owners did not inhabit their homes in downtown West Troy. Living elsewhere, businessmen purchased the buildings as rental income properties. I encountered several pieces of information that revealed the owners lived across the Hudson, in Troy, and Lansingburgh, and had tenants on-site in West Troy.

Fortunately, I later determined that future occupation, as well as ownership of 207, was kept in the same family for several decades. This made for a much more productive search for its residents.

I found a Mr. Robert Wood listed as a resident at No. 20 Genesee Street (207), for the year 1868. This led me to the first recorded death having occurred at 207. Sadly, it was a child.

On Saturday, August 22nd, 1868, Robert Wood's 11-year-old daughter, Philamela Wood, died. Her cause of death remains unknown. Her funeral was held at 20 Genesee Street. More than likely, due in part to the era, there is a high probability that the little girl died in the home, as was the case for most residents throughout the 19th century. Regardless, it was a very disheartening find.

Her obituary in the Daily Whig states: "DIED . . . WOOD – Saturday, August 29, Philamela Wood, daughter of Robert and Anna Wood, aged 11 years and 4 months. Friends and acquaintances are invited to attend the funeral this Monday afternoon at half past 4 o'clock, from the house No. 20 Genesee Street, West Troy." (Daily Whig, 1868)

For purpose of interest, Robert Wood was a chair maker, who worked for the renowned the *Troy Chair Company*. The manufacturer produced chairs, wagons, and other elaborate, wood-carved objects.

I thought this to be of peculiar interest, given that 207 had several fireplaces. The mantles were decorated with ornate, hand-carved wood features, which can be viewed on the "Book Photos" page of my website (www.jillmariemorris.com). Additional research revealed that Mr. Wood holds the patent for a rocking chair that was quite popular back then.

207 changed hands yet again, going from Emily Mc--,

to Mary Cunningham Campbell. Bearing in mind that the house was either sold to, or inherited by Mary, as opposed to her husband Robert Campbell, it is strongly suspect that Mary may have been a relative of Emily.

Mary's husband Robert, was listed as living next door to 207, at No. 18 Genesee, until approximately 1873. Decades later, this dwelling was widely known to many as *DeLollo's Wine & Liquor.*

It is at this juncture that the meat and potatoes of my investigation really took shape. With records prior to this time proven to be sketchy at best, future archives and databases provided higher levels of accuracy. Just prior to the turn of the century, the village also welcomed the opening of the Congress Street Bridge.

Continuing with my quest, it was discovered that that Mary's husband Robert, died sometime after June of 1875, and before May of 1876. Unable to find anything relative to his death, such as an obituary, or cause, it is presumed that he died in his house: 20 Genesee Street (207).

In 1877, Felix Cunningham, brother of Mary Cunningham Campbell, lived at No. 20 Genesee Street, along with his widowed sister, Mrs. Campbell. Felix was a successful businessman for his time, and owned another home at nearby No. 26 Genesee Street. This location is just west of No. 20 Genesee, and close to Ohio Street (3rd Ave.).

Mary Cunningham Campbell died sometime after June 14th, 1880, and before September 24th, 1880. It is presumed that she too, died at her home: No. 20 Genesee Street (207).

Justin was able to access Mary's Last Will and Testament. He states that she left a considerable sum of money to St. Patrick's Church, and directed the funds: "To be expended as William F. Sheehan deems best." Justin states that the remainder of her estate was bequeathed to her "Beloved brother Felix Cunningham." (Albany County Surrogate's Court, 1880)

Her estate consisted of Lot 18 Genesee Street (205 19th St., aka: DeLollo's Wine & Liquor), and Lot 20 Genesee Street (207 19th St.). Both properties stayed in the family for several decades following Mary's death.

This is the first bit of evidence that shows a direct correlation between the residents of 207, to Sheehan, and St. Patrick's Church. As with most families, inclusive of modern times, priests frequently visit homes for dinners, counsel, and other varied reasons. I have strongly speculated that Sheehan visited 207 on numerous occasions.

Felix's niece, Winifred (Cunningham) Moran, lived at No. 20 Genesee Street, circa 1881, and is thought to have relocated from Brooklyn, to West Troy in approximately 1880. Her move north, was more than likely due to the death of her husband, Michael Moran.

Michael and Winifred appear to have come from Ireland, and then settled in Brooklyn. They had the following children: Mary, Annie, and Katharine, as well as fourth daughter, Dorothy. Dorothy was born sometime after 1870, and died prior to 1892.

On an aside; throughout my research and investigation into the Moran family, I had encountered many obstacles. Sending out messages on social media sites such as Facebook, I asked if people were descendants of the Moran family, of Watervliet. I also emailed various individuals through Ancestry.com, yet did not find anyone who was willing to discuss their heritage.

One afternoon, I decided to revert back to traditional gumshoe ways, and simply looked up telephone numbers in the *White Pages*, for anyone named Moran that lived in the Watervliet area. Not wanting to cause a ruckus, I picked only one, and left a voice message briefly detailing the reason for my call.

Gut intuition led me straight to the correct descendent. Later that night, I received a call back from a pleasant man, who offered quite a bit of information on his line. One of his comments resurfaced, and tied his family to the Moran family of 207.

The man discussed that most of his family were buried in St. Agnes' Cemetery. He detailed approximate locations of headstones, engraved with the family surname. When I asked him about Michael and Winifred Moran, he stated that his family had passed down a story that an ancestor named Michael Moran had died, after falling into a body of water, but he did not know where, or when. He also stated that he was told Michael was drunk at the time he fell into the canal. Interesting, I thought.

Since Winifred and Michael did not have any sons, it is through the paternal lineage of Michael Moran's family, that my source is related. I was quite thankful for his contribution, and noted the conversation. A few months later, Justin stumbled onto an obituary in the *Brooklyn Daily Eagle,* which confirmed my source's story.

Michael Moran, drowned in 1875, at the young age of 35. He fell into the East River, under the influence of alcohol. According to Justin, Michael and Winifred lived at the corners of Little and United States Streets, in Brooklyn, New York. This location was close to the area where Michael's body was found.

Widowed with a clan of small children, Winifred and her family moved north, into West Troy, to start a new life. Her Uncle Felix proved to be the person who not only helped her, but more than likely prevented her children from being taken away from her upon arrival in the village.

Single parents, especially mothers, were not 'allowed' to keep their children, due in part to Sheehan's control of the orphanage, and town. Further details as to why are addressed in Chapter 6.

Approaching the end of the 19th century, mass migrations into the U.S., were in full swing. Locally, the canal had provided a point of enormous growth, which correlated with other socio-economic issues.

1888 was the year I jest at being the year of *great*

enumeration in the village. In the course of the transition, Genesee Street was renamed 19th Street, and Erie was changed to 2nd Avenue. No. 20 Genesee Street had officially become: *207 19th Street.*

Felix Cunningham died on December 29th, 1889. As with many of the earlier residents and owners of 207, a cause and place of death were not found. Reasonable conclusion can be drawn that Felix also died at his residence.

His Last Will and Testament states: "I give and devise unto my niece Winifred Moran of West Troy, NY a house and lot known as lot number Twenty (20) on the north side of said Genesee Street." (Albany County Surrogate's Court, 1890)

He also left his niece $500.00, along with a portion of residuals from his estate. This was a modest chunk of change for Winifred to put in her nest egg.

Since Felix identified the property by its lot number, along with the street name listed as Genesee, it is indicative that his papers were drawn prior to 1888. As previously mentioned, the house numbers, and street names changed in '88.

Based upon an earlier plat map, along with a tax record from 1893, Lot 20 Genesee Street, and 207 19th Street, are of the same. As a refresher, this also attributes to the fact 18 Genesee St., was changed to 205 19th Street (aka: DeLollo's Wine & Liquor).

For the next several years, Winifred Moran resided 207 19th Street. Living with her daughters Mary, Annie and Kate, she ran a grocery store at 205 19th Street.

An entry appearing in the *Proceedings of the Board of Supervisors of the County of Albany*, from 1884 states a "Mrs. Winifred Moran" as owing ". . .unpaid school tax for School District No. 20, Town of Watervliet, for the year 1893." (Argus & Greenwood, 1894)

The location and description of the owed taxes reflect 205 19th Street [lot 18] with an assessment of $800, resulting in a tax equal to $1.76. The assessment of 207 19th Street [lot 20] was listed as $1,500, owing tax in the amount of $3.30. It is reasonable to assume Felix deeded her Lot 18 (205 19th St.), prior to his passing, as early as 1881, but no later than 1888. (Argus & Greenwood, 1894)

By the end of the 19th century, 207 had at least 8 owners, and was the target of an arsonist. Philamela Wood, Robert and Mary Campbell, as well as Felix Cunningham, had died while living in the house. There remains a slight possibility that Dorothy Moran, fourth daughter of Michael and Winifred Moran, died at the house too, as Winifred first appears in West Troy in 1888. Dorothy more than likely died in 207 sometime prior to 1892, as no information could be found on her, after that year.

Bittersweet for sure, the close of this chapter's history brought about a rather nostalgic thought. I found myself pondering over the name Felix; yet another random happenstance that prompted me to contemplate the great mystery of life.

* * * * * * * *

Ever since I was a young child, I have loved the name Felix. Inspired by the television show *Felix the Cat*, I use to run through the house, singing the show's theme song at the top of my lungs, and to the point my mother begged me to stop. I couldn't help it. I loved the name *Felix*.

In adulthood, I found a great sense of peace emanating from the unusual name, and have often wondered if it held any significance to my life. At one time, I had even considered naming my youngest son (Kyle) Felix, but my husband thought the fate too cruel for a child. The feeling was reciprocated when he wanted to name him Chet. We compromised, and chose Kyle – a far cry from Felix, and Chet.

To me, Felix is a cool name, and for some weird reason, inspires me. I love to say it, and I admit, even as an adult, I still burst into song, and sing the silly tune.

It wasn't until I had finished researching Mr. Felix Cunningham, that I became more intrigued by it, as by all accounts as stated in his will, was a stand-up man with a big heart. In moments such as these, I relish the good that comes from such a sad, and tragic story. A pillar of strength, Felix Cunningham will forever remain a bright light in the wicked history of that dreadful home.

Case #7: Name Withheld, 1957.
Location: Same apartment building as Case #6.

This was the first, of only two suicides that I am aware of involving females. A young woman living in the same apartment building as the man described in Case #6, hung herself, just shy of one year from the date of the male who shot himself. To my knowledge, the deceased individuals did not know one another.

This case was also confirmed by the same, retired Watervliet cop, in addition to multiple sources who lived near the dwelling. The deceased was less than 20-years-old at the time, and lived with her family. Based on witness accounts, the girl became despondent; reasons unknown. Her mother came home, and found her hanging in the apartment.

Case #8: Thomas Adams, 1964.
Location: 18 13th Street.

The Knickerbocker News, Albany, Monday [illegible] 3, 1964 states: "Fire Escape Plunge Fatal. . . A Watervliet man, described by authorities as despondent over the illness of his wife, plunged to his death from a third floor landing of a fire escape at the rear of Albany Garden Nursing Home on North Pearl Street, early today.

Thomas Adams, 63, of 18 13th Street, Watervliet, suffered a broken neck in the fall, Coroner Elmer M.

Parker said, in issuing a verdict of suicide.

The man was discovered by Miss Theresa Dumont of 8 Lincoln Avenue, Cohoes, a nurse at the home, when she arrived for work at 6:30 a.m. Patrolman James Glass, who responded, ordered him taken to Albany Medical Center Hospital where Mr. Adams was pronounced dead on arrival.

Coroner Parker said Mr. Adams, a retired employee at the Watervliet Arsenal, apparently had climbed the fire escape to the third floor, taken off a jacket and overcoat, and leaped about 40 feet to his death. The coats were found on the third floor landing. There was no note.

A member of the family told Coroner Parker that Mrs. Adams had been despondent since his wife Catherine was stricken ill recently.

Other survivors include three sons, Joseph, Edward and Thomas Adams Jr., and a daughter, Mrs. Mary Razzano." (Knickerbocker News, 1964)

6. ASYLUM

"There can be no keener revelation of a society's soul than the way in which it treats its children." Nelson Mandela

The business of religion has deep roots in many organizations, some of which began to prolifically spring forth in early, 19th century America. The establishment of these institutions were part of the movement that in my opinion, was a money making front, using *'kids for cash.'* With little law, or ordinance in place to monitor business practices, these institutions rapidly grew in number, most under the auspice of a church, or religious society.

The awkward development of the United States throughout the 1800s presented with both ambition and danger, grappling with an astounding influx of immigrants and respective families who came to seek a better life. Very few schools were present in most areas, and many villages lacked designated care for its residents.

West Troy was one such location that fit this historical

profile, as it was destined to become the location for *Saint Colman's Orphanage*. The home was incorporated, and built by Rev. William F. Sheehan.

The advancement of immigrant populations in America often became a burden on small towns, and villages. Although locations such as West Troy offered numerous, and lucrative job opportunities, they were also besieged with crime. Various health issues also plagued the residents. Contemplating the out of control ways of the villagers, mainly due to alcohol, drugs and other societal woes, West Troy was the 19th century poster child of community dysfunction.

Lack of reprimand for law-breaking criminals, or care for the ill, became an even larger problem, especially in this century. Parents who had substance abuse issues kept little watch over their broods. As a result, those children showed little respect for discipline, and authority.

The same applied to parents who could not physically, or financially care for their children. Be it out of frustration, hunger, or misdirection, their young often found themselves in trouble, after resorting to delinquency, and other unfortunate acts, as a means of survival.

In an effort to quell these issues, some founders established designated homes, or asylums, to send wayward children – and adults. I like to refer to these places as Victorian pokies. The pokies were places to restore peace to the community, and (hopefully), rehabilitate offenders, as well as those whom were ill.

With time, children placed in the confines of an asylum, were separated from the adults. It was difficult enough to control the adults, but a population mingled with kids, meant larger problems. Separating the two groups, orphanages became the springboard for 'kids for cash.'

Reasoning leads most to the conclusion that an orphan is a child who has lost one, or both of its parents. Many orphans in this era did not match that criteria. Back then, orphanages were regarded as an institution of convenience, used to send, or place a child for a number of reasons. It did not necessarily matter if he, or she, was parentless.

Most orphanages were comprised of children unjustly, and heartbreakingly so, taken from their homes to serve a purpose elsewhere in society, be it within the local community, or in lands afar. The more children enrolled, equated to increased revenues provided to the establishments, by residents, and state-run organizations.

Greatly depending upon the governing body, some 'orphans' received religious instruction, and a rather rudimentary education. Functioning like large, militaristic reformatories, many children ran away, only to be captured, and returned to the asylum. There, they faced severe punishment. Some later died under mysterious causes.

With this said, who exactly were the designated, responsible parties for admission to, and screening of the inmates? Priests, and sometimes nuns, were the primary decision-makers when it came to assisting their communities. The more privatized the poorhouse, the more control its officials had over their flocks, inclusive of the children.

Considering the large Irish immigrant population that exploded in West Troy, the very same issues plagued the village, thus leading relative, societal concerns to weigh heavily upon the shoulders of its priests and pastors. The village was a 19th century, hot mess.

Not to be overlooked is the fact that all through the first part of the century, women were not allowed to own property, nor could they vote. Single, or widowed females were also considered unworthy of giving care to their child(ren).

Even youngsters living in two-parent households were at risk of being taken away. Most orphanages worked in tandem with officials to determine the fate of life's most innocent. Once deemed unfit, the parents were ordered to hand over their flesh and blood to the local institution. More times than not, a religious official, or priest, was in charge of making the rules, and ensuring such 'transactions' took place.

These establishments frequently changed their admission criteria like the wind. They accepted anyone: sick children, children with financially destitute parents, lawbreakers, and an *occasional* orphan. St. Colman's Home was no exception.

If a husband died, the wife was was commonly left without an income, and thus ordered to surrender any children. Out of desperation, most women in that situation literally rushed to remarry, immediately following the death of their spouse. It was a common solution to a heart wrenching problem, and considered one of the more viable options that remained. Forget about romance; they were mothers on a mission.

I can say with certainty, that given the above situation, the thought of having my children taken away from me would have warranted a fierce fight on my part. Practically any arrangement was a more suitable solution, with the one exception being having to send them off to an asylum. That would be simply heartbreaking.

Scarier is the fact that had my husband committed suicide in the 1800s, I may have had my son taken away from me. Being of Catholic faith, and having lived at 207 back then, he might have been placed in St. Colman's.

Primarily dependent upon country of origin as a means of favoritism, those in-charge determined what to do with the community's young. If an orphanage was a blend of nationalities, slightly less occurrences of partiality to an ethnicity took place, however, if the institution was managed and controlled by one nationality, favoritism towards children of that particular descent, was commonplace.

Many of the orphanages were biased. West Troy was no stranger to the idea, targeting to extrapolate children of

Irish descent from their families, while more favorable outcomes were afforded to children of other nationalities.

Sadly, once any child had been placed in an orphanage, they became wards of the institution, and at the mercy of those providing them care. Safe to say, most institutions ran a tight ship, and showed little kindness to the residents.

Reprimand in the orphanage was harsh. Every type of corporal punishment was fair game to those handing down the sentence; beatings and humiliation were geared to break the child. The goal was to make the child subservient to, and fearful of, their caregivers. This method worked all too well.

Another occurrence that became all too customary in the orphan environment, was that of sexual abuse. It only stands to reason that the younger, often handicapped, were singled-out, molested, raped, and beaten. Not only did the employees assault the children, but the residents battered one another as well.

As time passed, and more institutions were built, less than appropriate care became the norm in many of the orphanages of the 1800s. Care of the children was frequently overshadowed by greed. Money was spent less on resources for the children, such as food, medicine, and hygiene. Instead, it was lavished on incorporators, and officials.

Indentured servants became the money-maker of the time, and girls in particular, were trained to become domestic servants. Young girls typically lived with well-to-do families, working as maids, cooks, launderers, and tailors. With little restriction imposed, many were also sexually abused by members of the household.

Another degrading attribute endured by the servants had to do with the fact the orphanages took almost every penny of the child's sparse salary. Every cent went to the pimping asylums. This placed both boys and girls, at the mercy of the orphanage, as they were unable to support themselves.

Young boys were often sent to learn a trade. Masonry and plumbing were among the common crafts taught at some institutions. Their fate was commonly the same as their female counterparts: cash for kids, at any cost — any age.

By the mid-1800s, orphanages had popped-up all over New York. The bank accounts of the church continued to swell, as orphanages proved to be a profitable industry. The children continued to be victimized, practically every way imaginable.

Given new-found religious freedom in 19th Century America, Catholic priests established a number of orphanages throughout the eastern United States. This practice lasted well into the mid-to-late 1800s.

One example of the Catholic orphanage movement of the 1880s is exampled by Rev. Sheehan. Shortly after taking charge of St. Patrick's Church, he opened a school for boys, followed by a convent for girls. Both of the schools housed hundreds of children.

In 1884, Sheehan incorporated *St. Colman's Orphan Asylum*. His intent was "to obtain a charitable, industrial school; to instruct the inmates in useful trades, and occupations, and to take care of and educate orphan and half-orphan children." (New York State Board of Charities, 1906)

Conflicting dates are reported relative to the actual incorporation of St. Colman's, with some listing January 8th, 1884, and others showing July 26th, 1884. Most of the information was derived from the New York State Board of Charities.

Pertaining to the incorporation of St. Colman's, Sheehan was listed as both the President, and the Treasurer of Saint Colman's. Interesting: he controlled who was admitted, and the home's finances.

Shortly after incorporation, Sheehan sent an invitation to the *Sisters of the Presentation of the Blessed Virgin Mary*, to work at the orphanage. Be it known that the Sisters of the

Presentation also hailed from the village of Fermoy, Ireland. Sheehan picked this group specifically, due to their charity towards his mother, and seven siblings.

In turn, the sisters asked the bishop to pay for Sheehan's theological schooling. This does not make sense, as some insinuate that Sheehan came from a family of wealthy architect.

The Sisters of the Presentation were organized in Cork, Ireland. The first round of Irish nuns from the presentation arrived in the western U.S., sometime in the mid-1800s. Within years, the convents made way their way east, and into Watervliet, NY.

The nuns' request for Sheehan to receive education was granted. After becoming a priest, he was sent to the U.S., and moved between a few churches in Upstate New York, eventually settling in the Capital District.

In the same manner by which Sheehan had designed his most marvelous church, the priest embellished St. Colman's. A considerably large facility, it was surrounded by acres of rolling hills, and woodlands. Sheehan himself, paid for the land, and the home's development project.

Upon the arrival of the good sisters, *St. Colman's Industrial School and Orphan Asylum of Watervliet*, opened its doors for business. One final detail remained: he needed to fill the place. West Troy's young and defenseless, were at the mercy of the priest, and the presentation nuns.

As for the admission of children into the home, Sheehan himself, is noted to be the sole person with permission to do so. According to the New York State Board of Charities, Annual Report, Vol. 2, the "Terms and Qualifications for Admittance" are listed as: "Orphans and half-orphans are received; boys under 10 years of age, girls of the legal age. . . Application to be made to the President." (New York State Board of Charities, 1904)

With concurrent, and continued enrollment, the home managed much like a well-oiled, self-sustaining machine. In a manner fashioned very much like the new St. Patrick's

Church on 19th Street, St. Colman's was like a hilltop beacon, where it vigilantly kept watch over the residents of West Troy, and the Hudson River Valley.

The main structure is a large, brick behemoth that towers over seemingly innocent, green pastures. Speckled with outbuildings used for various functions, its expansive space brimmed with fresh, country air and beckoned a *come hither, we care* ambience, back in the day.

Be it a symbol of charity for those left orphaned or destitute, or as a strategically mounted money-maker, the home was feared, and has long been deemed *eerie*, by many.

The children whom were placed in care of the nuns were supported by public funds. Curious, is the fact that the admission criteria changed, placing greater restriction on females, than males. This was noted in subsequent review of multiple New York State Board of Charities publications, as provided in their Annual Reports.

With the primary focus of the home to provide shelter, education and care for inmates in seemingly dire straits, one cannot help but wonder: exactly how so many of these children were true orphans? Considering many were sent into the community as indentured servants, in turn surrendering most of their pay back to the home, it is a fair supposition that the children were eyeballed as an end, to a means.

The use of the term *inmate*, in conjunction with anything charitable, not-for-profit, or meant in any type of other loving, compassionate context, seems a bit foreshadowing, and rather unsettling. Such was the case at St. Colman's.

In view of what a gracious and caring man Sheehan was said to be, in every sense of reality, there could have been a number of more appropriate words chosen to better describe the plight of an orphaned child needing refuge. Only much later in my research, did the term inmate resurface, and in turn, completely disfigure the once pristine image of both the founding father, and the home, itself.

Not too long after its incorporation, many children escaped the care of the sisters. One of the earliest articles I found relative to an escapee, is dated August 2, 1890 (The Daily Times, Troy, NY). This situation continued for decades to follow, and includes claims made by my late husband Jim, as well as his mother.

I was told that Jim had been briefly placed at St. Colman's for *foster care*, sometime in the '70s. Having wanted to verify that information, I met with resistance after calling the home, and asking to speak with someone about obtaining records. A gruff woman urged me to send a written request, by which one followed. To-date, I have yet to receive any confirmation, or denial, of Jim's placement.

Truth be told, both Jim and his mother had stated that he had run away from the home due to issues involving abuse, and hunger. In the course of our courtship, Jim had confided in me that it was one of the *scariest places* he had ever been. If there is any merit to this, he stated that he ran away *twice*. After the final time, he was placed with a private family in Rensselaer County. I was able to confirm the latter.

Many times, those who absconded were found, returned, and even relocated to another facility, however, some were not. Several seemed to vanish into thin air; never to be seen again.

Given the sheer volume of children in the home's care over the duration of many decades, it does not shock me to hear repulsive stories detailing poor living conditions, substandard food quality and portion, as well as instances of neglect, abuse, and even death. What my husband did share with me was unsettling, as he described belt whippings, constant hunger, and other methods of punishment; all of which caused him to flee.

Through my research, I came across two different, yet highly compelling and publicized cases that made my heart break, and my skin crawl. The first case, one of which I had been aware of prior to writing Saints, has to do with a little boy named Gilbert Bonneau. The second, came from the source of a book written by Susanne Maloney Robertson, a former St. Colman's orphan.

Although both stories are completely different, the underlying theme is similar, and strikes a disconcerting chord. Together, both sets of allegations taint the legacy of both the Sisters of the Presentation, as well as Sheehan.

The tragedy of Gilbert Bonneau began in approximately 1947, and is highlighted on the website: www.justiceforgilbert.com. I did email Mr. Bonneau via the email listed on the website, and asked for an interview. I have yet to receive a response.

In short, Gilbert's mother took ill. Left a single parent, his father was rendered incapable of caring for his children. (Bonneau, 2013)

This is quite an absurd and archaic way of thinking, even for the late '40s. I was amazed the trend continued.

Understandably so, this was heartbreaking to learn of, and more so for the Bonneau's. The entire family was ripped apart, against will. Many times, I have thought about how tragic and awful it must have been for strangers to tell a parent that they were not allowed to raise their child(ren) in a single parent household.

Unfortunately, this was a recurring theme in Watervliet, since Sheehan had established orphanage protocol, decades prior. To think of the sorrow this situation caused the children, and parents, is almost unbearable – and all due to a shameful decision to remove the children from a loving home.

In late November of 1953 – the 27th, to be exact – it appears that the child had fell ill. Make note that this date too, is yet another coincidence of dates added to an ever-growing list.

Relative to the date, it was be the week of November 27th, 1988, that the most inexplicably putrid odor that I have ever experienced, invaded 207 19th Street, forcing evacuation of the entire building. The date itself - November 27th - was also the date my son Jimmy, was baptized.

Documentation shows that the following day, Gilbert's father received word that his son's condition had worsened. The problem is: nobody really knows what happened. The child was barely alive.

Gilbert succumbed to his wounds, and died a short while later. It was also noted that the child had a head wound that was covered with a dressing, indicating he had suffered some type of head trauma. (Bonneau, 2013)

Decades later, a whistleblower contacted the family, and stated she lived at Saint Colman's the same time as Gilbert. It is alleged that this female bore witness to the child being assaulted by a rage-filled nun.

It is incredible how one phone call, all those years later, was enough to cast doubt upon St. Colman's. I cannot imagine the guilt the woman carried with her for all of those years. It was truly, a disturbing, and deadly secret.

The family's quest into Gilbert's death was unfairly met with resistance by the church, and orphanage. From what I have read about the case, the family's hands were tied.

Gilbert's highly publicized case resulted in many others stepping forward. For the most part, each one of them shared personal particulars of similar incidents while having formerly lived at the home. Several of those victims detail being suffocated, beaten, and sexually abused.

Patterns of heinous attacks on children continued to come out of the woodwork, and from every angle in the tri-city region of Upstate New York. St. Colman's soon found itself under a well-deserved umbrella of suspicion.

Another very notable claim of abuse comes from reports made by Susanne Maloney Robertson, who publically announced her experiences while living at Saint Colman's, in a book titled: *The Throw Away Child*.

Placed in the care of the nuns at Saint Colman's

beginning in the late 1950s, Robertson graphically details multiple forms of abuse, and down-right torture. The author also interviewed former residents of the orphanage, and included their respective stories of sadistic cruelty.

Robertson claims that as a child, she suffered almost a dozen broken ribs while living at St. Colman's. She also asserts to have copies of hundreds, upon hundreds of reports relative to abuse that other, former St. Colman residents bore. She asserts that almost every allegation was filed with the Colonie Police Department. (Robertson, 2007)

In an alarming mention, Robertson believes that the investigation lasted days from start, to finish. Given the very large number of alleged complaints, a short-lived examination is quite frankly, suspicious. In my opinion, I think that an investigation of that length is absurd, and is indicative of someone in the department, looking the other way.

Such disturbing allegations of abuse at the home sickened me. There are even accusations that the same nun who allegedly beat Gilbert Bonneau, remaining an employee of the home, as recently as 2009. Should this be true, it is an outrageous example of injustice towards the victims, their families, and the community as a whole.

So what happened with the so-called investigation by the police department? With a church that held the community in its strong, and far-reaching grasp, I guess that one shouldn't be astonished to find that *some* policemen, investigators, as well as other city officials, more than likely turned a blind eye on the allegations. Sleaze knows no boundaries, and often invades every aspect of politics, even in a small town like Watervliet.

For objectivity's sake, I must also report that there are true stories of compassion on behalf of those who were cared for at St. Colman's.

Although the positive accounts are nowhere near as plentiful as their negative counterparts, some individuals have confided to me, both publically and in private that their overall experience while living at the home shaped their lives for the purpose of doing good. Some former orphans received a 'calling' to work in the fields of medicine, healthcare, and social services.

A few stated that although their experiences were nurturing, there were a few nuns that had "a less than stellar reputation." Some also added that "it was a known fact" if residents did what they were told, they could avoid the wrath unleashed by a specific handful of nasty nuns. As one source stated, "there was one sister who could make your life a nightmare, if you were disobedient."

I do not think that all of the nuns providing care at the home were, or are immoral, but as with most aspects of life, there is good, and there is bad. Any work the good seeks to do, is too frequently overshadowed by the bad. It's a precarious power play that occurs on a daily basis.

The home, and Sheehan, seem to have an air of sin, and scandal. To me, as a medium-psychic, there exists a very common thread between the two.

Aside from Sheehan being the most obvious, there is a black, mist-like, shape-shifting element that not only I have seen at both the church, and orphanage, but two current employees, as well as one former worker, have as well. A friend of mine also shared a story she had been told by an employee, however, I was not privy to the name, and cannot tell if it is someone who had previously contacted me. I found all sources to be credible.

Two of the employees experienced the sightings together, and on multiple occasions. There are "certain areas" in the main home, where a "black mist" is known to appear. Both employees stated that on more than one instance, it manifested and appeared to "charge" towards them. As a result, they took off, and fled the room.

Appearing to be quite fearful of the mist-like apparition, I suggested they use spiritual protection and most importantly; *do not show fear.* Those types of *things* thrive on fear.

The personal testimony of the former worker, gave me goose bumps. The source shared specific information relative to their own experiences, which resulted in the individual speaking with a supervisor. I can reveal this individual is: older than age 65, and a devout Catholic. They were an employee at St. Colman's prior to 1980.

At one point in time, my source saw the black mist appear at the end of a hallway, and move rapidly towards a coworker. Within moments, the coworker began to experience acute nausea, and lightheadedness. Going to the aid of the stricken coworker, my source urged them to seek medical attention. They declined. After spending some time in an office chair, the coworker went home.

Witnessing two, additional events such as the one aforementioned, and sensing a feeling of dread each time the mist appeared, the source again, privately spoke to a supervisor. They were told several people have complained in the past, but there existed "no proof the stories were real," suggesting that for years, reports have been fabricated by attention-seekers.

With a well-established working relationship in place, my source stated they confided in their superior, and shared details of witnessing the mist approach the worker, followed by a sudden onset of illness. The source also divulged they had a very bad feeling about its presence in the home, more so fearful it could affect the children.

Without saying a word, the source's supervisor stood up, and left the room. A few shifts later that week, my source was approached by the administrator, and told that stories have indeed, circulated for decades. My source was told that many believe *it* – the black mist – is either Sheehan, or one of the original nuns that helped to run the home.

Hearing those words in particular, made me uneasy. So many times I have questioned the makings of the black mist. For purpose of identifying this anomaly, I asked my sources if they, or anyone else have been able to notice any semblance of the vapor, to that of a person. Not a single one has.

Personally, I do *not* think it is Sheehan, or a nun. I think it is something that was conjured sometime after St. Patrick's Church was built, perhaps in an exorcism gone badly. Regardless, it is foul, and feeds off those weak in body, mind and soul.

* * * * * * * *

I will never forget that black, mist-like cloud I saw hanging in the direction of St. Colman's Home. It was there every time I had gazed out of 207's second floor, kitchen window. It was tremendously unsettling, and foretold of death.

Recollecting a most frightening spirit contact that occurred in my sleep, soon after the release of *207*, (and prior to my delving into the disputed and unsavory stories of abuse allegations at St. Colman's), I cannot help but feel the darkness that hung in 207, as having dual residency at St. Colman's.

I have shared the following experience with some family, and close friends. Troubling, it is something that I will not easily forget.

As with some of my spirit contacts that take place while I'm asleep, I was approached by a white light that was pure, and radiant. It had a strong, yet soothing, maternal quality. It told me that I needed to "go see *something*."

After initiating contact, it plucked me up, and placed me in front of 207. I had been transported back to 19th century West Troy. In one, swooping motion, we soared through the air, to the north, and then slightly west. Swiftly, we made our way to a large structure surrounded by trees.

Glancing down, the property was making me extremely

anxious. As I expressed my concern, the light communicated that I was going to be okay, and enveloped me in a shield of its warm glow. It further advised me that I was not to speak – only to observe.

On approach, I felt my heart race. A feeling of doom shrouded the building, as a changing, ink-black form oozed across the land, down a hill, and back towards the direction of 207.

As we approached, I noticed a smaller building attached to the front, left side of the larger home. The stillness of the night was punctured by occasional cries from children, as a dim, amber light was visible in a window of the affixed, brick structure.

Although I was warmly embraced by the shield of spirit, I remember the buildings were fortressed by an arctic chill that tried to permeate my protective bubble. Gently lowered to the ground, I crouched below an open window of the smaller unit: I heard people talking.

There were three, hood-cloaked, black figures. One commanded another group member to fetch a shovel, while the other was ordered to go along with the leader, towards a wooded area located to the rear, and left of the home. Lifted once more, the light whisked me off to a different location, somewhere on the property.

A rather rundown building stood at the far edge of some woods. The commander and its protégé entered the dwelling, and waited for the other shadow figure to return with the spade. A flickering lamp was placed on a table; the room was dank, and smelled stale. Comingled traces of dirt, dried grass and a mildly, rotting scent, filtered through the air.

Towards the back, a white-hot woodstove was burning, as a number of long tables were staggered in the center of the room. An inferno before my eyes, I still felt an ice-cold chill trying to invade my safe space.

Protected, I managed to avoid detection, and watched as one of the cloaked figures prepared each of the tables by laying a white sheet over its top. The commander walked between the tables, raising and lowering its billowing, robed arms, as though it was pulling something up from the floor, and then slowly, pushing it back down. The third cloaked figure appeared with the tool, followed by others who were hastily dragging stuffed, sacks along the ground. They set a parcel next to each table.

Fear began to course through my body. The light restored a sense of calm in me, and told me that I needed to, "see this for the children."

A cloaked figure stoked the stove, as the leader instructed the others to place the sacks onto the tables. One by one, they untied the bags.

To my horror, the satchels contained bodies of dead children. I wanted to turn and run, yet could not. Unable to move, I watched as the figures cracked crisp, clean white sheets over the children. The head figure then commanded others to line the tables at the door. The tables were actually old-fashioned stretchers.

Two of the figures wheeled their carts to the burning furnace, forcing the children into the fire, while the others lined up at the door, and followed their leader outside, and into the woods. I begged and pleaded for the light to make it stop.

Terrified by the unfolding spectacle, I wept. My heart broke into a million pieces, as I witnessed such barbarity involving children. The light did not release me, but transported me to another location.

Hidden behind thick shrub, I watched the dark figures dig shallow graves. The commander left, and returned to the room with the woodstove. There, it began to speak in another language that may have been Latin.

It was a deep, old voice, riddled with evil. It was neither male, nor female. It chanted, and watched as the others prodded the fire. The stronger the fire grew, the more frenzied the leader became, while once more, raising its robed arms up, and then down.

Back in the woods, some of the figures had positioned their carts next to the freshly created crypts. The human-like shadows pushed the children into the graves, and then covered the bodies with dirt. More than I could stand to witness, I shouted for the light to take me home.

Pulled upward, and sent high above the large home, the light escorted me back towards the city. As we flew away, the sounds of a maniacal chant was heard, interspersed with the screams of children. The reverberations gradually evaporated into the night.

Landing in the middle of 19th Street, and in front of 207, I sobbed. What was the lesson? Nothing good can come from such a sight. The light then told me that I had seen the truth, and regardless of doubt, or scrutiny, nothing – *nothing* – could ever take that way.

Releasing me from its protective bubble, the light instantly vanished. I immediately sat up in my bed, quivering.

With my heart pounding, I tried to make sense out of what transpired. I knew that I had been in the presence of a loving and protective spirit, but why did I *need* to see *that*? Why did I *need to know*? The horrific vision of yesteryear has since remained a mystery.

Case #9: Name Withheld, 1978.
Location: Third Avenue & 21st Street.

In September of 1978, a 67-year-old man shot and killed himself, for no apparent reason. Multiple sources state that the man had been the caretaker for the then vacant, *St. Ann's Maronite Church*, located on Third Avenue and 21st Street – the small church once owned by my former landlord, just to the northwest, and rear of 207.

After leaving the church, the man went to the basement of his home, and shot himself in the head with a shotgun. I do have the name and address of the individual, and will not release it, as his obituary did not state a cause of death, only that he died *"suddenly."*

7. IN SICKNESS & DEATH

"The life of the dead is placed in the memory of the living."
Marcus Tullius Cicero

Working through the previous century's history was an unusual experience. It was as if the walls and floors, enveloped in the blood-red brick exterior of 207, had come to life, as I learned about its former inhabitants.

Understanding that the preceding decades had lacked modern medicine, or institution to treat illness, I expected to find death had knocked a time, or two, upon 207's doors. Although I had uncovered the deaths of four residents at the house, the range of the hellish nightmare did not grow until my investigation leapt into the 20th century.

At times, the writing of this book left me cynical. I mulled over an intricate web of coincidence, curious of the cause to the tragedy and mayhem that was uncovered. Indeed, there were times in the course of this project that I felt almost too drained to continue.

Every time that I wanted to throw in the towel and walk away, I reminded myself that those who died within the confines of the towering structure, needed a voice. Collectively, their stories had to be shared to instill a sense of faith, as well as bring about an awareness that there is more to the world we live in; something we cannot see.

On one such day that I was feeling quite drained, I reflected upon a profound moment that occurred when I was a teen. It's funny how a conversation sticks in the back the brain for recall.

Exasperated from the culture shock of moving to the middle of nowhere (literally), I told my father that I wanted to quit school. They were empty words; I was exercising my given, adolescent right to complain. My threat was idle, but my words sure hit a nerve with my Dad.

My father's words resonate to this day. Retreating to my room to simmer down, he opened the door and said, "Don't you ever say that you will quit, or give up – on anything! Do you understand? *Do you understand me?!* As hard as it may be, you figure things out, and keep going. Got that?"

So many times throughout my life, I found myself thinking about that afternoon. Forever embedded into my psyche, those words, along with numerous examples of courage that my mother, and grandparents have instilled, carried me through the most difficult of times.

That message, so many years ago, became clearer, with every passing hour that I worked on this project. I could not give up, no matter how much adversity, frustration, and emotional fatigue the research, and investigation had caused.

It was the death of the little, 11-year-old girl that lingered with me. Having blocked any spirit activity while living in 207, I almost feel responsible that I did not look into the realm, to see if she was troubled, or stuck. I felt like an earth-bound mother, who had let her spirit child down – as strange as that sounds.

Given the unfolding mayhem that was filtering through via records, research, and online queries, I did find a unique source of inspiration, perhaps at a moment when I needed it most. Getting to know Felix Cunningham brought positive light to my investigation, as I yearned to find more stories that could dim the home's nefarious past.

A man so caring, he took his niece and her children underneath his competent wings, and provided them with refuge. His love allowed Winifred an opportunity to secure a respectable, well-paying job, which kept the family together, and away from the dark grasp of Sheehan, and St. Colman's.

By 1900, Winifred Moran owned her home, free of mortgage. This was no easy feat for a widow, in such rough and tumble times. I often wonder if she ever feared Sheehan, when it came to her own brood. After all, she was a single parent.

Winifred acquired additional property when her sister, Dora Egan, died on March 18th, 1908. The property was located in Brooklyn, indicating that perhaps her late husband was related to the famed Moran Towing Company family.

Identified as "a sister of the said Dora Egan, deceased" in estate papers filed in Brooklyn Surrogate Court, March 24, 1908, Winifred was noted to be "Known Next of Kin" residing at 207 19th Street, Watervliet. At the time of her death, Dora resided at 128 Summit Street, Brooklyn, New York. (Brooklyn Surrogate's Court, 1908)

If curiosity interests you, I suggest googling "128 Summit Street, Brooklyn, New York," and taking a gander at the house. Built after 207, it holds a striking resemblance to the dwelling in Watervliet.

Unknown if Winifred's husband was a relative, tugboat Captain Michael Moran, owner of the renowned *Moran Towing Co.*, resided mere houses away, at 143 Summit

Street. That was also the general area by which Winifred's husband Michael Moran, had drown.

Bolstering evidence that we had accurate information relative to our research, Dora's death certificate identifies her parents as "Thomas Cunningham and Ann Boyd of County Sligo, Ireland." Thomas Cunningham was found to at first be employed as a grocer, and later as a Constable for the police force in West Troy, much earlier in the 1800s.

As previously mentioned, name variations and misspellings frequently created a hassle. Throughout this monotonous process, I developed an even greater respect for die-hard genealogists, who spend countless hours racking their brains on such matters.

Par for the course, Winifred was no exception to the name game, as various publications noted the spelling of her name as: Winfort, Winfred, and Winne. All indicate that she was the mother of 4 children, and was the wife, and later widow, of Michael Moran.

Mary Moran's name remained consistent. Her middle name began with "L." Variations of Anna Moran include: Annie, Ann, and Ann.

Catherine also underwent a series of name changes, which proved to be a challenge at times. Additional spellings of her given name are listed as: Catharine, Katharine, Kate, and Katherine, with a middle initial "V."

Investigating the place, and dates of death for tenants became a usual course of business, seeing that it was important to know the names, and causes of death for 207's tenants. Although resident Henry M. Taft did not meet his demise while living at 207, he did have a rather unfortunate encounter at the canal bridge, just north of the house, and near the Upper side cut. More weirdness, but it was almost expected, if you lived at 207.

Henry took a nasty tumble on a set of concrete stairs in the summer of 1908. Seriously injured, Taft was not killed during the fall, and recovered.

A handful of residents have heard about Henry Taft living at 207, and relayed the story to me. They were under the impression that the man died at the house.

I am certain that he did not, as Taft moved to another residence shortly *after* the accident, and lived long enough to sue for his injuries. The case was dismissed. (Attorney General's Office, 1911)

According to examination, life at 207 remained quiet up until Winifred's death. The Moran matriarch, and grocery store owner died on March 25th, 1915. She was 68-years-old.

Her obituary, as posted in the Troy Times, March 26, 1915, states: "Mrs. Winifred Moran, a native of Ireland, and a resident of Watervliet many years, died last night at her home, 207 19th St. She was a member of St. Patrick's Church whence the funeral will be held Monday morning. The survivors are three sisters, Misses Mary, Ann and Katherine Moran." (The Troy NY Daily Times, 1915)

A second announcement featured in the Troy Times on March 29th, 1915 states, "The funeral of Mrs. Winifred Moran was held this morning from St. Bridget's Church. Rev. Edward T. Reilly, Rev. Frank McMahon and Rev. Stephen Kiernan officiated at the solemn high mass. The bearers were Arthur Kennedy, Michael Broderick, John Ball, Frank Baker, Joseph Parker, Charles Barnes, John McManus and John J. Loughlin." (The Troy NY Daily Times, 1915)

I felt a deep sadness when I realized Winifred had died in 207, especially at such a fairly young age. She embodied so many things: strength, perseverance, motherhood, and was a hard-working immigrant who raised her children under the watchful eyes of the community. She surmounted so many obstacles.

As discussed earlier in the book; I was blocking, and unaware of her presence. If in fact her spirit was in the house, she was more than likely part of the force that protected us.

Justin's request of probate records indicate the home was kept in the Moran family until halfway through the 20th century. Additional resources, such as obituaries listing 207 19th Street as a resident's address, led to the discovery of Irving, and Margaret LaLiburte (aka: LaLiberte, LaLiberty). More name variations to sort through.

An interesting parallel was noted relative to Winifred Moran's sister; Dora Egan. Margaret LaLiburte and Veronica (Vera) Allen, were sisters (nee Egan), and very possibly related to Winifred. At the very least, they were related to Dora.

Justin discovered that Winifred Moran's Watervliet estate was appraised at $7,150. She bequeathed the estate to daughters Mary L. Moran (Executrix), Annie A. Moran, and Katherine V. Moran, all residing at 207 19th Street, Watervliet. She also had been the owner of the house on Summit Street, in Brooklyn. The Brooklyn property was valued at $8,500. She was quite well-off at the time of her death, given her holdings.

Not all information was ascertained through obituaries, but random newspaper clippings as well. On May 13th, 1933, an ad in the Albany Evening News states a permit issued to the "estate of Winifred Moran." (Albany Evening News, 1933)

I believe this to be the addition that was built onto the rear, and side of 207. The permit ad is an interesting mention, as I had previously explained in my first book that back of the home always felt more clear, compared to the main structure. It felt as if there was a dividing line between two, alternate, coexisting universes. In fact, the rear bedroom was far larger than the front bedroom.

Upon moving into the house, I did not want the nursery located in the main house because it felt *unsafe* and dark, thus leading me to select the larger room in the addition, for the baby. This never made sense to most people who came to visit, as several commented that my husband and I should have taken the bigger room. Odd, yes, but I am very glad that I listened to my intuition when making that decision.

Mary and Annie appeared to have stayed out of the city's limelight. Mary was a dressmaker, while Annie did not appear to have any type of employment, thus adding to my theory she may have had some type of health issue.

Every so often, I stumbled across a small article, or two highlighting Katharine Moran's social undertakings, and job duties. Through these time capsules, I learned that she served the Red Cross, and provided instruction for public health classes. The findings were little snippets of time that breathed life into the names of the departed.

A bit controversial, an article in the September 11th, 1935 edition of the Troy Times Record states: "Mayoral candidate Charles Parker accused City of Watervliet officials of padding payrolls, being well over-paid in comparison to Cohoes officials and, of corruption." (Troy Times Record, 1935)

Apparently, Parker scorned the Watervliet Police Department for looking the other way when it came to solving a large heist. Several articles mention that numerous bags of flour inexplicably disappeared from Moran's office. Sounds to me, like someone had help, as flour sacks are a hefty lift.

At the time of Parker's complaint, Katharine was the city's *Charities Commissioner*. Katharine is noted as having later retired from that position. Interesting that corruption had surfaced its ugly head, yet again.

Another find that I have been asked about on occasion, has to do with Katharine V. Moran owning 218, and 220 Nineteenth St. I was contacted by multiple residents of the city who shared this information with me. Initial efforts to find documentation relative to her acquiring the property turned up nothing, however, does not remove speculation that she was as a possible owner.

As time passed, I rapidly learned that derailment from 207, in order to follow some of the more trivial matters, often led to a colossal waste of precious research time. Choosing my battles wisely was a strategic maneuver to completing this book. Otherwise, it is quite possible that spending time on issues involving other homes, could have lasted years, and further delayed its release.

Without rhyme or reason, Annie Moran vanished sometime after 1930, but before 1942. Justin and I, searched high and low to find an obituary, or newspaper article that accounted for her whereabouts, yet did not find one. Taking her age into account, Annie was between 60, and 70-years-old at that time. This makes it likely that she too, died while living at 207.

Personally, I feel a very somber, almost child-like quality when I think of her (Annie). I sense a degree of protection around her, possibly indicating she may have been sickly, or handicapped.

The second *confirmed* death having occurred at 207 in the 20th century, is that of Mary L. Moran. On June 16th, 1942, at the approximate age of 57-years-old, Mary passed. Her obituary in The Times Record, Troy, New York, June 17th, 1942 states: "Miss Mary L. Moran, a well-known resident of Watervliet, died last evening in her residence, 207 Nineteenth Street. Daughter of the late Michael Moran and Winifred Cunningham, she is survived by a sister, Katherine V. Moran, of Watervliet. She was a member of Saint Patrick's Church and the Rosary Society of that church. The funeral will be held from the residence Friday at 9 a.m. and thence to Saint Patrick's Church, where a solemn requiem mass will be sung. Burial will be in St. Agnes' Cemetery, Menands." (The Times Record, 1942).

Noticeable is the fact that only Katherine is the sole, surviving sister, and Moran family member. This bolsters my hunch that Annie died before Mary, as she is not listed in the obituary.

The Times Record, Troy, New York, June 19th, 1942 states: "Funeral services for Miss Mary L. Moran were held at St. Patrick's Church, Watervliet, today at 9:30 a.m. after prayers at the home, 207 Nineteenth Street, Watervliet. Rev. Gregory M. Connolly celebrated requiem mass, with Rev. John C. Carey as deacon and Rev. Joseph A. Honan, sub-deacon. Miss Agnes Dundon played organ selections and John Fogarty and Miss Alice Fogarty sang "Domine Jesu Christe" at the offertory and "De Profundis" at the conclusion. Bearers were Arthur R. Allen, Irving LaLiberte, Dr. Charles D. Rancourt, Thomas F. Horan, Daniel Baron and *Joseph C. DeLollo*. Father Connolly officiated at interment in St. Agnes' Cemetery, Menands." (The Times Record, 1942).

Joseph C. DeLollo was a well-recognized individual relative to 207's history. Approximately one decade after Mary's death, Joe purchased the house.

On December 4th, 1950, tragedy struck the Moran family one last time, when Katharine died. There is conflicting information relative to her actual place of residency at the time of death.

Presuming she had acquired both 218, and 220 19th Street prior to death, it is quite possible that given no remaining, immediate relatives were present when she passed, the newspaper made an error by reporting she died at 218 19th Street. It would not be the first time incorrect information was printed in a newspaper.

Objectively, it also possible that for some reason, she left her life-long home just prior to her passing, and lived briefly at another one of her properties. The Polk City Directory does list her as residing in 207 19th Streets consecutively, from 1943, *through 1949*. The same directories show two other families lived in the house which makes sense, as there were three flats (apartments). (Polk City Directory, 1941-1987)

The reader needs to be made aware that strangely, the 1950 directory was missing. The 1951 directory shows a new tenant by the name of Karl Shibenger, along with previous tenants Arthur Allen, and Irving LaLiberte. (Polk

City Directory, 1941-1987)

With tomfoolery taking place throughout my investigation, Justin and I noted that various annual directories typically made available at onsite facilities, vanished at times when there was a changeover in the ownership of 207. It prolonged the investigation, but the discovery of other resources made it less painful.

Regardless, Katharine's obituary in the Times Record, dated December 5th, 1950 states: "Miss Katharine Moran, Watervliet City Clerk for twenty years, died yesterday at her home, 218 Nineteenth Street, after a brief illness.

Appointed city clerk Jan 1, 1920, Miss Moran served for two decades under three different administrations until she retired December 29, 1939.

In her capacity as city clerk she also served as welfare commissioner, secretary to the civil service commission and secretary to the city council. Before entering the city's service, she was a business college teacher.

Miss Moran was named city clerk by Mayor Michael L. Wash when the city manager plan of government was first adopted in Watervliet. She served for two years under Mayor George R. Halpin and for eight years under Mayor James F. Donlon.

Born in Brooklyn the daughter of the late Winifred Cunningham and Michael Moran, she lived most of her life in Watervliet. She was a member of St. Patrick's Church, the League of the Sacred Heart and the Rosary Society.

There are no immediate survivors.

Funeral services will be held at 9 a.m. Thursday from the Parker Brothers Memorial, Watervliet, and at 9:30 a.m. from St. Patrick's Church, where a requiem mass will be sung. Interment will be in St. Agnes' Cemetery, Menands." (The Times Record, 1950)

Her ownership of the properties may very well predate the early 20th century, but a deed search was not conducted on the properties. With the focus on 207, I wanted to avoid writing a book that could have been well over 500 pages.

The only point of interest that stems from her ownership of the additional properties, is that two Parker family members lived at Katharine's rental properties. Josephine M. Parker, who died in 220 19th Street, on January 11th, 1940 (brief illness), and Thomas F. Horan, on October 22nd, 1944 (long illness).

Highly speculative, but with good reason, it is believed that there exists distinct possibility tenants James H. Keegan (1898), Thomas C. Parker (between 1920 and 1925), and Joseph S. Egan (1928), also died in while living in Katharine's rental.

Katharine's death signified the end to the Moran era, as well as an immigrant family's legacy. Enduring tremendous loss, matriarch Winifred appeared to have raised responsible, respectful adults, who stayed afloat when at times, the world around them seemed to crumble.

It was only 1950, and the shadow of death lingered, giving way to an unsettled feeling. I could not help but ponder; *how many more deaths in the house?* There remained a helluva lot of ground to cover.

* * * * * * * *

God bless those who spend their days at the County Clerk's Office, researching deeds. That is a tedious job.

Having never undertaken such a huge research project, I found myself swimming in a sea of new terms, and fumbling my way through methods of property reference. From maps, to plats, to microfilm, I was on a self-taught journey, surrounded by an occasional well-imbedded hooligan, waiting to intentionally steer me down the wrong path.

In some instances, the moment I stated who I was, the demeanor of certain individuals grossly changed from that of being openly helpful, to walling me off, as if I were a Leper. With a "we're happy to be of assistance" sign hanging in the background, these people shut down faster than a government office on a Friday, going into a three day weekend. Oh, the stories that I could tell.

One party had me driving all over Albany County, when with hindsight, I should have never had to leave the original location. Another became quite adept at sending out secret bat signals to family and friends, alerting them of my whereabouts.

Family members, as well as friends of some of the city's key players showed up at times, and asked me a battery of questions. It is now very evident to me, not only is blood thicker than water, but the community water in Watervliet is pretty damn dense, too.

In some cases, these individuals surfaced in research venues, striking up seemingly innocent conversations, and hawked over my every move. On more than one occasion, some of the minions answering to their ambiguous overlords, actually tried to befriend me, literally sitting directly across from me at the desk, asking obnoxiously invasive questions. At one site, one of the cronies watched everything that I wrote down for nearly *five hours*. Yes, it was that ridiculous. Never mind the continuous texting, and occasional retreat outdoors, to make a phone call.

The next piece of information came by telephone. Encountering a discrepancy as to who became 207's next owner, I decided to take to the phones once again. Sometimes old fashioned investigative techniques end up working the best.

Mustering courage, I called retired Judge Warren DeLollo. I was pleased by what transpired.

Judge DeLollo is of the same DeLollo family as my 207 landlord, Phil DeLollo. At the time of my interview, he was 95-years-old. One year prior, he had broken his hip, and was being cared for by his lovely daughter, Nancie. Warren felt best to have Nancie speak with me, while he answered questions.

The conversation revealed that Joseph DeLollo (Phil

DeLollo's brother), had owned 207 prior to Phil, and the other siblings. Both Warren and Nancie stated that "Joe purchased the home sometime between 1950, and 1953." 207 had been listed for sale, and was next door to Joe's barber business (later DeLollo's Wine & Liquor). It is believed that 207 had been put up for sale at some point after the death of Katharine V. Moran, in 1950.

Warren and Nancie informed me that Joseph rented one of 207's flats to Alfred and Camilla (nee DeLollo) Aulisi. I was aware that the two had resided in 207, for a few years.

Joe became quite ill, and the rest of the DeLollo siblings joined their brother in ownership of the property sometime between 1970, and 1987. Joe died at home (not at 207), after a long illness, in 1987.

I also asked Warren if he remembered if anyone had committed suicide in 207, by which he could not recall, yet stated he was "unsure." He then suggested that I contact Ann Riley.

Ann is both Joe, and Phil's niece. Phil was Ann's Godfather.

Warren and Nancy were quite interested in my research, and passed along Ann's information. For a man of his age, Judge DeLollo took an active part in helping me track-down information, looking up phone numbers in the phone book. It was a pleasure to have both he, and Nancie, take time to discuss some of Watervliet's history. I am very grateful to them for doing so.

As mentioned in a previous chapter, I did contact Ann Riley. Ann and I, discussed the church property that Phil had purchased, as well as discussed interesting morsels of information about family history, and 207. Unfortunately, not much was known about 207's history, other than when Ann mentioned that she felt Joe's faith kept things "at bay" in the house, as he was strongly grounded in his religion. I told her that it was a very distinct possibility it kept him protected.

Based upon verbal accounts by Judge Warren C. DeLollo, his daughter Nancie, and niece Ann Riley, along with some documentation, it is believed that Joe DeLollo did acquire 207 between 1950, and 1953. Records indicate that a majority of 207's tenants remained stable throughout the '40s, and '50s. This includes the Aulisi, Allen, and LaLiberte families.

The next recorded death to occur *at* 207 was that of Margaret LaLiberte, who died at home on January 24th, 1958. Her obituary in the Troy Record, Saturday Morning, January 25th, 1958 states: "Mrs. Margaret LaLiberte of 207 19th St., Watervliet, died suddenly at the residence Friday following a short illness. The Watervliet Fire Department inhalalor (sic) squad was summoned but the woman was beyond aid at their arrival. Although she had been ill in health, her death was unexpected. Mrs. LaLiberte was born in Albany but had resided in Watervliet the greater part of her life where she graduated from the old Watervliet Academy. She was a communicant of St. Patrick's Church where she was a member of the Rosary Society, the Women's Guild and the League of the Sacred Heart. She is survived by her husband, Irving L. LaLiberte; a daughter, Mrs. Frank Slichko of Watervliet; and a sister, Miss Mary A. Egan of Watervliet, and two nieces. The funeral will be from the Parker Brothers Memorial, 2013 Broadway, Watervliet, at 9 a.m. tomorrow and at 9:30 a.m. from St. Patrick's Church where as Solemn Requiem Mass will be celebrated. Interment will be in St. Patrick's Cemetery." (The Troy Record, 1958)

Fifteen months later, another tenant died in the house. On April 29th, 1959, Mr. Peter Capozzelli is listed as having died at 207 19th Street. No information could be found relative to the cause of his death.

Seventeen months after Peter Capozzelli's death, tenant Christopher Carroll also died in 207. His obituary in the Troy Record, Friday Morning, September 1st, 1961 states: "Christopher F. Carroll, a retired machinist who lived in

Watervliet for the last three years, died at his residence, 207 19th Street, Watervliet, yesterday after a long illness.

A native of Holyoke, Mass., he was the son of the late Christopher and Mary Jane L'Esperance Carroll. He was a communicant of St. Patrick's Church in Watervliet.

In addition to his widow, the former Nora A. Hansmann, he is survived by five sisters, Mrs. Charles Herliby, Mrs. Jeremiah Herliby, Mrs. Harry Frazier, Mrs. William Doyle and Mrs. Henry Germain, all of Holyoke; and two brothers, Thomas of Long Island and Howard P. Carroll of Holyoke.

Funeral services will be held Monday at 9 a.m. from the Marra Funeral Home, Remsen and Columbia Sts., Chotoes, and at 9:30 a.m. from St. Patrick's Church, Watervliet, where a Solemn Requiem Mass will be celebrated." (The Troy Record, 1961)

Research into the next two decades proved to be a challenge. Again, documentation mysteriously went missing at one public research institution. This made constructing a timeline of tenants in the house, an unpromising task.

The Polk City Directories made available at the Hall of Records in Albany, begin in the early 1940's. Many different years were missing from the collection. The last directory made available, was for 1987.

This meant having to rely on digging through pages, upon pages, of internet documentation relative to newspapers articles, using keyword searches for the house. There is a good possibility that other people may have died in 207 as well, given turnover in tenant residency. It is highly possible that some families did not publish the deceased's address in the newspapers. Very little information was found for the years the City Directories were missing, causing great speculation that there were indeed, additional deaths.

Regardless, I was absolutely stunned that by 1970, there had been so many deaths in the house. It still gives me the chills.

Other notable findings relative to burial grounds, and early cemeteries being covered and left to the way-side, include the old Gibbonsville Cemetery. The Gibbonsville Reformed Church established a burial ground soon after its incorporation, circa 1815. Abandoned, it was the final resting place for many who lived in West Troy.

In April of 1979, the Watervliet Arsenal was in the throes of a modernization venture. Human remains were found on the grounds. The project was halted for a while, and the remains were relocated to the Rural Cemetery. (Swantek, 2009)

The remains found on a previously designated area on arsenal grounds referred to as the *Old Arsenal Burying Grounds,* also went through a similar situation in the early 1900s, when a resident found an abandoned cemetery. The headstones, and the skeletons from that site were relocated to the Albany Rural Cemetery.

These two cases alone, illustrate how burial sites, cemeteries, and graves contained within Watervliet city limits, have long been neglected, and sometimes shifted. Between church plots, consecrated grounds, Native American burial and massacre sites, as well as Potter's Fields scattered throughout the city, there is definite concern and indication of, significant unrest in the spirit world.

The repeated, wanton treatment of the city's oldest, deceased inhabitants is enough to create a great deal of negativity in the realm, leaving little doubt that this factor alone has to be considered when looking at the city's spiritual health. Many times throughout the writing of this book, I have questioned if 207 was built upon such a spot, as the house was tainted unlike anything else I have ever seen.

The energy in 207 was beyond heavy. The main energy - the one that I do think is demonic in nature - was controlling, and manipulative. I see where it had could have taken hold of Sheehan, and wonder what hand it played in some of the other deaths.

The haze in the living room seemed to represent a vortex of sorts, and a down-flow at that. Typically, there are two types of vortices: an up-flow, and a down-flow, (also known as an *in-flow*).

An up-flow vortex moves from beneath, to above, and is quite often associated with positive feelings, and sensations. It is frequently described as emanating excitement, but in a good way.

As a visual: an up-flow has an ascending, spraying motion. Many up-flow vortices enhance psychic abilities, functioning like a tapped point in the environment that releases endorphins, and stimulates the senses. There are several, naturally occurring up-flow vortices around the world, specifically in Arizona. Although I have never visited any of the popular sites in Sedona, I have spent time in few, inclusive of one located at a friend's home in Beverly Hills, California. It is an amazing experience!

In the case pertaining to my friend's house in Beverly Hills, the vortex was activated in the course of a construction project, and remodel. My house reading confirmed this. It is one of the most active, and exciting up-flows I have visited. The energy is incredibly powerful!

On the other hand, a vortex with a down-flow tends to be heavy and oppressive, and is often associated with feelings of fear, and dread. Many people have complained of sudden fatigue, lethargy, depression, and even falling ill with physical symptoms such as shortness of breath, confusion, chest pressure, and negative changes in mood.

Although negative energies, or entities may manifest in a down-flow, it does not mean the energy is demonic, but there are times when a demonic force may be present in the direct area of a down-flow. Rush to judgment that there must automatically be a demon present, needs to be avoided in order to stop further confusion during any type of investigation, in addition to instilling fear in someone that may live, or work in one.

With this clarified, I do think that there was an in-flow at 207, specifically in the living room. It acted as a syphon, pulling in all things dark; an attractive spot for a demon.

While living in the house, I felt the master energy – the demonic force – having power, or trying to gain power, over everything in the house. It seemed to circle the exterior of the vortex, as if it were a pit to toss souls of those it consumed. It seemed like the front room was a black hole, and the closer one came up to the landing of our second floor apartment, the stronger it could be felt.

The flat also became ice cold in some spots. Jim noticed it, too. One of those occasions took place not long after moving into our apartment. We did not have air conditioning, and the change in temperature went from chilly, to frigid within a matter of minutes. I do not remember it lasting very long each time, but it was quite strange.

Most times, random pockets of icy air occurred in the living room. I can specifically think of it happening twice in our bedroom, and once in the dining room; never in the back of the house.

The main door to enter our second floor flat opened into the dining room. I was never comfortable in that room, and more so uncomfortable in the living room. The dining room floor was marked by a set of average sized shoe prints, darker than the flooring. I looked like someone had taken several steps, and then exited the apartment.

My guess is that this occurred before any sanding machines existed, due to the actual shape of the shoe, and density of the stain patterns. By the time the floor was stained its amber color, the shoe prints appeared dark brown, almost black; the result of a heavy liquid. The prints led from the living room area, into the dining room, and then out the door.

It has often bothered me to think of the origin, and

cause of those shoe patterns. With the lighter colored floor in the living room, I am certain that the floor in the other room was sanded, and coated at least twice; the second sanding was conducted by my late husband Jim, who had done so prior to moving into the flat.

Disturbed by the spectacle that we found upon viewing the apartment for the first time in 1988, it also struck me as odd to see a circular pattern having been left sanded in the middle of the living room floor. What could have possibly occurred in that room to result in that random blemish? That question may have been answered in late, 2011.

Not long after the release of *207*, I received an e-mail submission from my website's contact page. It had an alarming subject line. Catching my attention, I responded, and asked the sender to please elaborate on his rather encrypted inquiry.

Shortly thereafter, I received a small book of information pertaining to strange happenings at the house, in days of yore. In the correspondence, I was informed there *may* have been a pentagram, or satanic symbol, drawn onto the floor, perhaps by the former tenant, or someone who had access to the apartment, before we had moved into it. Reading that statement made me ill, as I can only imagine how damaging – and damning – that could have been to a site already suffering an infestation.

By early 2012, I had received two more claims that there was a satanic cult in Watervliet. Neither e-mail listed names, only a generalized area by which they practiced.

The first e-mail mentioned a group of Pagans, who currently hold gatherings to conduct their practices, while the other e-mail (from a different source) claimed an older sect, very close in proximity to the other, still practices black magic, and satanic worship. I thought this to be quite strange, given the earlier e-mail I had received about the possible pentagram on 207's floor. The location of both groups is a matter of blocks away from 207 19th Street.

It is not my job to reply with a comment on what someone may, or may not be doing, so I thanked the parties, and did not feed in to, or ask any additional questions about their statements. For safety's sake, I also deleted the latter two communications, as it was quite disturbing for me to even keep them in my in-box.

With prospect that something such as satanic worship, or witchcraft, having been practiced in the house prior to our arrival, in addition to the extremely alarming history and death tally, it must be taken into consideration that a bad situation may have been made worse. I will also share a situation that presented itself, relative to an individual who showed up at my very first book signing at Stuyvesant Plaza, in the summer of 2011.

With witness, I was approached, and questioned by an individual who asked if I was aware of a 'witch coven' that exists in the city of Watervliet. At the time, I had not. Since I was at the signing, I was a captive audience for this person, and endured several minutes of creepy details, relative to their childhood adventures in the city.

They later sent me an unsettling email, relinquishing particulars that involved physical, and sexual abuse. They claimed the abuse was part of the alleged coven's ritualistic practice. It was at that point when I had to ask the party to refrain from sharing that information with me, and suggested they contact the police.

Should some type of ritual have transpired in that house, particularly in my former flat, it could explain for what was unleashed the instant we moved in. The entire conversation, followed by such a sensational email, was completely disconcerting.

Sensing impending doom, in addition to a frightening sequence of dreams that began prior to stepping foot in the apartment, I disputed our move into the house. Not only did I lose the argument, but within a year's time, I also lost the love of my life.

After relocating to 207 19th Street, things changed at an

alarming pace. Unable to make rhyme or reason as to my husband's bizarre behavior, or the dread that I felt and had to deal with on a daily basis, even friends and family were uncomfortable visiting us, and all with justified reason.

Trying to recall any paranormal activity that may have escaped me in the writing of *207,* the one thing that my best friend Carol reminded me about, was the weird knocking at the front door of our apartment. I somehow had forgotten to mention these events. I may have repressed them, because they really frightened me.

To the best of my ability, I can trace the first knocking to the late summer of '88. I was almost due to deliver my son, when I was startled by some zealous raps on the door.

Our couch was first positioned on the west wall of the living room, blocking a door that led into the stairwell of the house. This door was literally around the corner from the main entry door to the flat.

Not feeling well, I had been laying on the couch reading, when I heard a rather loud set of knocks on the main door. Odd, I had not noticed anyone climbing the loud, creaky, wooden stairs behind me.

Managing to hoist my very pregnant self from the sofa, I waddled to the door, and opened it. Nobody was there. I was speechless. I knew that I heard a *knock, knock, knock.*

Staring into the hallway, I looked downstairs, into the foyer: I did not see anyone. Looking upstairs, towards Betty's landing; nothing.

I shut the door, and stood in the dining room slightly puzzled. They had rapped on the door with moderate pressure, which was quite rude, I thought. I had mentioned the incident to my husband later that night. Jim found it rather amusing.

The second knocking occurred after our son was born, sometime in the late fall. This time, Jim and I heard it; *knock, knock, knock.* It was loud, and fairly forceful, prompting Jim to spring out of the chair quipping, *"Who the hell is that?"*

He opened the door and came face to face with - nothing. Insisting someone was playing games, Jim charged upstairs to Betty's, and then downstairs to Vinny's. Baffled, I reminded him that the very same thing happened to me a month or two, prior. This time he didn't laugh.

More knockings were heard late winter, into early spring, but these were noticeably more violent, to the point the door rattled quite loudly. One of the times we were home together, but the remainder transpired when I was alone, with my son.

It was beyond strange. There seemed to be no specific pattern with the occurrence of the ghostly bangs, but they were increasing with intensity.

I believe it was the close to the last knocking when I picked upon on something. I was in the kitchen when I heard a ferocious rattling just before three loud sounds: *bang, bang, bang!* The succession was followed by a strange vibrating sound. Immediately after the noise, I had a lucid premonition.

Startled, and staring at the door from the middle of the kitchen floor, I saw Carol's friend; he was grieving over the loss of a relative. It was as though the door was a portal into time. The hallway looked grey. I saw a tall, black figure standing in the background. I recognized the blackness as *death*.

Having grown uneasily accustomed to the occasional knocking, I blessed myself, and walked into the nursery to check on my son. Seeing that he was asleep, I stood by his crib, and prayed.

That weekend, I contacted Carol, and told her what I saw. A few days later, she called to tell me that her friend had informed her of a relative's passing.

What was going on in this God forsaken house?! I had been blocking, yet somehow the colossal knocks broke through, resulting in the premonition. I was at a loss for words.

Jim's conduct continued to change. Everything from

strange obsessions, mind-slips, escalating violence, supernatural fits of strength, alteration of physical appearance, and even changes to his voice and speech patterns, along with a true abhorrence for anything Godly, good, or faith-related, only grew in intensity.

A culminating act of destruction took place on the night of June 28th, 1989. Forever, it will remain a night of the most unspeakable tragedy that I have personally known, and bore witness to.

After a foiled triple murder-suicide plot, and a game of hide-go-seek between the police forces of Albany and Rensselaer counties, Jim returned to 207. There, he shot himself after making a final phone call from Angie's Pizza Parlor, across the street. He could battle the demon(s) no more.

Sitting in the very spot that our Christmas tree had stood just six months before, and in the exact spot that Sheehan had first appeared, Jim pressed the trigger of his grandfather's antique, shotgun, and killed himself. It was a ghastly scene.

The blast rang-out through all of eastern 19th Street, causing some to think a big-rig had blown a tire. Vinny identified what remained of Jim, while neighbors scrambled to their windows, and out into the street. It wasn't until the late winter of 2012, that I spoke with former neighbor Dom Denardo, about that night.

I was informed that the police had to use a generator for lights in the flat, as the power had been turned off. I had left Jim several weeks prior, and was living at my mother's, in Troy. As a result, I was unaware of what he was doing in that dreadful place.

Dom saw the coroner take my husband out of the house on a stretcher, and could not believe what had happened. Dom stated that it is still unsettling for him to think about that night.

I personally, continue to suffer from PTSD (Post Traumatic Stress Disorder), as a result of the events of

June 28th, 1989. Twenty-four years later, and my heart still skips beats, and my palms and forehead become sweaty. I also cry when I think about holding my infant son in my arms, begging, and pleading for my husband not to shoot us.

All too well, I can picture the shotgun inches away from us, as well as the look on my son's precious face, throughout the ordeal. Those thoughts also dredge up the memory of my husband's demon-possessed face, as he pinned us into a corner.

Amidst the ungodly actions of a man possessed, my mother saved my son, and me. Love won for a moment, but in another, the devil was no competition for a weak soul. Yes, we were spared, but the beast was too formidable an adversary for Jim.

The months that followed were the truly the most difficult in my adult life. Loss, grief, change, becoming a widow, and single parent caused unbelievable stress.

That August, a matter of just two months since his death, Jim was spiritually freed of the torment he endured. This, I am most sure of.

From that point forward, Jim has been a messenger, and a protector. This unexpected turn of events in the spirit realm further enhanced my sense of faith, and has grounded my Spiritual Self in many ways.

I always asked God to protect those who lived in the house following Jim's death. I did not want to find out that anyone else had fallen prey to the house, and spent many nights saying my rosary, asking the Lord to protect Betty, Vinny, as well as anyone else who called that vile place *home*.

One of the reasons that I prayed for protection, came the moment I ran out the door, after stopping by 207 to retrieve personal effects after Jim's death. I sensed *it* wasn't over; there was an insatiable appetite for death that hung in the air. The malevolent energy was supercharged, and ready to annihilate another family.

Leaving the Capital District in 1991, I had been told that nobody else lived on the second floor after Jim's death. Even though I had been told so, I knew otherwise. I had also noted the time when I saw a young family sitting on the steps, while on my way through town. I was advised they were friends of Vinny, but intuition told me differently. I was afraid for them, and I was equally concerned for anyone within feet of that house.

Evidence of Jim's warning me about Jerry's suicide from the *other side,* was followed by the news of his death on November 1st, 1989. The chain of events further reinforced my intuition.

Although Jerry did not die in 207, he had been spending hours in the vacant flat, after Jim's death. He told several friends that he went there to talk to Jim, and claimed to have seen him in the house. After a few months of increasingly strange behavior, Jerry took his life, too.

Evil does not have a discriminating palate; it will eat whatever it wants, so long as there is a meal to have. As physically strong as both Jim and Jerry had been, they were ensnared by the most profane.

In a true story, filled with more twists and turns than the world's largest rollercoaster, it only seemed appropriate for something to knock me for a loop. That hard ball hit me in July, 2013; two years after *207* was published. It came in the form of two Facebook 'friend requests.'

A husband and wife had messaged me on the social media site, and stated they needed to discuss something important. Intrigued by the last name, and urgency of their request, I obliged. We exchanged telephone numbers, and were speaking on the phone within minutes.

After a brief introduction, the two informed me that *they were the family whom had moved in to 207's second floor flat after Jim's death.* I described the young family that I had noticed on the steps of the house years ago: it was them.

I experienced a flood of emotions, as I listened to their encounter. It was surreal, to say the least.

Days after Jim's death, the male (husband) had been informed by Vinny that he could make some money on the side by helping out Phil DeLollo; 207's landlord. He was asked to clean up the apartment where Jim had committed suicide. Young, and somewhat naïve, the man agreed to the task, only to realize it was one of the worst things he had ever dealt with.

It was a mess. With help from a friend, they did the best they could, given the fact that Jim had obliterated his entire head. He said that it was a very difficult undertaking, but fulfilled his duties, and left.

His voice trembled as he recounted the past. Respectful of the fact that I did not want to hear gory details, he summarized the ordeal, and continued with the events that later took place in the house.

By the winter of 1989, he and his wife were looking for a place to live. Vinny advised them of the remaining vacancy in 207's second floor apartment. After contacting Phil, the couple moved into the house.

Coincidentally, the wife was pregnant at the time they took residence in the house, just as I had been. As a matter of fact, her due-date was within *three years to the date of my son's,* when we had moved into 207.

Almost immediately, the couple did not have good vibes. Admittedly, they both agree that their initial feelings had to do with the knowledge that Jim had committed suicide in the living room.

The wife stated that she didn't want to read too much into the situation, but did notice that her husband's behavior started to change, shortly after moving into the flat. For some unknown reason, he could not sleep in the master bedroom, located off of the dining room. Not only that, but he did not sleep more than 3-4 hours at a time, and could only do so while on the living room couch. He also began to have a nightmare about *a dead body in the basement of 207.*

He stated that the dream never changed, and detailed

how he was always "called into" the large, crushed stone floor basement, to "attend a wake." In the empty room, he walked up to a casket that contained a "decomposing body" of what he believed to be a male. The nightmare always left him feeling unsettled, and literally, unwilling to go into the basement again.

The woman spoke of how her husband, a once calm and rational man, became irrational, and increasingly violent. He started drinking more heavily, and began to use drugs, which was evidently out of character for him before moving into the flat. Family and friends noticed the change in her husband's behavior as well, leaving them to question the family's safety.

When I had asked about any type of unusual activity in the house, they both described instances where the dining room sconces "turned upside down." The wife states that she, not being receptive to anything paranormal, was quite upset by these events, and grew more concerned.

They also mentioned a "strange knocking" at the front, *and* back doors. This was startling to hear, bearing in mind I too, had experienced weird knocking, but limited only to the front door.

Sure enough, they heard sporadic pounding. At times, the back door opened on its own. They described one instance when Vinny actually heard the banging, and showed up at the door with his hunting rifle, fearing an intruder. The two explained that it was an anomaly, which stumped Vinny.

They went on to explain the day that Betty, the woman on the third floor, came home and went about her daily routine. The following day, a neighbor across the street noticed that Betty had left her front room light on all night, which was out of character. Concerned that they had not heard her leave earlier that morning, the male tenant ventured up to the third floor, and found Betty deceased, sitting on her living room sofa.

Summoning the paramedics, there was nothing they

could do. She died the day prior, after she had returned to the house. They were told that she suffered a massive heart attack after her pacemaker had suddenly stopped working.

A dear, sweet woman who always checked on me and Jimmy for the duration of our year's stay at the house, Betty died sometime in 1991, or 1992. A dozen residents that live in the area also informed me of Betty's death, and believe '91, or '92, to be an accurate timeframe. I was unable to locate her obituary. She was the last confirmed death to have occurred in 207, before the house was demolished at the end of the millennium.

The conversation took yet another crazy turn, when the couple had mentioned the crucifix they found after moving into 207. *Could they be talking about Jim's grandfather's crucifix?*

After Jim had taken the crucifix off of our bedroom wall during my grandmother's visit in the spring of 1989 (detailed in *207*), I had left it in the dresser. Any attempts to place it back over our bed were met with fierce adversity. I decided it was best not to stir the pot, and no longer tried to force the issue.

Jim's attitude towards church, the cross, even my rosary beads and bible, was extremely destructive, prompting him to fits of violence, whenever I questioned him. When I finally fled the flat, I did not take the crucifix, and had always wondered where it had gone after his death. I also lost my rosary beads.

Tucked away in a box, in the back bedroom closet, the husband and wife tenants found the cross. They kept it with them for all of these years, and took it out, as we talked on the phone. I was shocked.

Feeling rather uncomfortable upon hearing the story about what happened the day Jim removed it from the wall (after my grandmother had proudly showed him a photograph of she, and the Pope), they questioned if I wanted it back. Without hesitation I said *no,* for one, primary reason: Ann Fisher had warned me to never take anything left in the house. As much as I was happy that someone had cared for the crucifix, I had to heed Ann's advice, and listen to my instincts.

The couple questioned if they should throw it out, however, I did not feel that was appropriate. After a brief explanation as to why, they agreed, and said they were going to look for a new home for the relic. It was then that they stated they had always felt something was 'off' with the crucifix.

Following Betty's death, the couple's relationship continued to deteriorate. The woman watched as her husband spiraled out of control. Unwarranted outbursts, peculiar behavior, and hellacious battles ensued. This was completely out of the ordinary for the pair. Specifically, the husband's family grew gravely concerned for the wellbeing of the family. This was later confirmed when I interviewed one of the male's family members.

After almost three years, the woman and her children fled the house, when her husband *tried to kill her*. They explained how he picked up his wife, and threw her across the room with an unhuman-like strength. He briefly remained at 207, and then followed his wife. They never returned.

Once again, something had gone very wrong in 207. The blessing: they all escaped.

It was interesting to hear the male describe how within two months of leaving the house, he started to feel better. His wife corroborated this information.

With hindsight, they knew it was the house, and wanted to know what type of sinister entity was dwelling in the structure. The male further explained that he has struggled with the events that transpired at the flat. To this day, he feels terrible when he reflects on his uncharacteristic tirades, and insane behavior. He also shared a poignant anecdote about what happened to his sense of faith and spirituality, while living in the house.

According to both husband and wife, the male pulled

away from anything religious, and doubted God's existence. He said that "something happened" to him when he moved into the house; it wore him down physically, mentally, emotionally and spiritually, to the point it has taken years for him to recover in a spiritual sense. This was very difficult for me to hear, as I completely believe my faith and spirituality were what kept me from getting killed, while living there.

I tried to encourage him, and make him see how fortunate he really is. No matter how much the demon tried to break him, he had enough reasoning ability left in his head to prevent him from reaching the point of no return. He did not succeed in taking his wife's life, nor did he take his own. He got out alive: *he won*.

The husband accredits his survival to his mother, who had passed before they moved into the house. He believes that she was probably the guiding force behind the protection they received, even considering the dangerous, and often tense situations that transpired.

Broad-sided by the outreach of this couple, I reflected: it is odd how life can thrust you head-on into a bond with a complete stranger. Sharing the sentiment, the three of us agreed.

So, how did the two find out about my book first book? Through a family member, who was informed by a coworker.

She immediately reached-out to her brother when she heard that the story had taken place in her brother's "old, haunted apartment." After connecting with her sibling, she advised him to contact me, given what occurred in the house during the course of their tenancy.

The male admits that it was extremely hard to bring up the past, as it has all but destroyed him. I do not doubt that, as I could hear it in his voice.

He stated that it was very difficult to revisit those days, yet at the same time, had found a bit of relief knowing that he and his wife were not alone in their plight. They finally found someone who could relate to them; someone who understood. This was important to them, as they had grown accustomed to being teased about their haunting ordeal at 207, by several people, including family.

Relative to tenants, the two were able to fill in gaps up to 1996. I was told that someone else moved into the second floor flat, after they fled.

According to the couple, the tenant, a woman, experienced problems with her boyfriend, but they were not privy to details. Apparently, a tenant moved into Betty's apartment following her death, but no further information is known.

In 1999, the city commenced with the revitalization project along the 19th Street corridor. 207 was completely vacated, and slated for demolition.

At almost 150-years-old, the house that once stood as a symbol of the American dream, was roped-off with yellow hazard tape: its shattered windows gazing onto 19th Street, holding a dark secret. Physically empty, the silent moans of lost souls were left swirling in the confines of the hell house.

The number of residents confirmed to have died while living at 207 19th Street, total: *14*. They are: Philamela Wood, Robert and Mary Campbell, Felix Cunningham, Dorothy Moran, Winifred Moran, Anna Moran, Mary Moran, Katharine Moran, Margaret LaLiberte, Peter Capozzelli, Christopher Carroll, my husband Jim, and Elizabeth "Betty" Keenan.

There are also two, unconfirmed, male suicides (aside from my husband), that are not included in the numbers. The number confirmed to have actually died *in the house:* 8.

Citing incomplete, and missing records (intentionally removed, or otherwise) as plausible reason, there are probably additional residents who took their last breath in the house.

Case #10: Name Withheld, 1983.

Location: Second Ave., and 25th Street.

In the fall of 1983, after struggling with a long illness, a much-loved, and well-known businessman, and member of the city, killed himself with a shotgun wound to the head. It is said that he had been suffering a terminal illness. Today, his family legacy and business, remain a big part of community.

8. RAZING HELL

"Be sober-minded; be watchful. Your adversary the devil prowls around like a roaring lion, seeking someone to devour."
1 Peter 5:8

I have truly tried to think that 207 19th Street was anything other than a house of horrors, but each time I attempted to find one reason to give it such credit, I thought about the lives that were lost while living there. It seemed to have transcended any normalcy in the life of most homes.

The deaths of *at least 14* residents is astounding. Expecting there to be perhaps a few throughout the history of an older home, it is perplexing, and very bothersome to survey the list. Sudden death, long illness, brief illness, suicide, and a few unknowns makes this a disconcerting, as well as remarkable finding.

The existence of multiple causes of death do not implicate demonic possession of every life lost, but it does indicate an infestation. The house, and land, are *sick*.

After the DeLollo family sold the property to Columbia 19th Street Development, the site was eyed as a prime, commercial property. Not only did 207, and the adjacent DeLollo properties meet their fate with at the claw of a backhoe, but the same destiny befell Sarah's homestead, as well as one of the Denardo family homes.

With 207's actual demo date remaining of particular interest, I sought the help of Columbia 19th Street Development. Initially, the secretary stated that I needed to speak with Mark Goldstein. After numerous telephone messages, I again, hit a wall of silence.

Despite the glitch, several sources imbedded within the city, corroborated information that the homes were razed sometime between late 1999, and early 2000. Other witnesses attest the demolition crews remained on-scene, working through the winter of '99.

A photograph of the house, as posted on the Facebook page of the Watervliet Historical Society, shows 211 19th Street (yellow brick), 207 (red brick), and a section of 205 (grey), 19th Street as vacated. A handwritten description of the photo reads: "19th Street – 2nd Avenue 10/1999." This information authenticates the verbal accounts relative to the approximate demo timeframe.

A peculiar piece of information came about by way of a discussion with community members. Many recall standing alongside 19th Street, and 2nd Avenue, watching from across the street, as the wrecking crew made its way through the old homes. Collectively, there was an air of sadness that I sensed in each individual; memories – mostly good – being yanked away. The city was undergoing more change.

Having heard some rather spine-chilling stories from the residents, I was not quite prepared for one witness account. According to a very reputable source who had watched the rigs take down the homes, 211 and 207 19th Street, were among the last to be taken down on that section of the block.

At one point shortly after 207 crumbled to the ground, the demo crew was halted by what the source described as "a foreman." Additional vehicles arrived on-site, and secured a perimeter by placing "sheet barriers," around a particular section of 207's lot. The witness also described seeing men wearing "paper suits" carrying "large pillow cases" to a certain spot. The witness stated that the men pulled "several items" from the debris.

The same source specifically saw what appeared to be "men's clothing – jeans and shoes," pulled from the rubble. These items, along with several others, were placed into the cloth bags. The witness states that they could not see what the other items were, but reiterated that their view afforded clear identification of the pants, and shoes.

After a few hours, the men in paper suits left. The barriers were removed, and the construction crew resumed with the task at-hand. To my source's knowledge, this type of situation did not transpire on any other section of the construction site. The witness was present, daily, all through the flattening of the block.

This witness account is quite incredible for a few reasons. The first is due to the fact that a *possible* body was found underneath the house. The second applies to the strange set of photographs that Carol and I took during our investigation of the lot, and surrounding area in November of 2011, that is detailed later in this book.

Lastly, two former tenants had experiences involving the basement. The tenant that moved into 207 after Jim's death, had specifically described his strange, recurring dream, relative to a dead body in the cellar.

The basement floor was unfinished, and has often been described as crushed gravel, or compact stone. It is quite possible that someone may have been intentionally interred there, or even buried in the cellar to cover-up a crime.

Discussion of the jeans and shoes does raise yet another question: if a body was found, was it entombed in anything? This is necessary to ask, due to a body's exposure to the elements.

An earthen grave would have more than likely caused extreme damage to the garments, making them next to impossible to identify. This was not the case; they were unmistakably described as a pair of dungarees, and a pair of men's shoes.

What I find fascinating about this situation, is the fact that the area was sectioned-off, and obscured from view (for the most part). The crew stopped; someone had to have made a call, or two, advising of a discovery. Aware of this story prior to contacting Columbia 19th Street Development in Albany, it was at the top of my list of questions for Goldstein.

There are laws relative to the unearthing of remains, and they entail strict protocol. It is a detailed and lengthy process to sort, measure and assess a scene, especially if it is rendered as part of a crime scene.

Typically, the coroner is alerted to investigate, and if need be, law enforcement, forensics, and even museum staff, if the site pertains to an archaeological find. The paperwork, and investigation can take months, even years, to finish.

In my opinion, I cannot help but think that the development company and crew, were given the green light to bypass standard protocol. Although several sacks of 'objects' were collected and removed from 207's lot, it is again, in my opinion, highly debatable that the situation was properly handled.

Think about it: the discovery of remains could have indefinitely put the project on hold, with fair chance that it may have completely sidelined the revitalization efforts. Was this yet another example of *looking the other way*, relative to the city, and its history?

With evidence of Indian encampments, as well as makeshift burial sites scattered throughout the city, there is reason to question why little-to-no documentation exists as to remains found within city limits. It is a reasonable question to ask, especially when to the north, south, east and west of the town, there *is* recorded evidence.

Even with the brief disruption, the demolition was finished. Pieces of the structures, inclusive of 207, were heaped into trucks, and carted away to the dump. The only remaining evidence as to the homes, or businesses which once lined the eastern end of 19th Street, is house number 215.

The site was then prepped, and the slate appeared to be clean, but not according to things existing on the spiritual plane. Oblivious to 207, and the surrounding land's history, the newly erected pharmacy settled in to its fresh environment.

With many sources feeding me a constant stream of information about the commercial property, I consulted an (unnamed) attorney. Making a determination that it was in my best interest to forgo any mention of the activities at the store, I have chosen two words for this topic: *no comment*.

People of all ages have confided in me, sharing their stories relative to the block. A very sweet, 85-year-old, life-long resident of Watervliet, came to one of my book signings. In front of others, she stated that for her *entire life*, she has never walked in front of 215, 211, 207, 205, or 203 19th Street. She, and her sister, always crossed the street at 3rd Avenue, and ventured along the south side.

She also described their aversion to looking at 207. She stated that the house was "very strange." The woman also spoke of having heard "some stories, years ago" relative to the house, but did not elaborate when I questioned her about them.

I have also spoken with an 87-year-old man who came to see me. He too, shared his family's experiences. Raised very close to 207, the kind man stated that he and his family had experienced decades of paranormal activity at their home. He elaborated by telling me that his mother and sisters religiously blessed their home twice each year, yet it never seemed to keep things quiet. When given the choice to keep the house himself, or pass it onto his sibling, he opted for the latter, as there were too many weird occurrences that took place. He was not comfortable there.

He also made mention of the fact that his family agreed to keep things hushed, and did not discuss the happenings with neighbors and friends, due to scrutiny and ridicule. That was a common statement spoken by many of the city's elderly. Those things were not to be shared, for fear of scorn.

What was extremely frightening for me, were the two individuals who came forward to tell me that a family member, two and three generations back, underwent a supposed possession, resulting in an exorcism. Only in one account, did the individual heal, while the other person was never quite the same.

In each instance, the family did not discuss this with outsiders, or community members. I sensed the embarrassment and fear in the voice of each source, and knew not to push them for additional details, in as much as I would have liked to. Underlying elements rang familiar with each; unusual behavior, bizarre, and unsettling acts.

Neither of the cases were like anything you see on television. Both spoke of unusual posturing of the bodies, but nothing freakishly contorted. Both victims appeared to denounce God, and went out of their ways to lash out at anything holy.

One source stated they were told the voice of the affected family member was distorted, and in each case they mentioned that the eyes were "black," or "dark." One source stated that they were told the relative "attacked family members, and scratched them." This individual was also said to have made very "unnatural motions," with their limbs.

No pivoting heads, projectile vomiting, scaling of the

walls and ceiling like a rabid cat, or obscene gestures with religious artifacts. I believe their stories are genuine.

Each story tied my stomach into knots; nearly vomiting from a few, disturbing details. After hearing one account, I had an awful nightmare, and had a very difficult time going back to sleep.

To this day, I have not been able to sit through *The Exorcist*, or anything similar. Ever since living at 207, I cannot even stand to see a commercial portraying demonic possession. I will turn the channel faster than a flash. Some laugh, but as I have said a thousand times; you cannot appreciate how terrifying something like that is, until you go through it.

Many stories surfaced, with a high number having transpired long before Jim's death, and prior to the release of *207*. I did find a handful of kooks that spouted nonsense, be it to get a rise out of me, or to gain written acknowledgement in this book. Luckily, it didn't take long to figure out who was legit, and who was not.

The more I heard throughout the course of my research, the more my feelings were validated. It was also growing more apparent that whatever had invaded 207, had possibly taken up residence very close by.

With discussion having taken place between my family and our former priest, it is highly suspected that Jim may have undergone an oppression, and possession. Whatever lurked in the house, or upon the land, certainly found a weak link in Jim's psyche, and quite sadly, wormed its way in. It took less than a year for it to career my husband down a path of death, and destruction.

Conversation relative to this aspect has taken place several times. Strangers have remarked that Jim's behavior and suicide was due to drinking, and drugs; that there is no way he was possessed. What many fail to understand is that demonic forces *target* those whom are weakened. It is through these *fractures* that they seek to enter a person.

Drugs, alcohol, mental illness, physical illness, and

even sleep deprivation are fractures that lower a threshold. An addiction, or propensity to indulge in ways that actively lower the gate, invite-in trouble. Living in the wrong environment can be disastrous. This is exactly what happened with Jim.

The following is an excerpt from my blog. It is a good summary of demonic oppression and possession:

"Depending upon different religious doctrine, the premise of demonic energy is the same: it stems from a lower order of angels that fell to Earth from God, or from the Creator's grace. Most religious doctrines agree that no matter the origin, demonic energy is malevolent and inhuman, governed by hatred, and looks for every means possible in order to obliterate anything in its unholy path.

Demonic energy fears anything Godly, and therefore reacts by creating aversions to all that goodness and God represents. An example of this is illustrated when a blessing, or exorcism takes place: the demonic energy is fearful of being cast-out and fights the actions to expel it from the host, or environment.

Demonic oppression is a blend of a human's free-will and lack of control over the physical, mental and emotional state of their Being. In theory, it is something that happens as a result of what an individual does – and does not do. An oppression is something that can over an abbreviated, or longer duration of time. The venue is often due to exposure to dark, or demonic energy whether intentional, or not.

There is a laundry list of intentional actions that can open the channels and create a conducive environment for a dark, or demonic energy to inhabit a space, or attempt to form an attachment on a human. Instances of intent include a willingness to conduct unholy chants, recite Satanic spells or incantations, use of Ouija Boards, actively seeking Satanic or dark energies for entertainment, and misuse of Tarot or other divination tools. Each of these actions opens the door for a demonic force to cross, and makes way for horrific, and often tragic, opportunity.

Once an exposure to a demonic energy occurs, regardless of reason, the facilitation can take on a number of characteristics in the host, including but not limited to: absence, or loss in the belief and, or fear, of God, conflict with authority, lack of life purpose, committing acts of hatred and, or violence, irrational fear, anxiety, lack of self-control, a hunger for power and attainment through cruel means, hopelessness and depression that is not a result of a medical condition. Through time, these characteristics can worsen and in turn, lead to a full-blown demonic possession.

Once an individual has been oppressed, the function of the demonic energy is to fulfill its desire to annihilate. Symptoms of a demonic possession include, but are not limited to: extremely reckless behaviors such as violence, lack of self-respect and respect for others, extreme verbal and sexual vulgarity, obsessively wielding power, uncontrolled sexual expression and behaviors, obsession with pornography, split-personality, changed appearance (black, or soulless eyes), distorted vocal annunciation, denouncement of all that is Godly, affirmation of Satan, mania, despondency, and thoughts of committing murder and, or suicide.

Regardless, the basis of oppression and possession remain the same: a demonic energy will seek out a weakened individual and attempt to take over the physical body in order to carry-out their work. With every oppression and possession, the ultimate goal is to destroy, be it by means of murder, death, suicide or the will to create mass chaos.

Some people are shocked to find out that men take the lead in oppressions and possessions. When I state that the "host" – or physical body – in which a demonic entity will seek is weakened, I am referring to the emotional, psychological and spiritual states of the individual, more than the actual physical state of the host. A person may appear to be physically strong, but that does not mean they are protected from an oppression or possession. On the same token, a physically weak individual does not equal susceptibility. There are many factors to consider and each leads to a common ground: weakening the host.

Drug and alcohol abuse, inclusive of prescription medications abuse (such as narcotics and mind-altering, or brain chemistry altering drugs), can weaken an individual's mental and emotional state, thus making them a candidate for an oppression and possession. Every instance of drug or alcohol abuse alters mental status and leads to the inability to maintain mental and physical stability. The impact from abused drugs and, or alcohol, and even misuse of OTC (Over the Counter) medication and herbs, lowers spiritual energy. When the spiritual energy becomes weakened, the dark, or demonic energies can overpower the host.

Those who have histories of drug and, or alcohol abuse tend to have self-destructive tendencies, by which demonic energies thrive upon. Additionally, self-doubt and impaired reasoning, become a perfect environment for the initial oppression to take place. Remember: the main goal of a dark, negative or demonic energy, is to create as much conflict and destruction that it can.

By attaching itself to the host, the demon seeks out fulfillment of these desires, and can cause the host to take-part in increasingly bad, and unhealthy behaviors. In cases where an attachment has occurred in a host whom has had issues with drug and, or alcohol abuse, the host's addictive behavior will likely progress, and even worsen. The demon has a "craving" that is sought-out by the host's physical ability to "feed" it. This also includes excessive, and increased smoking, and even severe cases of overeating.

Mental health issues and disease are very serious issues that need to be understood and respected; they can happen to anyone, at any time. Some individuals are more prone to them due to genetic predisposition, but certain life situations may also cause someone with no familial history, to find themselves depressed, or facing a mental health crisis. Either way, an individual who may be afflicted with certain mental health issues, are mentally and emotionally more likely to be eyed as a host.

A demonic energy will try to mentally "break" the host, or in other words, wear them down, in an attempt to control their thoughts, feelings and actions. In an oppression the energy will try to manifest in various ways such as: hallucinations (auditory and visual), sleep deprivation, anger and isolation of the host from family and, or friends, create false perceptions, lack of trust, paranoia, fatigue, and intermittent loss of control and awareness relative to the host's body/mind function (memory lapse).

Personal faith and spirituality in an individual is perhaps the best defense against an oppression and possession. As expected, a demonic force opposes all that is Godly, and good. Every individual, no matter what their faith or spiritual belief, is subject to moments in life when they question their purpose, or direction, or even if God, a Creator, exists.

The determining factor in an oppression and possession relative to personal spirituality occurs when an individual crosses a threshold and denounces God, or their Creator. Individuals whom have been infiltrated by a demonic attack tend to spiral downwards to a place of spiritual darkness, hopelessness, pity, shame and fear.

A host suffering from an oppression and possession will "see" demons, and speak in a manner completely different than, prior to the attack. The host will have an outward aversion to what is perceived as holy, such as spoken and, or written words, photographs, likenesses or symbols that relate to God, a Creator, angels, Jesus Christ, the Holy Spirit, or even to prayer and blessings. Hosts will lash-out and verbalize their lack of respect and hatred to all that is Godly, and in turn, develop physical characteristics such as distorted facial expressions and voice inflections that can be deemed as maniacal, or other-worldly. The focus of a host is to rebuke any form of goodness, love, light and God.

To start, an individual who appears to be, or thinks that they may be suffering from an oppression and, or a possession must honestly evaluate every aspect of their life and be willing to accept light, love and God, or Creator, in to it. This includes a willingness to get rid of anything that is Satanic, or unholy in nature including books, documents, media, tools, clothing etc., that is used for, or in part of anything that is dark and, or demonic in nature. Additionally, one must seek forgiveness by those whom they have committed any atrocities towards, and ask that light, love and God, or Creator, govern over their physical, mental, emotional and spiritual Being.

In certain situations, a demon may need to be cast-out by means of an exorcism, in order to relieve the host of the possession. It takes someone skilled and versed in exorcisms, to safely conduct one. An exorcism should never be attempted by a lay-person, or novice. This is not fodder for the foolish. Many faiths believe in casting out demonic spirits and most faiths have specifically trained professionals to take charge of the task."

The history of exorcism relative to Christianity is quite intriguing. The New Testament paints Jesus as the most well-known exorcist (Luke 8:26-39, Mark 1:25, Mark 8:23).

Many religious instructors, theologians, and clergy members believe that the healings Jesus performed, were actually exorcisms. There is even reference to demonic forces having been exorcised from Mary Magdalene. I could not find any direct reference as to who may have cast them out, although it is suspected that it may have been Jesus.

The casting of demons was initially an honored tradition, and deemed a very special *holy gift*. In turn, exorcisms grew to become a significant part of tradition in the early church. In the end, it paved the way for the Catholic Church to develop laws relating to the *Solemn Rite of Exorcism.*

I spoke with a priest about this very practice. I was advised that the Solemn Rite of Exorcism is performed *only* by an ordained priest whom has been "granted permission by a bishop." It is important to note that other rituals of exorcism are practiced by many individuals and faiths, with less stringent guidelines. Interested parties must attend Vatican-sponsored classes.

As would be expected, the training of priests for the rite is highly rigorous, and intense. It involves a great deal of classroom instruction. Entrants must actively work underneath a credentialed exorcist.

The effectiveness of a rite depends on two crucial aspects: the faith of the priest performing the exorcism, and permission from a higher level church official. This is important to note, given what may, or may not have transpired while Sheehan was in charge of St. Patrick's.

According to my interviews with priests located in different states, the diocese has a designated priest whom has been specifically trained to perform an exorcism. This is fairly typical practice for most diocese within the United States. The names of the priest and the possessed, are kept guarded. The same applies to any relative church files. I can certainly appreciate why this is routine practice.

My sources state that a request to look into an oppression, or possession occurs when a member of the church speaks with their community pastor. Depending on exact location and specific protocol, most priests will interview the affected person, and send them to have a series of evaluations. In other words: they don't just jump in, and perform the ceremony.

In the case of my late husband, everything was addressed on the basis of hindsight, and no case had been opened. Time was not on our side, and the events that occurred in 207, came to a climax by means of a slow boil.

As detailed in *207*, any attempt to call our priest, even for a house blessing, was met with Jim's extreme hostility, as he deliberately prevented the intervention, thus masking the warning signs. This was just one sign.

There are many different types of demons, and each comes with its own calling card. The only commonality between the lots: their appetite for annihilation.

Aside from what I had outlined in my blog post, additional signs and symptoms that a demon may have invaded a person include: lack of appetite, a very cold feeling enveloping the room, physical outbursts and attacks, *cutting*, unusual strength, and the ability to speak another language (not learned).

The following information is to be used for perspective, and as a basic understanding of the process of an exorcism, relative to the Catholic Church. *They are in no way to be deemed as instructions.*

In no specific order: the ritual must be performed by an exorcist that has been granted permission by a bishop (or, priest of a higher order). Multiple witnesses need to be present at the time of the rite, and the ceremony is forbidden to be announced. This is a highly secretive ritual, which I was made well aware of, while interviewing the relatives of those who underwent an exorcism.

This contrasts greatly with all of the hype that modern programming features on some paranormal shows, whereas the more cameras and theatrics for the exorcism, the better. This approach often exposes those present, to potential physical, and spiritual hazards.

There is a specific order of events that transpire before, during, and after the rite. Prior to, the priest must go to confession. Anyone (family, or otherwise), who will be attending the ceremony needs to do the same. Since the priest actually conducts spiritual warfare with the demon, it is extremely important that he is physically, mentally, and emotionally capable to perform the exorcism. A health assessment is a big part of the preparation, prior to the rite.

As for rite attire: most priests wear a specially designated vestment, and scarf. The exorcist will also read from their personal bible.

Exorcisms can be potentially physically, as well as spiritually dangerous. More times than not, the affected party needs to be restrained before the ceremony. This is done to protect everyone in attendance.

From start to finish, the exorcist must follow specific rules as outlined by the Vatican, in order to perform the ceremony. With prayer, and the laying of hands, the exorcism commences.

Contrary to popular belief, not all exorcisms are completely effective on the first go-round. This is something that the general public needs to be leery of, when someone claims that a demonologist, or exorcist can guarantee the ability to cast out demons. The same applies to those that charge for the service. That is a red flag, indicating someone is taking advantage of people in unfortunate situations.

I was informed that there have been multiple cases that have taken priests weeks, up to years, to exorcise the demon(s). Additionally, there is *no known way to predetermine, or direct, where the demon(s) will flee, once it leaves the possessed host.*

This has long been a concern with the razing of 207. The number of deaths, high incident rate for suicides in the house and immediate, as well as surrounding area, indicate a heavy-duty problem. In my opinion, although the house was demolished, the demon(s) seem to have stayed.

Speaking about this aspect with many, most all agree that the danger of conducting an exorcism on-site, or nearby, could scatter the malevolent forces a couple of feet, a few blocks, or beyond. It is an extremely dangerous undertaking, and careful consideration is something that needs to be given in the event one is ever performed.

Removing religious affiliation from the equation, spiritual warfare is a must when faced with an infestation, or possible oppression, and possession. It becomes a literal battle of the wills, and can be exhausting.

Learning to say the Rosary was something my grandmother and mother taught me at a fairly young age. Catechism, or Sunday school, further instilled values. As an adult, I find great peace in the hours just prior to going to sleep, whereas I say my prayers, and count my blessings.

After moving into 207, an interesting dynamic took place: Jim pulled away from the church, while I held onto every ounce of faith that I could muster, relying heavily on prayer and meditation, to protect my family. My mother and grandmother were also a source of strength, and spiritual support.

Jim had been an altar boy in his church. Our dear priest had known him for many years. It was puzzling, and rather distressing to see my husband change, especially when it came time to baptize our son.

By November of '88, Jim had stopped attending church. He slowly began to act out against all things pertaining to religion, including religious items such as his grandfather's crucifix, and a photograph of my grandmother with the Pope. Additionally, he went through great lengths to prevent our priest from blessing the house. His anger and tone became hostile.

I have often thought about that night in 207, when I had a horrific dream. I was chased by pure evil. Flames licked at my feet and body as I ran, holding my infant son close to me. I was terrified beyond words.

Armed with my bible, I sat in 207's living room, and prayed. Unintentionally opening the book to *Psalm 11*, I felt the demon nearby, and needed to create an impenetrable shield. I recited the psalm out loud.

Years later, I can feel the strength of those words, as I have with many prayers that I still keep in my repertoire. It is not my goal to preach, but to point out the irony in message of the psalm. It could not have been more appropriate for that present time, or for the future.

My understanding of the psalm may be different than another, but the basis is more than likely similar. There is a great deal of irony relative the words, and what my personal interpretation imparts.

My understanding: when the going gets tough, the tough hold onto their faith, and keep going. Those who do not know God, tend to target those of us who do. It's an age-old philosophy of the battle between good, and evil.

In turn, it is spiritually important that one does not run away when faced with adversity, or challenged by those who seek to destroy; we need to stand, and fight for what we believe in. This strength comes from having the assurance in God.

As much as I wanted to run out of the house screaming that night, especially after Jim shrieked in his sleep moments after I had gone into the living room in a fright, I knew that I had to stay and protect my family. At the very least, I had to try. I believed with my heart and soul, that God was going to protect us.

Had I only knew that Jim was at the very least oppressed at that point, I may have been a bit more aware of what we were dealing with, and what I needed to do. Regardless, I knew that it was something unlike anything I had ever – and have ever – experienced. It was menacing, and extremely dangerous.

My grandmother gave me a prayer to recite after Jim's strange reaction to her photo with the Pope, and removal of the crucifix from our bedroom wall. *Saint Michael the Archangel's Prayer of Protection*, became part of my spiritual warfare, long before ghost hunting shows became popular.

As a medium, and paranormal investigator, it has been one of the first prayers that I say when going into a client's home, conducting a reading, or when sensing danger. It is a prayer that is also widely used in the paranormal community, in general.

It reads: "Saint Michael the Archangel, defend us in battle. Be our protection against the wickedness and snares of the devil. May God rebuke him, we humbly pray; and do Thou, O Prince of the Heavenly Host – by the Divine Power of God – cast into hell, Satan and all the dark spirits, who roam throughout the world seeking the ruin of souls. Amen."

Beyond a single doubt, I believe that Jim's lowered threshold from drinking, and smoking pot, created a fracture that allowed for the demon(s) to enter, thus turning him into a host. I find it no coincidence that the same situation presented itself with the husband and wife who moved into the house, just months after Jim's suicide.

Having been told of two other suicides having taken place at the house, I wonder if they too, had fractures. Understanding that physical illness can weaken the Spiritual Self, I suspect that perhaps someone with a serious illness may have fallen susceptible to a demonic attack, resulting in the inability to cope and deal with the sickness.

With fair certainty, there does not appear to have been a suicide in 207 between the years of 1972, and 1988. Based upon so many findings, it is interesting to ponder why things were so quiet back then.

Another incredible happening led me to the possible answer of that thought. It came by means of doing a happen-chance reading for a friend of mine named Angela, in April, 2013.

I first met Angela in the fall of 2012, at a book signing in Upstate New York. From the moment she introduced herself to me, I knew that she was a spunky, no-nonsense gal, with a heart and smile as big as the ocean. While on my trip, I conducted a private reading for her.

Periodically, I touch-base with Angela, to see how she is doing. It was no different on Saturday, April 13th, 2013, as we had once again connected thru Facebook. She had contacted me this time, asking if I was picking up on anything unusual that was going on around her. Already uneasy about something, I told her that I needed to wait a few days, in order to see what I picked up on. I told her that I was going to get back to her on Monday, or Tuesday of the following week.

That subsequent Sunday night, into Monday morning, I established spirit contact with a *priest*. Odd, I thought. I woke up and recorded the communication in my dream diary. It was approximately 6:20AM.

In light of the severity of the communication, I digested things, had coffee and went back to the dream diary at approximately 9:12AM. The dates and times are recorded in my journal.

I began to message Angela about the spirit communication, sometime in the neighborhood of 9:51AM, after I had finished recording the details in my book. As stated, the spirit who contacted me was a priest. He was associated with my friend in a very bonded, familial type of way. He gave me very specific details. I had no idea about her family's relationship with him.

His face was serene, and pure. His jowls were offset by a kind smile that seemed to be somewhat overshadowed by a burden. Behind a pair of modest reading glasses, his eyes showed concern. He exuded tranquility, yet carried a powerful series of messages. Angela told me that I described "Father Emery" to a "t."

Father Emery gave me three distinctly different messages. One was for Angela, another for two men that I believe to be Father Emery's family members, and the third was for his 'home' community. The overall essence of his spirit was strength, love – and caution.

Early into the communication, the priest had shown me a dark church. Inside, large groups of men gathered to listen to someone standing on a podium, dressed in a deep, red robe. The robes were not symbolic of anything relative to the Catholic Church, but were more archaic in design. Something felt 'off' about the attire; it was as though they were costumes.

A leader of sorts, spoke at the make-shift platform in

the altar section of the church. Robed men approached the leader and bowed down; their hands to the ground. Upon resuming the standing position, the leader gave them each a dark bag. When the two men turned around, I noticed that their faces were *painted* white, concealing a darker complexion from underneath.

The ghostly makeup ran down their faces in white streaks. Their eyes were dark. They did not smile. They took the sacks, and left.

Two, by two, other men dressed in red robes with white painted faces approached the head of the gathering, received their satchels, and left the church. I did not like the feeling. Father Emery insisted I watch.

The contact was also mingled with personal information pertaining to Angela that I will not reveal. The priest then showed me something that still stands out. The details are vivid, and have not faded with the passing of time.

Father Emery loved his hometown, his parish and his community, just as much as they loved him. In this particular portion of the contact, he seated me in front of a *packed* Catholic Church, while he conducted a large funeral service.

He waved a thurible to and fro, sending dense incense into the congregation. He prayed aloud, as the communicants wept.

Side, to side, the lantern swung on its chain. It seemed as though thousands were crammed into the church pews, clutching one another's hands, praying along with him. He was tending to his flock; I was sitting amidst a community in grief. I felt their sorrow. I felt his strength, and compassion: I also felt his pain.

Father Emery was wearing a white alb that flowed to the floor, but even he too, was surrounded by a sea of parishioners. Everyone was dressed in green.

Through prayer, Father Emery said that we were *to have hope, no matter how bad things would be*. Somehow, he was going to guide his flock through it.

Via Facebook, I asked Angela several questions, and also advised her that there was a very strong warning associated with this spirit communication. I told her as much as there was good that came through, there was also a heavy warning.

Throughout the late morning of Monday, April 15th, Angela kept in contact with me, answering my questions. She also shared how special Father Dominic *Emery* Parillo was to her.

Rev. Parillo, known to the Watervliet community as *Father Emery*, had been Angela's priest throughout her entire life. He was very close to her clan, and had baptized her daughter in 2006.

Many of the details that I had recorded in the dream diary were validated by Angela, although we were a bit confused as to why the priest gave me such a dire message. It seemed more global than personal, in relationship to my friend.

At 2:49 p.m. that afternoon, the Boston Marathon was crippled by two pressure cooker bombs. Three innocent people lost their lives, including a child. The city, and the nation, was devastated.

Within minutes after the bombings, Angela and I were able to reconnect. The two of us were in shock. Although the warning fit the tragedy, we did not understand the relationship between Father Emery, and Boston. We were stumped, and also disturbed by the terrible series of events that had just emerged.

On a quest to find out what the connection was, I began to google Father Emery's name. It then became quite apparent as to the association with his warnings, inclusive of the sea of green, relative to the good priest.

Father Dominic Emery Parillo was a native of Boston, Massachusetts. There, he served the Catholic community for several years, until he was transferred to Watervliet. Father Emery was the local priest for *Our Lady of Mount*

Carmel.

It was during this time that he became close to Angela and her family, and baptized her daughter at St. Patrick's Church. After retirement, he moved back to his beloved Boston, where he died in 2012.

I quickly messaged Angela the information. She had completely forgotten about the Boston connection!

It all made sense at that point. The two men with white paint dripping from their disguised faces were the terrorists. The sacks that they gathered were perhaps, the backpacks that carried the explosives.

They became radicalized, and with a leader on the pulpit, it was as though these two were following instruction, or inspired to carry out a heinous mission.

Sadly, there were many others walking to the platform, following the two that left with bags in-hand; paint running down their cheeks.

Father Emery came through with the warning. For some reason, he chose me as his messenger.

As for Father Emery's liturgy of hope and inspiration: he insisted that we remain strong. More so, that we unite, and show our strength in force. He was letting everyone know that he was mourning alongside Boston, and the nation. The same applies to his relationship with Angela, as Father Emery still watches over her.

That afternoon changed my life in so many ways. Angela stated the same. It was by far, one of the most powerful communications that I have had.

The more I heard about this kind priest, the more I felt as though I knew him. He was the fabric that wove the cloth of the community; he meant so much, to many.

Just prior to finishing *Saints*, I received a phone call from the sister of the husband-wife tenants at 207. She is also Vinny's sister. She wanted to share something with me.

A long while back, she had moved out of state, and occasionally returned to Watervliet to visit family. One of her routine stops included a visit to see her brother Vinny, and his wife, who had lived on the first floor at 207 19th Street.

Not too long after Vinny and his wife had moved into their apartment, the sister had come home to visit the couple, and was seated at the kitchen table. Vinny's wife took her out to 207's small, backyard lot. Passing by the basement door, Vinny's wife remarked that she hated the basement; it made her very uncomfortable, yet did not elaborate as to why.

I was told that something had disturbed Vinny's wife to the point that she asked her priest to bless the house on a *monthly basis*. The priest visited 207, and blessed their flat, along with the stairwell, and common areas of the house. Her priest's name: *Father Emery*.

Just prior to the time Jim and I moved into our second floor flat at 207, Vinny and his wife divorced. After she left the house, Father Emery stopped coming by to bless it. This is quite remarkable, as I have pondered the reason the house appeared to be 'quiet' for several years.

Someone was keeping the devil at bay, and I, along with many others, tend to think that Father Emery was just the person to be able to do it. He was a protector.

After more than two decades of staving-off a dark energy, his presence was no longer requested at the house, and all hell broke loose. One of its most violent outbursts occurred on June 28th, 1989.

Years passed, and the house was ultimately destroyed. Metaphorically speaking; the city had razed hell. For some, it's 'out of sight, and out of mind.'

Blessed be the fool who becomes complacent about such matters. For in the spirit realm, what we cannot see, tends to be far more powerful and dangerous, than what we can.

Case #11: Name Withheld, 1992.
Location: Third Avenue and 23rd Street.

In 2012, I was contacted by a man who had read my first book. He stated that the similarities between his brother and Jim, were uncanny and very distressing.

For years, he and his family have discussed the possibility that something had taken over their loved one, as they all saw a change in his behavior and appearance, shortly after moving from Cohoes, to his apartment.

The family member stated that he was always a social drinker, but not an alcoholic. He kept a fulltime job for years, and had two children that he doted on.

Upon moving into his second floor apartment, he started to isolate himself, and withdraw. His drinking increased, and he had a difficult time sleeping. More disturbing is the fact that he also began to hear what he called, a 'male voice.' The man states that no family members suffer from mental illness.

Just before his suicide, the man began to 'cut' himself. Trying to get his brother help proved exhausting, and unsuccessful. He also had sporadic bouts of anger, and lashed-out at family and friends.

In late summer of 1992, the middle-aged man shot and killed himself with a shotgun. He left no note. The last family members to speak with him said that he could not cope with the voice he kept hearing. The obituary that I was shown confirms his name, date of death, the location as *"at home"* and states *"unexpectedly, after a brief illness."*

JILL MARIE MORRIS

9. MADNESS & MURDER

"The world was getting dangerously crowded with crazy people."
John Dunning

It has been my heart-felt pleasure to listen to many members of the Watervliet community share their personal stories with me. The more nostalgic memories have included roller-skating down the middle of the streets, playing stickball, ice-skating at the rink, or on the river, attending large parades, dances and socials, and religious worship. Just like many other small towns, the community of Watervliet is an extended family, connected by a range of memories born from good times, and bad.

Most of their stories heavily rely on ancestral anecdotes that have been passed down for many decades. The spookier of stories seem to withstand the test of time.

Given the number of people that I have spoken with since I began writing this book, it has been interesting to find the community divided, relative to its knowledge of the city's history, and how it correlates with the spiritual, and paranormal worlds. Most of the elders are aware of the more unsavory stories, as are some of the more current populations. On the other hand, there are also some who remain completely clueless.

An interesting dynamic took place when I was approximately three quarters of the way finished with this project. Many discussions often led to heated debate as to documented accounts. I was shocked to find that a fairly large number of people – consisting of all age groups – do not believe that the Native Americans lived within city limits.

The same applies to other articles and documents provided to them, relative to Potter's Fields, and the treacherous canal period. For those that fall into a more skeptical mind; they think the stories of make-shift burial grounds are nothing but a bunch of rubbish.

Out of all the people whom I have interviewed, roughly one third have admitted to hearing stories pertaining to the seedier side of the city. These individuals also confess to being fully aware that something dark has loomed over Watervliet for hundreds of years – this according to familial tales, and encounters. Fascinating is the fact that nearly all of the elderly that fall into that category, have experienced some type of unexplainable, paranormal phenomenon.

Asking both groups as to their thoughts on the city's odd history, the elderly have mixed feelings as to the cause. Some believe the Native Americans once cursed the land, while others think that immigrants may have cursed the town; mainly the Irish.

A smaller number believe that there is something ancient, perhaps more demonic going on, confiding in me that they are very well aware of the city's high number of suicides, in addition to its murder-driven residents. Indeed, something extraordinarily wicked, this way comes.

I have been quite intrigued by the younger crowd,

given their interest in paranormal programming, and related movies that have surged over the last several years. Whether they are too young to appreciate the history, too scared to believe it could be true, or simply refuse to accept it, many think that it is hearsay, hocus pocus.

For those that do believe something is amok, they have either had an experience, or know of someone they trust, who has. There are also those who have been brought up listening to generational yarns, and as a result, hold a quiet respect for the spirit world. This includes people of all faiths, with a higher percentage being of the *Catholic* religion. Imagine that?

I admit to being intrigued, having been told about odd personal experiences, peculiar news stories, and secret goings-on in the neighborhood. After a few of the more senior members had mentioned the same stories, I could not but help, and look into them.

To truly comprehend the impact that history has had upon the town, I implore the reader to understand just how small Watervliet is. Covering less than 2 square miles radius, it is not an overgrown, excessively populated area. On the same token, even though the town is not known for million dollar homes boasting large yards, it isn't a shanty town, or slum-ridden municipality either. It's a middle class, white and blue collar city, with a large elderly population.

Upon commencement of digging into old tales told, I uncovered a pattern of murder, madness and mayhem, that I had previously been unaware. Together, these locally publicized stories further signaled the existence of something quite malevolent. They also demonstrate an increasingly violent movement.

The first story that I stumbled upon described the death of John Weston, in 1873. Weston lived in Brooklyn with his wife. Having survived the Civil War, his life ended on a rather gruesome, and extremely violent note in of all places: Watervliet.

For some unknown reason, in early August of 1873, Weston left Brooklyn with his neighbor, Emil Lowenstein. Lowenstein was Weston's barber. For reasons unknown, the two city boys, ventured north, and into Watervliet.

Weston was murdered. His body was discovered in an in a field, somewhere in Watervliet.

Practically decapitated, Weston's throat had been sliced open. He was also shot numerous times in the head, and upper body area. A gents' razor was found near his body, along with a card inscribed with the name of a Brooklyn barber.

Tell-tale signs of a deadly plan were uncovered, as the investigation revealed that Weston had drained his family's entire savings days before he vanished. On the other hand, Lowenstein did not.

Shortly after Lowenstein returned to the city, he spent a wad of cash. This made the barber climb the ladder of suspicion.

The smoking gun, appears to have been an actual gun. Lowenstein demanded his wife ditch one of his. If that didn't scream guilt, I'm not too sure what does.

Cops continued to investigate the case, closing in on Lowenstein. Unsure as to why the gun-stashing wasn't enough to raise doubt, his wife finally realized her husband was involved in the crime.

After a series of findings faulted Lowenstein, detectives arrested him, and took him back to Watervliet. He was later convicted of murder.

Professing his innocence up to the very end, Lowenstein met his fate by noose in April, 1874. He is buried in *St. Mary's Cemetery* in Albany, New York.

The exact location of Weston's murder remains unknown. Based upon description, my guess is that it occurred close to, or on, the old Bleecker, or Oothout Farms.

* * * * * * * *

Another peculiar occurrence transpired right along 19th Street, on April 13th, 1929. The newspaper article in the Troy NY Daily Times, Saturday Evening, April 13th, 1929 edition states: 'Find Baby's Body – Trooper Discover Nude Body of Child in Ditch on 19th Street – Had not Died of Exposure, Coroner Believes. . . The body of a baby boy, apparently three months old, was found this morning in a ditch on 19th street adjoining the property of William Armstrong. The discovery was made by Sergeant Walter F. Reilly and Trooper William Bonzyck, of the Latham Barracks, who were passing in an automobile. The baby, fully developed, was in a nude state. Coroner Edward J. Cusack was called and had the body taken to Parker's Undertaking Parlors. No marks of any description could be found on the body. The Coroner said he was dropped from a passing automobile and was dead at the time, he having found no evidence the child had died from exposure." (Troy Times, 1929)

This story completely sickened me. I could not find any reference as to whether or not, the child's body was ever identified.

* * * * * * * *

Apropos for such a disturbing chapter, the infamous story of Watervliet resident Joseph Mascari, once again, forced the city center-stage in 1942. Mascari was a truck driver who went on a murderous rampage with his lover Anna Gelina. Gelina was from across the river, in Troy.

Motivated by his affair with the younger Gelina, Mascari killed his wife Rose O'Connell. Her badly beaten body was found in the Town of Sullivan, in mid-December, of the same year.

According to reports, the woman was pummeled so severely, the State Police could only identify her through her eyewear. Family made the final identification, once the troopers discovered her name.

Believed to be the last to see O'Connell, Mascari and Gelina were arrested: Mascari confessed. In the course of interrogation, the animal admitted he killed his wife by bashing-in her head with a hammer.

Mascari stated that the events were not premeditated. He also claimed that he, along with wife (O'Connell), their daughter, and his lover (Gelina), left Watervliet, to go for a seemingly, innocent ride.

At some point in the course of the jaunt, an altercation ensued. Mascari whipped out a hammer – that just so happened to be in the car – and attacked her. The woman was left for dead, alongside the creek.

Mascari was indicted, however, Gelina was not. He was convicted of murder, and sentenced to death.

In January of 1944, Mascari was put to death by a juicy jolt from Sing Sing's notorious electric chair. A cold-blooded killer from Watervliet, he never apologized for his acts, nor did he display any signs of regret for the foul crime.

* * * * * * * *

In May, 1990, yet another Watervliet citizen derailed, and went off the deep end. Ronald Latham, a resident of the city, killed his former girlfriend, Marie Shambeau.

Latham, who was a nurse, claimed that he was terribly upset, and could not deal with the fact that Shambeau had ended their relationship. I'm sorry, but that is just pathetic.

Reports show that Latham viciously knifed, and strangled the woman. Shambeau's parents found her clinging to life, and called the paramedics.

Shambeau underwent surgery, but suffered a stroke. A combination of injuries from the attack, along with the stroke, Shambeau was paralyzed. She was later transferred to a long-term care facility. There, the woman continued to fight for her life.

Latham turned himself in, and was charged with Second Degree Murder, as well as First Degree Assault. Initially, he was sentenced to serve several years in prison. In my opinion, that seems like a rather light judgment, bearing in mind the brutality of the crime.

Sadly, just weeks after Latham was sentenced, Shambeau died from complications. Latham's sentence was changed, due to the circumstances.

Despite two, appeals, Latham lost, and remains guilty of murder. He is currently serving a 25-year term, in a New York State prison.

* * * * * * * *

Something else caught my eye, relative to mentionable happenings in the city. I was going to insert this into the *Asylum* chapter, but felt it was more appropriate to do so, here.

On February 10th, 1996, John Moran of the Daily Gazette reported the following: "Police probe another death at St. Colman's. 1943 case is third alleged fatal beating at orphanage; other complaints come in." (Moran, 1996)

This time, the Colonie Police Department looked into the death of Andrew Rada. Rada was only 6-years-old when he lived at the orphanage, in the early '40s.

As with many reports pertaining to children who died in orphanages, Rada's death was listed as caused by pneumonia. Reports surfaced that the child's true cause of death was due to beatings initiated by the nuns.

The police department did not question the orphanage's determination. How this is possible, given other mysterious deaths at the home, is beyond unbelievable.

I did not find any follow-up to these claims, and suspect the police department may have been overwhelmed, overburdened – or, quite possibly, told to keep quiet. What a terrible shame.

* * * * * * * *

The next story not only shocked the community of Watervliet, but has all the markings of a true scandal. The shock waves of the incident tore through the Catholic Church and its tightly-knit community, like a tornado.

The widely debated suicide - or murder - of Father John Minkler left the Albany Catholic Diocese in a lurch. It was far too soon after the sex abuse scandals had rocked Catholics, worldwide.

In part, Rev. Minkler's obituary in the Albany Times Union, dated February 22, 1994 states: "Father Minkler was born in Troy, N.Y. and attended Sacred Heart Elementary School in Troy and graduated from Catholic Central High School. He attended Mater Christi Seminary School in Albany, for his minor seminary (A.A.) and the University Seminary in Ottawa, Canada for his major seminary (B.A., B. Th. University of Ottawa and B. Ph., S.T.B., St. Paul University, Ottawa). Father was ordained a priest on May 13, 1972 by the Most Reverend Edwin B. Broderick at the Cathedral of the Immaculate Conception, Albany, N.Y. . . ." (Albany Times Union, 2004)

Minkler was a very active member of the Catholic community of Upstate New York, and served at churches in both Troy, as well as Rensselaer. He was also well-loved, by parish members.

On February 15th, 2004, Minkler's body was discovered in his Watervliet apartment. According to reports, his sister found the priest on the kitchen floor.

Story has it, that Rev. Sipperly told Minkler's sister to check on her brother. He alleged Minkler left him a message asking that she do so, because he was not feeling well. Upon her arrival, the sister realized that Minkler was dead. There was a bottle of prescription medication next to his body.

To some, this may appear to be a cut and dry suicide,

but to many, more specifically members of Albany's Catholic community, it was fishy. This is why . . .

The story behind this case originated nine years prior to the priests death, when Minkler had been connected to a tell-all communication addressed to Archbishop O'Connor. Basically, the letter detailed claims against Bishop Hubbard, stating that the priest was gay, and had abused community members.

The entire debacle may have contributed to Minkler's suicide - or murder. A few months after the priest's death, the Albany County Coroner stated that Minkler's cause of death was *suicide*.

What makes this case such a sore subject, is the fact that just days prior to his death, Minkler had requested to meet with Bishop Hubbard. He was going to tell Hubbard that he never wrote the letter, or made claims, as another priest had stated.

The letter infuriated Hubbard, and the others, as it accused them of abuse. Hubbard has long-maintained his innocence in these matters.

With a coroner-rendered verdict of suicide, little was done to appease Watervliet, and the Catholic community. After my own discussions with sources, many believe Minkler's death is at the very least suspicious, and more indicative of murder, rather than suicide.

Asked about my opinion on this case, my response is the same as when working on cold cases: I withhold comment for personal reasons. I have chosen to keep mine, to myself.

* * * * * * * *

Six years after Rev. Minkler's untimely, and highly contested death, Bryan Ashline committed one of the most atrocious crimes in the city's history. It was considerably heinous.

On Father's Day, 2010, one of Watervliet High

School's former star basketball players stabbed his estranged girlfriend Trieste Clayton, along with their tiny, 3-month-old son, Xavier, to death in Bath, New York. The animalistic crime repulsed the city, as well as the surrounding region.

Many reports surfaced that Ashline frequently abused Clayton, while intoxicated. The pregnancy upset Ashline to the point his temper spiraled out of control.

Clayton attempted to correct her life, and moved back to Bath. Her parents helped raise their grandchild. Clayton's relationship with Ashline continued to go south.

On Father's Day, the former star athlete left Watervliet, and headed to Bath. The visit went terribly wrong.

There are differing versions as to what transpired next: Ashline tried to claim self-defense. Regardless of who was responsible for initiating the attack, Clayton was stabbed to death. Xavier died in his mother's arms in the attack. He too, had been butchered.

Ashline was captured, and arrested after the State Police found him along the New York State Thruway. In the fall of 2011, he was found guilty of murdering Clayton, and Xavier. The verdict did little to heal the broken hearts of those left mourning the loss of Clayton, and her son.

The residents of Watervliet were stunned. The Ashline case became yet another tragic, and puzzling incident that heavily weighed-down the city's morale. Two more senseless deaths, at the hands of another Watervliet man-gone-mad.

* * * * * * * *

In the spring of 2013, Watervliet was on-edge, after losing the battle to preserve their beloved St. Patrick's Church. Messages frequently flooded my in-box, as residents and interested parties questioned if I was able to 'pick up' on anything in the spirit realm.

With good reason, the community was unsettled. I, on

the other hand, had confided in a few that something was about to go very wrong, and whatever it was, was going to surface soon.

Given the indicators for such situations, I prayed for the safety of not only my friends, but the community itself. Something was about to go down, *and in a big way.*

Adding into the mix: I had a frightening premonition, just after the Boston bombings. It was horrible, and it scared me for the simple fact that for the first time ever, I saw something *attack the city.*

A large, black mass swept-in from the south, and then perched itself on the bell tower of St. Patrick's Church. It was ominous. This was not something emanating from the church, but was using it as a lookout.

I heard people yelling, and watched as they ran for cover; the black mass leapt from the tower. It made broad, swooping passes at people who dodged for safety. I prayed aloud, asking for God to protect everyone.

Watching from the vantage point of mid-19th Street, the shapeless form searched for victims, catching a few in its unhallowed path. *Was this also part of Father Emery's message?*

I had to make the vision stop. Mustering the strength to deter the creature, I blessed myself, made the sign of the cross, and asked God to make it go away. In a flash, the vision was over. I shared the vision with a select group of family, and friends.

A few days later, I was contacted by one of my confidantes. They called to inform me that something frightening had occurred very close to the church grounds. Speechless, I listened as they elaborated on the details that occurred in the 5th Avenue apartment of Brandon Burritt, and David Hochsprung.

The police received a call stating neighbors heard a commotion in the Burritt-Hochsprung apartment. Apparently, an argument ensued. The two men pulled knives on one another.

The Watervliet Police Department found Burritt alive, and profusely bleeding, while other officers noted Hochsprung had succumbed to his wounds. Witnesses describe a scene so horrifying, there was blood splatter all over place. My source (who was on-scene) attested to this.

Burritt survived his *self-inflicted* injuries, and was later arrested, and charged with murder. The damn, black mist had struck again.

* * * * * * * *

Watervliet is a family-oriented community. Naturally, as with any locale, there are bound to be problems, murders, and suicides. The fact that the city is so small, and no longer as dense, is what bothers me, when comparing its history to others its size.

Just as explained by persons interviewed, along with information from my sources, and the survey of historical records, I have little doubt that a section of this city is spiritually contaminated. This impurity can be dangerously corrosive to specific individuals. These stories have been included, not to besmirch Watervliet, but to evidence that something is wrong.

Objectively, and as with most American cities, it has its pockets of problem areas, but overall, is an old, ethnic community presenting with a predominantly senior population. Mainly Irish, Italian, and German, many of the city's senior citizens have been life-long residents.

From local reporters, to former communicants of St. Patrick's Church, to a couple of families with long-ties to Sheehan, the group that has harassed and threatened me, are indeed, primarily 65-years-old, and younger. This astounds me.

Ignoring any willingness to at least look at the evidence, or listen to my side, many have taken to public message boards, social media outlets, and have even resorted to telephone calls made to me, in a direct attempt to silence my efforts, and put an end to the release of this book. Sources also confide that age-old allegiances to Sheehan and the church are behind the movement, while a couple have cited lineage to the 207's Moran family, as the driving force.

Above all, I will continue to maintain that the church was not evil, nor was Sheehan. However, I will state as a matter of opinion, that something very dark affected the priest, and over time, consumed him.

Relative to the house: a combination of people, and events adversely impacted the city, and turned 207 19th Street into a syphon that literally sucked the life out many of its residents. You don't have to be a rocket scientist to figure that out.

Appreciating the fact that there exists certain fractures of the psyche in many, inclusive of clergy, it cannot be ignored that it is through these gateways that dark entities invade the soul. After prolonged exposure, regardless of the type of fracture, or the quality of character, the unholy are able to take control. When this occurs, even the most logical, and gentle humans, can snap.

Case #12: Daniel Reinfurt, 1997.
Location: Woodbine Court.

On August 5th, 1997, after a long battle with depression, beloved Coach Daniel Reinfurt died, after hanging himself in his garage. He was 45-years-old. The community of Watervliet, as well as much of the Capital District region, was devastated by his loss.

Dan, also affectionately called *Coach Reinfurt*, was a pillar in the city, and a well-respected teacher, as well as football coach for the Watervliet High School football team. Prior to his death, and as noted in Chapter 5, Dan had also worked with the family business (Parker Bros. Memorial).

Within mere minutes after learning about his death,

hundreds of people gathered in front of Dan's house, for a vigil. In the days following, the entire community packed into the school auditorium. Wisely, they took the opportunity to educate the public, relative to Dan's known battle with depression. The goal was to save a life, by addressing what happened to their beloved coach.

Not only did I hear countless stories of Dan's compassion from mostly everyone I interviewed for this book, but my own brother Will, also knew Dan through football, and coaching. He too, stated that Dan was one of the nicest guys he knew, and confirmed what others have shared with me.

Without a doubt, his legacy, and memory will live long in the hearts of those that knew, and loved him. Personally speaking, it is in my opinion that the community of Watervliet will never be the same. Rest in peace, Coach Reinfurt.

10. DEAD RINGER

"For fate may hang on any moment and at any moment be changed." Jeanette Winterson

Since Sheehan's death, the cost, care and upkeep of St. Patrick's Church was largely left in the hands of the community, and diocese. City-wide, the parish population continued to decline, leaving the diocese struggling to keep the church open.

The first hint that the church was at risk came in 2005, when the Catholic Diocese of Albany consolidated Saint Brigid's, Sacred Heart of Mary, Our Lady of Mount Carmel, and the Church of The Immaculate Conception of Watervliet, along with Green Island's St. Joseph's, and the city's beloved St. Patrick's Church. Slowly, they were pooled together to form the *Immaculate Heart of Mary.*

In September of 2011, Saint Patrick's Church closed its doors. The upkeep alone proved too much a burden for the diocese, and community. Regardless, there remained a strong interest among parishioners, to keep the church open. In the long run, their efforts were met with great resistance by the diocese.

In early spring of 2012, a group of residents formed the *Citizens for St. Patrick's*. The group's intent was to preserve both the church, and its long legacy. In the months that followed, their fierce loyalty, and unyielding spirit led many to refer to them as the *Preservationists*.

Understanding that all decisions pertaining to the church were the responsibility of the Albany Diocese, the Preservationists and bishopric, began an emotional battle of wills; each stood firm in their perspective. The activists were more than willing to be the voice of Watervliet's Catholic community.

Not too long after the Preservationists became vocal about their stance, unfavorable reports on the church's structural issues surfaced. Following a series of studies, a determination was made, rendering the need for a highly unattainable, multi-million dollar stabilization effort. This was a huge blow to the Preservationists.

Willing to raise money to save the church, the predicted figures exceeded any realistic hope. The group continued to hold public forums, reaching out to residents for their support.

That spring, the City of Watervliet hired an independent group of engineers for advice on the potential redevelopment of the church property. Noteworthy, is the fact that the city Mayor, Michael Manning, is an engineer by profession.

Almost instantaneously, John Nigro, of the *Nigro Companies*, headed the redevelopment project, eyeing the church's location as the site of a future Price Chopper. Price Chopper is a supermarket chain owned by the Golub Corporation. The owner(s) of the Golub Corp., have roots just west of Watervliet, in nearby Niskayuna.

The Albany Diocese and John Nigro, somehow managed to hold a rather secretive series of meetings. Initially, the Preservationists, along with the general public, were broadsided when the two cohorts, had produced and publicized, a negotiated deal.

Seemingly out of nowhere, Nigro purchased the church property. Preservationists, as well as peripheral community members, debated the prior engineer reports that were presented by the city. Rumors flew that the engineers had grossly exaggerated the church's state of repair, to bias the findings, and sway the diocese into selling the structure, and land. Some have complained Manning used his professional connections to influence the outcome in his favor.

With the inevitable destruction of the church looming in the distance, tempers flared. In addition to various reports by local news agencies, and papers, I was informed of several volatile debates. Sources revealed that some of the meetings were so heated, that the police stood on-guard, escorting disruptive attendees outside, even threatening them with arrest.

With the transaction complete, Nigro announced their pretentious plans to develop the church grounds into a Price Chopper grocery store. It was a bitter pill to swallow, since a market with the same namesake sits just blocks east, and south from the church.

Many questioned why the city, or the Golub Corporation, wanted both venues to run within such close proximity of the other. A large number were worried that another store could further destroy the city's historic district. Overlooked, was the damage being done to the city's Catholic community.

With this decision, many painted both the developer and the diocese as uncaring, materialistic corporations. Others turned on the city officials, and stated that the underhandedness of the mayor and his associates, resulted in a massive 'kick-back' for the bogus structural reports.

Either way; something smelled, and the war between those in favor, and those against the destruction of St. Patrick's Church, was fueled to new heights. It wasn't pretty.

In order for the city to proceed with the plans to rezone, a vote needed to take place. Backed by the mayor and other officials, the vote commenced in-favor of the revitalization effort. Meanwhile, the Preservationists dug in deep, strategizing on ways to keep the church from an unfair demise.

By mid-April of 2012, the *New York State Office of Parks and Recreation,* announced criteria had been met to have the church and grounds, listed as a national, historic landmark. This only proved to be a short-lived victory for the driven church supporters.

Unfortunately, the group faced further frustration due to the coalition between the City of Watervliet, the Nigro Company, and the diocese. Rubbing salt into the wounds of the Preservationists, the diocese refused any negotiation efforts to have the church listed as a historical monument. In turn, the Preservationists unfalteringly demanded an independent review of the previously inflated, structural reports.

Almost in premeditated fashion, the city responded. Their excuse was by far both ridiculous, and insulting. It also wreaked of corruption. Their answer: the city could not find the documents. The reports used to sell the property to Nigro had conveniently disappeared.

The Preservationists remained determined. For the duration of the battle, some of them bore unbelievable stress: this was not a little spat, but was a full-blown war.

Other oddities unfolded, eliciting further exclamations of dishonesty, as one individual found themselves dismissed from their position in the city. The former employee maintains her association to the church preservation efforts as the real reason behind the discharge. She has since filed suit against the city's General Manager, as well as the Building Inspector/Assessor, and the Mayor.

At this point, it was clear that someone, or a group of

people, were out to destroy the Preservationists, along with anyone who sympathized with the church. Especially those vocalizing their views.

Discussing these issues with Christine Bulmer, a lead Preservationist, I was advised that the entire situation involving the church was extremely frustrating for the group. Bulmer also stated that backers were willing to put up quite a bit of money to purchase St. Patrick's from the diocese, however, no matter how hard they tried, they could not overcome the hurdles set before them.

In addition to superfluous trickeries, I was advised that the asking price of the church inched higher, prior to its sale, soaring beyond the reach of those that loved the church the most. It was an agonizing ordeal for the group.

As for their plans, the Citizens for St. Patrick's had some workable ideas for church's future, should they have had the opportunity. Included in their proposal, they discussed turning the main church into a community venue for musical events, art shows, weddings, and other ceremonies. They also deliberated the aspect of turning the rectory into a museum, showcasing the church, and town's history. All of the concepts seemed appropriate for both the church, and community.

In efforts to hear another side of the church conundrum, I reached-out to Nigro Companies for their perspective. After leaving a voice message, I received a return call from Lisa Nigro Ferguson. Lisa is John Nigro's daughter, and the corporate attorney. Our conversation was surprising, to say the least.

Ms. Ferguson described the emotional impact that the entire ordeal had caused. Raised with strong Christian values, she personally felt (in a spiritual sense) that it was not the best decision to tear down St. Patrick's, however, from a business perspective, it had to be done.

With no uncertainty, do I think that she was trying to deceive me, as her words were peppered with pain. She was truly torn, but could not let it get in the way of corporate decision-making.

At the time of our conversation, Ms. Ferguson also stated that Nigro was trying to work on an arrangement to show respect for the church. There was mention of allowing residents to take church bricks as mementos, but even that met with scrutiny, and created its own set of issues.

After the discussion ended, I felt for this woman being placed in such a precarious position. Her father was seen as a crude, and soulless man for his decisions. He refused to allow the Preservationists any tangible shred of dignity, relative to the church, and its property. At the same time, he was her father; someone she loved, and admired. He was also her boss.

I also spoke with Rev. L. Edward Deimeke, who was sent by the diocese to handle the affairs of St. Patrick's. Rev. Deimeke is also part of the *Administrative Advocate for Priest* at the Roman Catholic Diocese of Albany.

On all three occasions I had found him candid, and helpful relative to my inquiries. His quick response to call me back after leaving a message was startling, given I had been told that it was difficult to get in-touch with him.

Our conversations primarily pertained to his role in church affairs, and his viewpoint relative to the situation at St. Patrick's Church. Learning that he was a Chaplain in the Armed Forces, I sensed that he was open-minded to discussion on many controversial topics. His no-nonsense attitude, mingled with compassion, was quite impressive.

I will state that Deimeke's position is also a bit unique. As pastor to *Immaculate Heart of Mary*, for Watervliet and Green Island, he has encountered quite a bit of resistance, relative to the consolidation of the local churches. Shortly after the merger, he was delegated the task of finalizing the fate of St. Patrick's Church.

Simply put, Deimeke stated that his job was to oversee the parish, and ensure a supervisory role relative to matters concerning the razing of the church, and property. When I had asked him if I could visit the church to take photographs, he kindly advised me that I was allowed to step up to the chain link fence that had been erected, but did not have permission to enter the structure.

Detailing the condition of the church as the main reason for the denial, he advised me that the site was considered hazardous, due to the demolition. By that time, many sources stated that it may not have done any good to see inside, as most of the church's interior artifacts and structural objects, had already been removed.

We also discussed how he felt about being in the hot seat, relative to the church. It was no secret that many were upset with him, judging him as the decision maker to tear it down.

Graciously, he explained how upsetting the situation was for the community. I will attest that his voice almost winced when he told me how he felt.

Much like Ferguson, Deimeke was between a rock, and a hard place. He mentioned that although he knew it wasn't going to be easy, he was up for the challenge.

Leaving our conversation open to future discussion, I thanked him, and advised that I enjoyed learning a bit about him. In my heart, I know that he cares for the people of Watervliet and St. Patrick's, even if they do not think he does.

In spite of any outside support, in late July of 2012, the City Council voted to rezone the church property. Not only did was it a crushing blow for the Citizens for St. Patrick's, but it was a punch in the gut for the community's spirit.

The sale of the church and property was granted by early December, 2012. Nigro prepared for the demolition of St. Patrick's, along with its outlying structures, inclusive of the rectory, and school.

Church supporters continued to pay homage to the site. Many persisted in protest, while others wept, embracing family members for support. The structure had been a part of thousands of families, for well over one century.

Rallying for one, last fight, the Preservationists petitioned the *New York State Supreme Court*. The court denied their bold request. Out of ammunition, they were not going to give up just yet.

In mid-December, 2012, community residents, along with the mighty Preservationists, held a candlelight vigil. I was touched by the photographs that made headlines in the local papers, inclusive on the walls of some of my Facebook friends. The church was truly their heart, and soul. Together, the young and old began to mourn.

I felt for the Preservationists, as I had seen the corruption, relative to my own retrieval of historical information pertaining to research of this book. Sources informed me that specific requests made by the group, relative to the documents needed to certify the church as a historical landmark, were intentionally blocked.

I too, encountered a manipulation of resources when it came to some of the city's history. It is appalling to learn that collectively, we were not allowed access to historical documents.

The church bell was lowered to the ground. Arrangements were made to place it in care of the Watervliet Historical Society. Several sources, inclusive of the individuals whom advised me of Ragosta's order to ignore me, believe that the bell itself, was used as a token prize if the curator kept his mouth shut. In all honesty, and as a matter of opinion; I agree with that theory.

Piece by piece, the 124-year-old church was dismantled, and knocked down. All but the bell tower.

As if holding its last breath of life, the steeple resisted the initial wrath of the crane that tried to make it tumble. After a few more rounds, the tired tower fell to the ground, taking the hopes and dreams of the community along with it.

I have tried to remain objective throughout my

investigation into all things relative to this book, but perhaps the most difficult time I have had, has to do with the fate of St. Patrick's Church. I have voiced my opinions many times, and always come to the same conclusion.

From a historical perspective, St. Patrick's Church was built in a time when Watervliet was in dire need of transformation. With attempts made by many other pastors and faiths, no other church was able to do what the church had, relative to the community.

Saving the founding priest's influence for future discussion at the close of this chapter, a basic fact can be proven: the enormous, and beautiful structure was erected as a beacon of hope for a city that was gravely scarred by centuries of turmoil, and violence. It gave them something to be proud of.

It also stood for the perseverance and devotion of the Irish Catholic community, who had endured especially difficult hardships both in the motherland, and upon settling in Watervliet. Discrimination knows not age, gender, or color, and the Irish were looked down upon for decades following their arrival. The church became the center of their world.

Perhaps not the wisest business venture, the construction of the church did instill a sense of pride, and belonging. City streets turned less violent, and crime began to dissipate. The literal, and metaphorical authority and respect it commanded, was revered by not only Catholics, but many residents of differing religious views.

From a spiritual perspective, I am less impressed, due to Sheehan's odd fascination with Lourdes, as outlined in previous chapters. A man who had seemingly good intentions, was quick to lack future insight as to the gigantic building's upkeep. In my opinion, there was absolutely no need to build a church that large, in such a small community, be it due to selfish motivation. Ultimately, the size and cost of repair to the church, is what brought it down.

I do not think that Sheehan was a bad man with ill intention, but I do feel that he succumbed to the negative forces of the land, through a previously described fracture. It is also of my opinion that he allowed his power as a religious leader on the community level, to overstep boundaries.

Sources with elderly family members who have heard of the priest, along with various documentation, show that he was not only the pastor; he was the governing police force. He also joined, as well as divided, families. He exuded, and demanded respect. That admiration helped the community in general, but was not spiritually healthy.

Sheehan was all about power. The church was erected under a desire for control, and was torn down due to an indirect show of power.

Additionally, his role in building St. Colman's Home is also suspect, given what occurred. The church was not only the focal point of the city, but symbolized Sheehan's personal mecca, jumbling faith with private agenda that was likely influenced by the land's dark energy.

Even a good man with a fracture can fall victim to darkness, and all that it entails. The land *used* Sheehan in his capacity as a priest. No matter what anyone else thinks, I do believe the church, its bell, and St. Colman's, to be symbolic examples of just that.

St. Patrick's was a magnificent church that bonded together residents and communicants for 124 years. The decision to sell it, with no respect for the community it had embraced, sends a pathetic message. It is hard to believe there was nothing that could be done to allow the community to honor its legacy.

Told by many that the sale and demolition practically killed them, all that these anguished residents have to hold onto remains captured in photographs, and fading memories. Fortunately, but of little console, those cherished remembrances are not for sale.

The   marriages,   baptisms,   First   Communions,

Confirmations, funerals and countless hours of worship that took place under the rooftop of the church vanished into a pile of dust, and rubble. Generations, upon generations, lost a member of their family when St. Patrick's toppled, and as do most who have lost a loved one; they grieve.

Case #13: Name Withheld, 2002.
Location: Rectory parking lot, St. Patrick's Church.

The sensitivity of this case cannot be stressed enough. It involves the death of the second female; a young woman, who ended her life when she should have had the world in her hands. She was only 20-years-old.

Several sources in the city advised me of the rather bizarre circumstances surrounding her death. The scene was so macabre that I can completely understand why the family chose to keep things quiet. I chose to keep the exact day, and month of death private, as there are other sources of information on the internet that can identify her by the date.

In late summer of 2002, a young woman's body was found inside of her car, in the rectory parking lot of St. Patrick's Church. She had somehow managed to fashion a hose to the exhaust pipe of her vehicle, and died from asphyxiation due to inhalation of fumes. The first responders made another gruesome discovery: sources state they found words carved into her arms. She had extensive blood loss, as well. Nobody seems to know for sure, what those words were.

Some sources state that the young woman's family had forced her to terminate a relationship with a young man. Others have stated the family was never quite sure what drove the girl to suicide.

When I asked my sources why she chose the rectory parking lot, several stated that her family were members of the church. Initially informed of this case, my heart skipped a beat, as I could not believe the words I was hearing. It is unquestionably, a terrible and tragic ending, to a life once full of promise.

11. GIVE US THIS DAY

"If man is to live, he must be all alive, body, soul, mind, heart and spirit." Thomas Merton

Case #14: Name Withheld, 2011.
Location: Third Avenue, south of 19th Street.

In spring of 2011, a 54-year-old man shot, and killed himself in his home located in the vicinity of Third Avenue, south of 19th Street. Sources state that even family members were shocked by this act, as there were no indications of trouble.

Hardworking, he left behind a somewhat large family. Many questions still remain surrounding his decision to commit suicide. The date of death, and his name have been withheld. His obituary gives no details as to cause of death, or place. All information came from credible sources, and has been corroborated by investigation.

In addition to the 14 cases mentioned in this book, there are three other suicides that have occurred within direct vicinity of 207. One of those allegedly took place on Second Avenue, near 21st Street, when a despondent male ran into the street, and shot himself. I could not find any corroborating information on this individual, as the name was not available, nor could my source remember what year it took place. Source stated that the events took place sometime within the last 10 years.

The two suicides, other than my husband's, that were said to have taken place in 207, also remain a mystery. More than a dozen different people confirmed this information, inclusive of retired police officers, and an attorney.

One retired Watervliet officer stated that he was at the scene, when the male was cut from the rope he hung himself with. He told me that the man was hanging from 207's third floor, between the second, and first floors, in the middle of the opening of the stairwell.

The second man was said to have shot himself with a shotgun, in the same living room as Jim did, approximately 30 years prior. This information was conveyed to me, by my landlord, Phil DeLollo. Phil was in complete shock over my husband's death, given the fact the same situation transpired when his brother Joe, owned the house.

Adding into the count is the suicide of my late husband's best friend, Jerry. It was a known fact that Jerry had spent a tremendous amount of time, even in the dark, at 207, following Jim's death. He too, began to act strangely and heard voices, specifically stating they were Jim's. Jerry committed suicide at his home on November 1st, 1989 – 126 days after Jim.

* * * * * * * *

The two, primary pieces of Watervliet's history that need the utmost consideration are that of the significance of religion, and the journey of the Native Americans. Both are equally as important as the other, when forming an opinion.

Religion has long been the enforcer of what is sacred, and sacrilege. Upon further examination, it can be found that the focus of most doctrines have served as social organizations, largely based upon a host of personal, as well as global agendas.

Religion has also been viewed as a means of exercising power and authority over a growing world population with variances dependent upon geographical location. Pertaining to Watervliet, the Dutch and English, as well as the Shakers, shaped the community, and cast foundational values upon its residents. In turn, the ultimate sacrifice to deliver a message, led to war, bloodshed, violence and corruption.

Referencing 'seat money' and church burnings, (regardless of cause), in addition to the extermination and removal of Native Americans in the region, one can develop a basic understanding of the damage that was done. Methods used to scare people straight, in a location that was supersaturated with crime, violence, death and venality, were both inconspicuous, as well as obvious.

By the mid-19th century, religion was rooting itself in the trenches as a mechanism of control. It was also in the early stages of incorporating itself as a *business* – and a very profitable one at that.

The establishment of the church symbolized power, greed and corruption. It also represented the resurgence of Christian Mysticism, throughout the mid-1800s.

It was no coincidence that Sheehan sent his architect to Lourdes, France, to model the structure after the Upper Basilica. The entire premise of Lourdes was built upon the apparitions of the Holy Mother, and was based upon a series of those visions.

Bernadette Soubirous made her first claims of the visions in 1858. A fledgling priest, Sheehan's duties were shaped by the events transpiring in Lourdes. Throughout the course of his residency in western New York State, he absorbed the full impact, and effect of the resurgence. Transferring to Watervliet, he built himself an empire, based more so on a personal agenda, than anything else.

The priest's heritage also needs to be considered. European clergy members, specifically Catholic priests, were very much involved with mysticism, and the revival. This can be demonstrated by mysticism's foundation with the Druids, as well as the Pagans, and their overall influence it had on the Irish. European priests, most notably the Irish-Catholic priests, were known to carry those values, and associated beliefs, into America.

By mid-century, the era of the Golden Dawn had ushered in an entirely new branch of mysticism. Having attended monastery in Ireland, Sheehan was instilled with a strong business sense, early in his training. The Trappist Monks were adept at crafts, and food goods, yet they were widely known for beer-making.

Reiterating a former point; the monks were allowed to make a profit for their wares, so long as the money was allocated directly to the monastery. This is an important aspect to consider, as conflicting information exists as to where Sheehan gained his alleged fortune.

Sheehan acquired a fortune by some means. In my opinion, he collected it on the side, probably through risqué endeavors. None of the church communities that he had worked prior to heading to Watervliet were affluent, so I do not think he was the recipient of gifts.

I have considered an inheritance by a family member, but again, it does not account for the excess of funds to finance all of his endeavors. Sheehan handed the properties over to the congregation, but still ran them. Additionally, he bequeathed a large sum of money at the time of his death. Conflicting records as to his family, make the matter at the very least, interesting. This is why I strongly feel there *may* have been an attachment to organized crime.

Another point worthy of thought has to do with the

Sisters of The Presentation (Fermoy, Ireland). Given they petitioned the bishop, and asked for the diocese to pay for his seminary school in exchange to bring Sheehan to America, is understandable, but still indicates a level of poverty in the family. Even if Sheehan "inherited" a small fortune, who was it through, and did he have to pay the diocese back? So many questions surface, relative to his wealth.

Regardless, in just over a decade, he built an ostentatious church, and a large orphanage. Records indicate that he also paid for the land by which both were built. This was not an easy achievement, for a relatively new priest.

Weighing all of the evidence, reasonable conclusion can be drawn that construction of the church, orphanage and schools, garnished the priest with a great deal of respect – *and power.* Several historical documents illustrate this point, and literally make reference to Sheehan as the sole, acting authority, relative to keeping an upper hand on a rather barbaric community.

Highly motivated, Sheehan did transition Watervliet from a state of chaos, into one of civility, but not without a price. He controlled families and children, and lavished the community with enormous buildings. This reflects a lack of foresight, and even hints at delusions of grandeur. Again, it also symbolizes his penchant for Christian Mysticism.

His keen business sense was grossly overshadowed by an internal pursuit of authority. In time, that power led to the demise of the church he built, and a huge scandal involving the orphanage.

I will argue that Watervliet did not need such a large church. Not only did his actions financially embarrass the diocese, but they also crushed a community that loved the church. Pushed to the wayside, they watched it fall to ruins.

I will restate that it is my opinion, Sheehan had good

intentions to start with, however, submitted to the darkness of the land. I have no doubt that he was used as a vehicle to accomplish both immediate, and long-term damage to the community. This is evidenced in the suffering of children whom were torn from their homes, and thus abused, as well as the anguish that church members have endured as the result of the closing, and demolition of the structure.

Adding to a growing list of correlating, and 'coincidental' dates that have woven together a strange past, another unusual occurrence transpired. The events were referenced to the actual date, with retrospect.

After receiving permission by the Watervliet Police Department to walk around the area of 19th Street, and Second Avenue, my best friend Carol and I, conducted a *mini* paranormal investigation relative to 207's lot. It was something that I had contemplated for a long time. I knew that it was imperative to seek permission from the police department, beforehand.

Advising the desk officers that we were setting out to take photographs on that night, I explained that we needed to utilize the sidewalks. We were given permission to walk around, and through the parking lot of the drug store, but were not go near the store structure. We were also instructed not to make any noise, or bring a lot of distracting equipment (e.g. cords, cables, tripods, etc.). I understood: they did not want us to make a scene.

Overall, this was good news. I was finally granted a window of time to conduct some research.

The Desk Sargent also stated that he was going to notify patrol as to our presence, in efforts to ensure everyone was on the same page. Agreeing to the terms, we headed into the city, armed with our cell phones, and a digital camera. Low-tech, but given our restrictions, it worked.

The temperature was approximately 37 degrees Fahrenheit; the sky was clear, and no precipitation was present. I *solely* functioned as a paranormal investigator, and intentionally blocked my abilities. I dared not allow anything to come through, given the situation. Another decision was also made well in advance: I was not going to step foot on the lot. I did however, agree to walk around it, paying careful attention not to cross boundaries.

Our investigation began at 11 p.m., and commenced with a series of photos as taken from the parking lot next to the old Angie's Pizza Parlor; now an attorney's office. Facing 207's lot from the south side of 19th Street, nothing unusual was noted. Carol snapped photos with her cell phone, and I manned my digital camera.

We moved across the street and headed east, and then turned north onto Second Avenue to ensure I was not going to cross the lot. We then walked through the parking lot, noting a few, empty, sporadically parked car.

The closer to the center of lot we walked, the darker it became. This made sense, as there was no lighting available in the lot. Simultaneously, and standing side-by-side, we took a series of photographs.

With intent, Carol moved onto 207's lot, and turned to face me. I said a few prayers, and took photographs as she stood directly on its lot. Nothing unusual was noted at the time. I switched to 'film mode.'

As Carol walked off of the lot, I talked about the chain of events that transpired the night Jim died. Shortly after I said Jim's name, a loud, metallic crash sounded from between the lot, and towards the rear of the sole house situated on property (215 19th Street). The house was vacant; no animals were seen roaming. The strange sound was captured on film. Not one car had passed.

I continued filming, as Carol examined the area surrounding the house. She did not find any loose object(s) laying on the ground that could have created the noise. We both remarked how strange it was, having occurred just as I spoke of Jim.

Moving back to the center of the lot, we did notice an

occasional patrol car driving by. Carol and I took another series of photos while facing the lot, as we discussed 207's nefarious history.

After close to an hour, we left the lot, and walked back to the south side of 19th Street. There, we stood directly in front of the lot, from across the street. More photographs were taken, while I described Jim's final movements on video.

Situated on the east side of the old pizzeria, I described the last minutes of Jim's life. Carol stood to my right.

Panning the camera between 207 and the pizzeria, I documented that Jim had left 207, and crossed the street, making his way into Angie's. There, he asked to use the telephone, whereas he phoned his best friend. Speaking with Jerry's girlfriend, Jim asked her to relay a bone-chilling message to me, hung up the phone, ran back across the street, into 207.

Within a matter of minutes, the shotgun blast shattered the summer night. I ended the filming at that point. It was too surreal and upsetting to be standing there, reliving his final moments of life.

Just as we had finished our investigation, a gold Ford Explorer pulled up along the curb, just west of the pizzeria. Turning off the truck lights, a dark-haired male, approximately 60-years-old, sat on the south side of 19th Street, and glared at us. He inched his vehicle closer, and closer, towards the edge of the street where were had been filming.

Despite our granted permission, it was evident that the man did not want us there. More so, due to the fact that I had just recollected some brutal memories, Carol and I packed up, and headed back to her house. As we got ourselves situated in the car, the Explorer drove east, over the Congress Street Bridge, and into Troy.

Once back at the house, we uploaded and reviewed the photographs, and videos. I was on a mission to find out what could have caused the crashing sound that took place between the lot, and house. There was not one bit of evidence indicating something had fallen. We estimated the impact to be approximately 20 feet from where I had stood, in the course of the video capture.

Nothing out of the ordinary showed up on my group of photographs, and most of Carol's were benign as well – until a series of photos showed a marked change. The interference in the photographs took place when the two of us had stood next to one another, both shooting pics, while facing the lot from the middle of the parking lot. Neither of us were using a flash.

Up to that point, both sets of photos as taken with the cell phone and camera, had been clear. While examining my own photos, Carol suddenly said, "Jill, you have got to see this."

For some reason, three, out of eight photos Carol had taken in succession, appeared as if it were *raining*. The photos showed a bluish, grainy glow. In one shot, there was an irregular, white spot that appeared to the right (not an orb). In another, a rectangular white object appears to the left, while in the same photo, the right side (by which I had been standing) reveals a blurred mass standing in front of me. Most startling, were what appeared to be three faces peering up from the ground *directly on 207's lot*. They were not in the grass.

After passing her laptop over to me, I immediately noticed the striking differences between the successive shots. The first few were clear and unaffected, the middle three were strange, and the last four, or so, back to normal. It was beyond strange.

To no avail, I fiddled with the contrast settings on the photograph to see if I could get better definition. It only made the faces more clear. It was as if three, skeletal expressions were looking up through the lot, directly at us. The blurred section of photograph was just as unnerving, knowing that something appeared to have stood right in front of me. In the next frame, everything was back to normal.

To this day, Carol will state that she was truly upset by the photographs. The normal succession of shots, interrupted by something so bizarre, was quite scary. I too, was puzzled and tried to (unsuccessfully) debunk the photos, making an allowance for everything from aperture, *pareidolia,* to movement; none of it made sense. There were several distinctly different things taking place in each of the three photographs.

To clarify a phrase most paranormal investigators are familiar with, pareidolia is a term used to define a psychological phenomenon that involves an image, or even a sound, to form another image, or shape. The human brain tends to turn random patterns into faces. An example of pareidolia can illustrated by recognizing a facial pattern of Jesus, in a grilled cheese sandwich (aka: *Cheez-us*).

With the understanding that a full investigation had not been conducted due to the limitations as imposed by the police department, it still proved to be quite interesting. A complete exploration of a nearby home, or even the store was desired, however, attempts made to initiate a dialogue for that to take place, were met with deafening silence.

As exampled by the lurking Ford Explorer that arrived on-scene in the course of our mini research project, so many other instances of disgruntled individuals have surfaced over the course of the investigation, and writing of this book. Some have been subtle, and some have been obvious. There have been snipped remarks, and outright threats.

An example of subtle antagonism against my efforts, can be found in a post that was added to the Citizens for St. Patrick's Facebook page. Someone had "shared" my press release that detailed my interest in filming a documentary about my book, and how St. Patrick's Church was a large part of the interest.

A reply to the press release was posted by an avid

church supporter, with long family ties to the St. Patrick's community. Listed was their singular response, with the link to a website. As of this entry into the book, the post is still listed on the Citizens for Saint Patrick's Facebook page reads: "Professional Insect/Butterfly Net . . . This sturdy butterfly net has a telescoping handle and long bag, making it easy to catch specimens. October 1, 2012 at 10:44am." (Broderick, 2012)

Several concerned individuals saw the post, and promptly contacted me, expressing concern. Each person viewed the response as a "veiled threat." A friend of mine who is a former law enforcement officer, was equally concerned.

With tension having mounted with the demolition of St. Patrick's Church, many community residents were at wits' end. For some, the thought of their beloved church meeting a cruel fate, was almost too much to bear. A handful chose to target me as a scapegoat, making ridiculous claims that my first book was the beginning, to the end of the church.

I have also been called a "witch," and some other, less than complimentary names, relative my being a medium, and psychic. Through such childish, often bullying behaviors, it has been made very clear that a specific group does not like me speaking of their church, or its founder.

By June 2013, the uproar over this book had reached an entirely different level. Having received information that a few misinformed, and rather illogical folk had actually plotted an attempt on my life, I was forced to cancel a sold-out event in Troy. This also prompted me to seek a security detail. It had gotten *that* out of hand.

Canceling the event just days prior to, definitely foiled the plan, but also created another set of circumstances. With most knowing that I do not live in New York, inquiries as to my whereabouts came flooding into email, and social media messaging accounts. I felt like a living *'where's Waldo?'*

People I have never spoken to in my life, were digging for information: was I still going to New York, even though the event was canceled? Where was I staying while in New York? The rumor mill was in full swing, as I fielded truly ridiculous questions.

In a creative effort for the plotters to figure out my next move, I was also inundated with more offers to meet for coffee in New York, than a burnt-out college student trying to survive exam week. The craftiness of some, was blatantly obvious.

Concerned not only with my own safety at that point, I was equally worried about the security of my family, and friends. One thing was clear: I had to do what I could to prevent people from getting hurt, even if it meant not going to New York, at all. That decision broke my mother's heart, and mine. It was far too dangerous a risk to go, so I canceled the entire trip.

There is also a camp of residents who refuse to believe anything sinister has taken place in their neighborhood. Even when presented with evidence, doors slammed, and phone calls abruptly ended: not here – not in Watervliet. That sort of thing doesn't happen.

Unfortunately, denial, revenge, and paranoia are common traits among the community relative to the misinformed, but the corruption that continues, is unreal. It is fairly easy to find sources that will talk, and are grounded enough to stand clear of the witch hunt, but it is very difficult to use public resources for historical research when efforts are made to construct roadblocks.

The political pollution is beyond help, and remains so thick and foul that it is no wonder the city is slowly, falling apart. Some things just never change.

Patience and resiliency, along with an ability to see the forest beyond the trees, helped me to plug-along. Admitting that I had to change my approach, I was finally able to obtain the information that I needed to finish the project.

The sheer frustration, as caused by the foolishness of those who played an active part in trying to deter the writing of this book, meant that I spent some considerable time blowing-off steam, behind closed doors. From first-hand experience, Justin knew exactly how I felt. Some of my family were also privy to specific information, and also expressed concern and worry, over the others' charades.

All of this only made me more aware. I learned that there was a book, within a book.

One of the most disheartening situations that occurred in the writing of *Saints*, was when I had been contacted by the family who moved into 207, after Jim died. It has been profoundly upsetting for me to know that another family endured much of the same.

Knowing that I have had to process through the tragedy is one thing, but to know an entire family also underwent a slightly similar situation, packs a powerful punch. Despite a few differences, there are too many disturbing parallels that transpired, all of which make my skin crawl.

Sometimes emotional and psychological scars are the most difficult to deal with, and I see that as being very present in the family that came forward. Always trying to look at blessings rather than misfortune, I have been able to motor-through it. Sadly, it is not the same for the family. It is clear to me, that they still struggle with their ordeal; specifically, the husband.

He states that he knows 'it' is trying to get him, even after all of these years. In many ways, he seems tortured by the hellacious dwelling that that tried, and frequently succeeded, tormenting the living. I pray that he, and his family, find the strength to see how truly fortunate they are, for the simple fact they are alive.

Speaking with so many city residents over the last two years, I have been fascinated by the fact that *207* opened up a discussion for others, who due to fear of ridicule, have kept theirs to themselves. Generational stories that impart a dark and deadly presence can be found in those that bravely came forward to share their experiences. Two such stories are of particular interest, given the location of the homes, and the length of time they have been family owned.

Contacted by an older male, I was advised of a well-kept secret relative to the family home. Since the early 1900s, there has been something very disturbing visiting the house. Located just west of 207, the house has witnessed one suicide of a family member, and multiple aspects of paranormal phenomenon.

Details of *door poundings* had every hair on my body standing up on end, as I, and the other family who left 207, are quite familiar with such occurrences. The source states that, "to this day, every time the knocking starts, someone becomes sick," and gravely, so. Just as in 207, the disturbances increase, and get louder.

A few weeks prior to the family member's suicide, the relative stated that he knew "the devil was out to get him." When another family member asked what he meant, he quietly walked away. Almost three weeks later, he pulled out his rifle, and shot himself. According to the source, he was not depressed, and appeared to have changed after moving into the home to stay with them. This home too, is still adorned with many religious statues, and undergoes routine blessings as a means of keeping whatever *it* is, at bay.

The second generational account goes back to the late 1800s. My source literally trembled, when detailing the activity in the home.

The family is convinced that whatever is affecting the area, is from the 19th century. As a result, they have been so afraid of what neighbors will think about their experiences, they have "a pact with one another," not speak of their experiences to outsiders. After reading *207*, they said they were relieved in a way, and felt validated; they are not going crazy.

This family also notes a very cold presence that comes, and goes, from the home. It is the only case that I have been advised of a putrid odor, such as the one that ravaged 207, back in 1987. The source states that the odor has occurred several times, and is untraceable. The family is extremely religious, and of the Catholic faith.

This individual also described "a hooded" figure which has appeared to various family members, throughout many generations. The man advised that Father Emery also use to bless their home, but after his departure from the city, the family has relied on doing it themselves.

There are many stories of paranormal activity in the city, especially between 14th Street, and 23rd Street. Most of the accounts involve poltergeist activity, at the northern end of the area. Noteworthy is the fact that this is the area of the Upper side cut, where most bars and brothels existed in the 19th century.

I have heard of everything, from objects flying off of tabletops, to disembodied footsteps, to more serious stories involving an uneasy feeling that changes the energy in a room, or house. For those that have come forward to share their stories, several are very aware of the multiple suicides that have taken place, noting that they do not think it is coincidence.

Oddly enough, many of the older residents remember 207 as a "strange house." It is often described as: uncomfortable, haunted, having bad energy, and as being odd. At least a dozen residents have stated they were happy when the house came down, given its vibe over time.

Yes, there was something about *that house*, but how does it impact the city? Sane, articulate, logical, responsible, and compassionate individuals have lost their minds. Be it madness, mayhem, murderous rampage, or suicide, something has continued to cause strange events, and wreak havoc in a small parameter of space.

Other common questions that I frequently field are:

why has 207 bore the brunt? Did something transpire in the house, or on the land? The answers are complicated.

I do not think it is coincidence that many families have had similar experiences within close vicinity of 207, and seeing that most will not share their plight with others, it is astounding to find others who speak of loud knockings, illness, suicide and odors, especially so close to the house.

Of interest, I do believe that a geological study on the area could prove beneficial. This may rule out, or in, naturally occurring, or manmade compounds, and even a contaminated water supply, as a source. With the Hudson River flowing heartily on the eastern banks of the city, it is logical that something could have physically tainted the town's water supply. The problem with this theory, has to do with the fact that this has been going on for a long time, and again, why was 207 a focal point?

Perhaps most importantly, the early indigenous people are a key factor as to what may have transpired, lending to the dark cloud that seems to hover over Watervliet. It may not be an intentional act, but very well may be more ancient in nature, prompting the Indians to honor the land.

The natives inhabited the area for centuries prior to Henry Hudson's arrival, and have truly suffered the most. Early-on, land thieves worked together for the betterment of their own interests, literally pushing out, and killing hundreds and thousands of Indians, through the 17th, and 18th centuries.

Going back to the original story of Skennenrahawi, great strides were taken to ensure peace and harmony, among not only the indigenous people as a whole, but in conjunction with the settlers. Nevertheless, and only after many massacres, their land slowly disappeared, leaving the natives to vacate what was rightfully theirs. Their numbers dwindled in the process.

With diseases such as smallpox and measles brought to America by the white man, it is no wonder why they thought the settlers, and even missionaries were intrusive, and a bad omen. Making matters worse, the trickery and deliberate attempt to kick them out of their homeland, created deeper pain, and more serious scarring, inclusive of spiritually.

Hundreds of years of tradition, and a natural way of living – and dying – were replaced by the ideals and philosophies of the Europeans. The Tree of Peace was cut down by hands of a white man baring an axe, leaving a culture to rely on its oral history.

Tucked-away, are precious memories and customs, most of which invoke an element of agony relative to the journey. Gone, was their sacred ground, specifically the stretch of land stretching from Port Schuyler and Watervliet, up to the Cohoes Falls.

In September of 2012, Brookfield Renewable Power donated a portion of the original sacred ground, to the *Hiawatha Institute for Indigenous Knowledge* (HIIK). Part of that land is situated next to the Cohoes Falls.

More importantly, this area is *still* considered sacred land to the Mohawk, and Iroquois. My very own great-great grandfather, named John-Bear, was a Seneca Indian (Iroquois). His wife, (my great-great grandmother) Gertrude, was a Chippewa Indian (Algonquian). Together, they settled in Ausable Chasms, New York. For its time, the pairing was considered disgraceful, but it worked. I am sure they knew of the falls, and its story.

Being that the Cohoes Falls region is one of *the most* sacred of grounds known to the Indigenous people of North America, the spiritual liberation that came from the land deal, is priceless. It was a small step to facilitate healing among the Iroquois.

Long overdue, the HIIK regained possession of a small portion of their hallowed ground, gaining back an even larger part of their heritage, and pride. I feel a sense of peace relative to my great-great grandparents, when I consider the outcome. I also cannot help but have empathy for what they endured; what the Native American people suffered through, and tolerated at the hands of greedy land thieves.

Frequently asked if I feel the Indians cursed the land, I always reply the same: no. I do not feel that to be the case, and sense that the darkness which looms over Watervliet, is something ancient; something dormant that was activated. Once triggered, it attacked with a vengeance.

The land is not just sick; it is infested. Objectively, I view the Native Americans as the nurses, doctors and caregivers who nurtured the land, despite their own warring. Somehow, after the settlers came to the town, a shift took place; literally, figuratively, and spiritually.

As with any perfect storm, there is a given recipe that can equate to disaster. Anyone who came, or has come onto the land with a fractured psyche, and a lowered Spiritual Self, can – and has become – an ingredient of that recipe. For certain, something menacing was summoned, or awakened, and has fed-off the community for centuries.

By presenting evidence, anecdotes, and personal opinion, a broader view can be seen relative to the city's tumultuous past. This information also affords insight into an unsettling aspect that for some reason, 207 19th Street, had a bull's eye on its back.

Without a complete history of tenants, and records of the house, it is extremely disconcerting to know that at least 14 people died within its walls. It also is interesting to note that since at least the late 1950s, the house was known to be 'haunted', by many in the community.

Without access to property tax records via the City of Watervliet Tax Assessor's Office, I was unable to identify the year the house was built, or by whom. Fortunately, other data afforded the opportunity to provide a more than decent glimpse at its past.

One thing is for sure, I tried to contact the Assessor's office (Mark Gilchrist), on multiple occasions, leaving both voicemail messages, and verbal. On once occasion that I spoke with a human being, I was told that the city *does* house the old records in a large room, stacked with boxes.

Offering to physically, help look for the property tax records, the message-taker flat-out advised me that the Assessor was not going to cooperate with my investigation. When I asked why, the individual did not directly answer the question, however, stated something to the fact that they could not get into it. They shared that they knew how important the information is to me, and had read *207*. The individual liked the book, but eluded that several residents do not.

The party wished me luck, and that was the last call I made to the office. More of the same. I had to regroup, and move forward. This was one of those times whereas I hung up the phone, and had a mini-meltdown.

As with most deeds at the Albany County Clerk's Office, and as advised by two lawyers, and Patrick Reilly, deed documents only illicit information pertaining to the lot itself, not the dwellings, or buildings constructed on the property. I agree with this, and noted it to be the case, after pulling several deeds on 207, through the online search database. Note: the online site only allows retrieval back to a certain date. Older records are not available via the website.

In almost every bit of advice I obtained, I was told that the only way to get information about when 207 was built, was to go to the Watervliet Tax Assessor's Office, or to call them. You know how well that went.

In order to continue, research strongly relied on Last Wills and Testaments, old newspaper articles, obituaries, and other public information to gain a guesstimate as to when the house was erected. Even with the adversity and direct attempt to block the information, I was able to narrow the timeframe of 207's construction to between 1840, and 1867. There also remains a high possibility that the original structure was torn down, or damaged by fire. If this were to be the case, the other structure existed *prior to 1868*.

I also contacted two, professional title abstracters, who after a few days of preliminary research, called me back to inform me that due to the age of the house, it was almost impossible to get the actual date the house was built. Okay; if they saw a big enough problem, then I didn't feel so bad. They also advised that they had to increase their fees quite considerably, should I have wanted them to go back as far as the late 1800s.

Justin Sanders proved to be a wiz at courthouse records, given his past experience. Once we had names, he was able to locate and order probate records for many of the home's owners.

Another example of having to navigate a circus ring, is illustrated by my contact with the Watervliet Historical Society. At first, Tom Ragosta was both congenial, and helpful. I will go as far and state that he truly seemed enthusiastic.

Throughout our initial conversations, I stated that I was looking for information, and had wrapped up *207*. Explaining my need to look into the history of the canal, as well as the house itself, Ragosta eagerly stated that he was going to "look around for information," and get back to me within a day, or two. He did post an old photograph of 207 19th Street on the Watervliet Historical Society Facebook page, which as of current date, is still listed on the page's wall.

Several weeks, and multiple unreturned messages later, lent me to discuss the situation with Justin. He too, found it odd that Ragosta had stopped communicating with me.

Worthy of another try, Justin reached-out to Ragosta at the Historical Society, and was able to initiate a 45-minute conversation, but only up to one point. Although he did not mention working with me relative to research, as soon as Justin mentioned the desire to know more specifics about the homes "at the intersection of 19th Street and 2nd Avenue," Ragosta changed his tune.

Justin stated that Ragosta asked him to call back the

following Monday, and gave him his cell phone to do so. As requested, he attempted to contact Ragosta by telephone, leaving a message, however, never received a response. Justin also states that he believes he may have also sent a follow-up email, which went unanswered. As with my encounter, Ragosta was initially helpful, but chose to close the door in our faces. Odd.

The most intriguing piece of information came to me in early summer of '13, when a source contacted me, and described a conversation they were privy to. Almost expected, it still frosted my cupcakes.

My source stated that their good friend, is friends with Ragosta. Evidently out for a Happy Hour toddy, the group began to discuss my book, *207,* as well as my research for this book. The person who is friends with Ragosta, stated that he (Ragosta) had confided in his friend that he was practically threatened by an unnamed person about the Historical Society's dealings with not only me, but some others. Ragosta was warned that the unnamed individual was going to "make sure and shut down the historical society," if they found out he cooperated with anyone on the "black list."

According to the source, Ragosta's initial reaction was that he felt compelled to give me the information. It was also stated that he found the entire subject of *207* fascinating. Ragosta was reminded that if he wanted the organization to remain operational, then he had best not speak with me, or anyone helping me.

I was amazed that someone had evidently gone to such great lengths to prevent me from obtaining information for my project. I also felt terrible for Ragosta, to have been put in that position.

If anything, it certainly explained the never-ending nonsense that had taken place relative to the research of this book. I was blocked on practically every level. As much as I tried to let it go, I kept going back to the conversation that I had with Mayor Michael Manning, in the spring of '13.

Sometime in late winter, early spring of 2013, the mayor *sent me* a 'Friend Request' via Facebook. This was not too strange, seeing that I had sent him a rather lengthy email through the city's website months prior, asking him to contact me relative to the book, and a public gathering that I was hoping to plan. In addition to the email, I had left a few telephone messages for him, regarding the same matters.

After a basic introduction on Facebook Messenger, Manning sent me his contact telephone number. The back-and-forth of telephone messages ensued. At the time, he was traveling, so establishing contact with him was tricky.

After approximately a month, or so, we were able to speak on the phone. More basic chit-chat, and then I explained to him that I had been encountering a host of problems relative to information pertaining to my research. His voice turned from neutral, to a more arrogant tone.

Asking me who had been uncooperative, I described a few of the scenarios, mentioning the historical society as the first. Paraphrasing, Manning responded by stating that the Watervliet Historical Society is a non-profit, and is not obligated to give me any information they did not want to. He added; if Ragosta did not want to give me information, or get involved with my project, then he did not have to.

I responded by telling Manning that Ragosta was initially cooperative with me, and then halted communication. I further explained that he was more than happy to help Justin, until he found out Justin wanted the same information as I did, and had connected the dots.

Adding that Ragosta had claimed himself to be a decent historian relative to canal and Watervliet matters, it was odd that he suddenly changed his mind, despite earlier interest. Manning, in a rather cocky attitude repeated the same information about it being a non-profit, and asked me about the other issues I had come across.

Sensing his overly self-confident response, I felt that it

was best not to go into the problem with the Assessor, and briefly explained a problem at the Hall of Records. Based upon the conversation, there was no doubt that he was well prepared for my questions. His replies were definitely calculated, as well.

It is a true statement: non-for-profit agencies do not have to follow the same information requests as other agencies, relative to my type of research. He had me there – and knew it. It still did not explain why the Assessor was not cooperating, and why I was blatantly told to give up. At that point, I was questioning the motive behind the denials, and realized that it was probably a combination of a few different things.

I had to pick and choose my fights carefully. I was heading into almost three years of research, and at this point, was not willing to expend another three, hiring a lawyer, and fighting the city. They knew they had bamboozled me relative to who built 207, and in what year.

Months later, it struck a nerve, to learn that someone threatened to shut down the historical society if Ragosta gave me the info. A raw nerve, at that.

I connected a few more puzzle pieces, and the picture sharpened. My, what a wicked web some weave.

* * * * * * * *

It has often been overwhelming to find that many others who lived near 207, had resorted to suicide. As the numbers climbed, and coincidence mounted, it grew more apparent that something has been very wrong, for an extraordinarily long time.

Just prior to this book's release, I was contacted by a source who shared an experience that transpired many years ago. A life-long native of Watervliet, he described a situation that took place sometime between 1958, and 1964. His memory is a bit fuzzy as to the exact year.

Providing me with details that Angie's Pizzeria was once a Dry Cleaning business, the man advised that he routinely took his mother's laundry to the cleaners. Even by then, the blood red, brick home known as 207 19th Street, had developed an alarming reputation.

The source stated that when he was approximately 12, or 13-years-old, he remembered a "remarkable event" at 207, when someone committed suicide. Shortly after, a friend that had accompanied him to the shop pointed to the house as they walked out of the cleaners, and stated to my source, "They say that the house across the street is haunted." Those words could not ring more true.

Back to my theory: I believe that long before the Native Americans dedicated the land as a sacred ground, something ancient called that location its home. As history has proven, that area has endured layer, upon layer of tragedy, beginning with warring tribes and massacres, and was followed by another century of murder, in the 1800s.

As a medium, I strongly believe that something was called upon, and energized. Specifically, given the resurgence of Christian Mysticism, and the impact it quite obviously had on Sheehan, I do think that a demon was unleashed in the course of an exorcism gone wrong. Unsure as to who may have performed the rite, it is in my opinion, that the exorcism took place in 207, sometime after it was built, and before the turn of the 20th century.

I speculate that it is also highly possible the spirit of a Native American may have been beckoned during a séance, or an exorcism in the house, adding further desecration to an already spiritually damaged land. Should this be the case, it is a disastrous violation to the spirit world.

That malevolence made its den in the living room area of the house, where I believe the exorcism took place. Trapped, it sought the closest victims first, and expanded its search outward, and into the neighborhood. This is exampled by the number of deaths having occurred inside of 207, and an exceptionally large number within its immediate vicinity.

As previously stated, without having records of every tenant that lived in the house, there is no way to determine an exact number of residents who died at 207, due to its age, and lack of proper records. I do think that the demon was present upon Sheehan's arrival, but its power grew.

An important piece of information has to do with the little girl who died in 1868 (Philamela Wood). She died in late August of 1868, the same year that Sheehan was placed in charge of St. Patrick's, however, Sheehan did not take over his formal duties until October, of that same year. It is unknown if Sheehan was in Watervliet by late summer, or not. Again, as a matter of opinion, I strongly believe that whatever evil had encroached upon the land, was there when he arrived, and had been resurrected.

Could Sheehan have performed an exorcism that went awry, contributing to an unleashing? Absolutely, but we will never really know. Is it possible that he was driven so far into the resurgence that his obsession with Lourdes prompted him to dabble with something dark, unaware that it could turn, and attack his congregation? Yes. He spent a tremendous amount of time, money and resources building a lavish church that symbolized the resurgence.

In my opinion, I know that Sheehan became its puppet. It is no coincidence that the black mist seen around the church, and in St. Colman's Home is strongly affiliated with the founder. It is also no accident that so many dates connect Sheehan to tragedy.

A series of strange, correlating dates factually tie the church, to actual phenomenon and tragedy. The following is a compilation, along with a brief explanation of key dates, as mentioned in this book:

Sheehan was ordained on June 27th, 1858. His Jubilee was celebrated in Watervliet on June 28th, 1908. This coincides with the date of Jim's death. Jim died exactly 81 years later, on June 28th, 1989.

The cornerstone for the new St. Patrick's Church was laid on July 4th, 1889. Strangely, Jim's burial was initially scheduled to take place on July 4th, but because of the holiday, was moved it to July 3rd, 1989. This is almost one complete century to the day of the laying of the cornerstone.

The new St. Patrick's Church celebrated its first Mass at on Christmas Day, December 25th, 1891. The ominous apparition of Sheehan standing in front of our Christmas tree at 207, took place sometime between Christmas Eve, and Christmas morning, 1988. That was also the exact spot where Jim committed suicide.

Gilbert Bonneau became gravely ill at St. Colman's Orphanage on November 27th, 1953. This is the date that it is alleged he was beaten to near-death. Exactly 35 years later, my son Jimmy was baptized. Mere days before, a foul odor penetrated the entire house at 207 19th Street, originating on the second floor. Additionally, and without any planning, Carol and I conducted our mini investigation at 207's lot, on November 27th, 2011.

Rev. Sheehan died on Easter Sunday, April 11th, 1909, exactly two years after the bell was first rung at the church (Easter Sunday, 1907). His sister, a nun, Mary Teresa (Sheehan), died in her convent in Ireland on April 12th, 1909, the very same day as her brother. The time zone change accounts for the difference in date.

So much history points straight back to Sheehan. This cannot be ignored from a historical, as well as spiritual perspective.

With many questions answered, there are an equally disturbing many that remain. The metaphorical can of worms that was opened, turned into a full-fledged bucket of snakes. Appropriate, bearing in mind that St. Patrick was said to have driven the wicked snakes out of Ireland. Making way from the motherland, those serpents found a home in Watervliet.

In conclusion, I leave you with much to digest. A

combination of research, historical data, personal anecdotes, and snippets of visions, and spirit contacts, condensed into a single book that covers several centuries of time.

I have grown, and *groaned* over this laborious, and often treacherous research project, in quest to shed light on one of the most tragic times I have ever experienced. Often disgusted and disheartened by threats, ill-will, and corruption, I have also been equally amazed by those with a true, and good spirit, who rose to the occasion and guided me through the labyrinth.

One person who can completely understand, and appreciate this rollercoaster ride, is Justin Sanders. It is only right that I thank he, and his wife Donna, for their time, and support over the last three years. Justin's patience, perseverance, knowledge, and love for historical research has been a Godsend. They are true friends.

I also want to thank my two sons (Jimmy and Kyle), as well as my best friend Carol, and my mother. Their love, light, and support have so many times been a guiding force, nudging me along when the going got tough.

With this journey, I have undoubtedly become stronger. In turn, I can also more clearly see that good will prevail over evil – even if it takes forever, and a day.

Spiritually grounded, I will continue to share my experiences with others in hopes that they too, will become rooted, and resilient. The hope and strength one gains through life experience, must be shared. By doing so, it will multiply, and become a beacon of light to others.

* * *

For centuries, a resurrected darkness has survived on a small stretch of land, in Upstate New York. Unknown, unnamed, and unholy, it remains on the prowl. In the end, the answer to what haunts Watervliet, undoubtedly lies somewhere hidden among the saints, the sinners, and the sacred ground.

REFERENCES

Albany County New York Estate Files. (1866-1923). *Letters of administration granted to petitioner, winifred moran.* Retrieved from https://familysearch.org

Albany County Surrogate's Court. (n.d.). *Will of katharine v. moran.* In (File No. 32718 ed., Vol. 91, p. 500). [Photo Copy]

Albany County Surrogate's Court. (1890). *Book of wills 1890-1891: Felix cunningham.* (Vol. 38, pp. 118-120). [Hand written] Retrieved from https://familysearch.org/pal:/MM9.3.1 /TH-1951-24568-22383-41?cc=1920234&wc=M9S9-PCP :n1035533697

Albany County Surrogate's Court. (1880). *Book of wills 1879-1881: Mary campbell.* (Vol. 28, p. 440). [Hand written] Retrieved from https://familysearch.org/pal:/MM9.3.1/TH-1951-24568-178 38-30?cc=1920234&wc=M9S9-PWW:n511947112

Albany Evening News. (1933, May 13). *Building permits issued.* Retrieved from http://www.fultonhistory.com/Fulton.html

Albany Times Union. (2004, February 22). *Fr. john a. minkler.* Retrieved from http://www.legacy.com/obituaries/ timesunion-albany/obituary

Argus & Greenwood, (1894). *Proceedings of the board of supervisors of the county of albany.* Albany: Agrus Greenwood Inc. Retrieved from http://books.google.com/books?id =GSYtAQAAMAAJ&pg=PA189&lpg=PA189&dq=unpaid school tax "winifred moran""Watervliet"1893&source= bl&ots=U2G_vq8c6i&sig=kIpslpLjCO9sKEX6r2Y_Vyv lVXk&hl=en&sa=X&ei=p3mEUuWmLOqe2QWZ0oDg Aw&ved=0CCsQ6AEwAA

Attorney General's Office. (1911). *Annual report of the attorney general of the state of new york .* Albany: J.B. Lyon Company, State Printers. Retrieved from http://books.google.com /books?id=eUQQAAAAYAAJ&pg=PP1

Baco, M., & Burghardt, L. (2013, October 18). [Web log message]. Retrieved from http://histpres.com/opportu nity/catholic-diocese-albany-ny-st-patricks-chuch-demo lition-price-chopper/

Bailey, E., Gay, W., Granger, E., & Granger, J. (1806-1827). *The iroquois: Six nations.* Retrieved from http://www.oswego.edu/library2/ archives/digitized_collections/granger/ir.html

Bechard, H. (1966). Tekakwitha, kateri. *Dictionary of canadian biography, 1.* Retrieved from http://www.biographi. ca/en/bio/Tekakwitha _1E.html

Bonneau, B. (2012, 2013). *Justice for gilbert.com.* Retrieved from http: //www.justiceforgilbert.com/

Broderick, S. (2013). *Church memorials & family names: St. patrick's church.* Retrieved from http://www.Rootsweb.ancestry.com/ ~nytigs/ChurchMemorials-StPatsWvlt.htm

Broderick,S. (2012, October 01). Professional insect/butter flynet [Online Facebook comment]. Retrieved from https:// www.facebook.com/Citizens.for.St.Patricks

Brooklyn Daily Eagle. (1875, November 06). *Drowned man.* Retrieved from http://interactive.ancestry.com/2469/2 490009/1216935205?backurl=http://search.ancestry.co m/cgibin/sse.dll?indiv=1&rank=1&gsfn=winifred&gsln =moran&sx=&f20=&f17=New+York&f15=west+troy &rg_f19__date=1890&rs_f19__date=10&gskw=&prox =1&db=usdirectories&ti=0&ti.si=0&gss=angs-d&pcat= 37&fh=0&h=1216935205&recoff=&ssrc=&backlabel =ReturnRecord

Campbell, T. (1910). *St. isaac jogues.* The Catholic Encyclopedia. New York: Robert Appleton Company. Retrieved from New Advent: http://www.newadvent.org/cathen/08420b.htm

Caswell, J. E. (2013). *Henry hudson.* Retrieved from http://www. britannica.com/EBchecked/topic/274681/Henry-Hudson

Cembellin, V. (1997, October 30). *Story of saint bernadette & our lady of lourdes.* Retrieved from http://www.medjugorjeusa.org /lourdes.htm

Cerri, L. (1989). *The history of watervliet, new york.* (1st ed.). Watervliet, New York: Watervliet History, 1989. [Notes]

Constas, R. (2013). Legend of the great peace of the Iroquois confederation. Retrieved from http://www.tsgfoundation. org/index.php?option=com_content&view=article&id=158 :legend-of-the-great-peace-of-the-iroquois confederation&ca tid=53:extended-book-reviews

Daily Whig. (1868, August 31). *Died.* Retrieved from http:// fultonhistory.com/Fulton.html

Deduce, A. (2012, April 10). Pulse of the people: Please don't pull the plug. *The Troy Record.* Retrieved from http://www.troyrecord.

com/general-news/20120410/pulse-of-the-people-please-dont-pull-plug

Department of State, Office of General Counsel, N. Y. S. D. O. C. (2013). *Cemetery regulation in new york state*. Retrieved from http://www.dos.ny.gov/cnsl/cemreg.html

Desmaizeaux, P., & Toland, J. (1814). *A new edition of toland's history of the druids: With an abstract of his life and writings; and a copious appendix, containing notes, critical, philological, and explanatory*. Montrose: Printed by J. Watt, for P. Hill, etc. Retrieved from http://books.google.com /books?id=zrnUAAAAMAAJ&printsec=frontcover&dq=thedruids &hl=en&sa=X&ei=OYlkUqTuEYPu9ATBvoDQAg&ved=0 CFQQ6AEwBw

Eastwood, L. (2012). *A new edition of toland*. Hants: Moon Books. Retrieved from http://books.google.com/books?id=vuV 0Qk96IKkC&printsec=frontcover&source=gbs_ge_summary_ r&cad=0

Encyclopedia Brittanica. (2013). *Thomas dongan, 2nd earl of limerick*. Retrieved from http://www.britannica.com/EBchecked /topic/169114/Thomas-Dongan-2nd-earl-of-Limerick

Finch, R. G. (1998). *The story of the new york state canals: Historical and commercial information*. (1st ed.). New York: J.B. Lyon Co. Retrieved from http://www.canals.ny.gov/history/finch_history_print.pdfy /finch_history_print.pdf

Guest. (2004, July 21). *Sex abuse investigations*. [Online community forum] Retrieved from http://factnet.org/vbforum/forum/religions-religious-sub-sects-and-religious-orspiritual-cults/christian-centered groups/catholic-sects/9619-sex-abuse- investigations

Harris, A. D. (1982). *Deganawidah: The two serpents*. Retrieved from http: //www.maitreya.org/english/PNative Americans/Iroquois Proph ecies.html

Harris, S. L., & Von Dehsen, C. D. (1999). *Philosophers and religious leaders*. (Vol. 1). Phoenix: The Oryx Press. Retrieved from http://books.google.com/books?id=25yC2ePhbXEC&pg=PA114 &dq="motherannlee"&hl=en&sa=X&ei=QGlkUvaSOoj28w Sd44Fw&ved=0CD0Q6AEwAw

Herwood, M. C. (2012, June 17). *The six native american tribes that dwell in new york state are known as the Iroquois confederacy*. Retrieved from http://voices.yahoo.com/the-six-native-american-tribes-dwell-york-11475476.html

Howell, G. R., & Munsell, J. H. (1886). *History of the county of schenectady, n.y., from 1662 to 1886* . (1st ed.). New York: W.W. Munsell & Co. Retrieved from http://books.google.com/books?id=eWThMMum H2QC&pg=PA190&dq=Schenectadymassacrehistory&hl=en&sa= X&ei=CDxkUqCOYXQ8wSY3IBY&ved=0CEEQ6AEwBA

Hutt, S. Department Of The Interior, National Park Service (2013). *Notice of intent to repatriate cultural items* (NPS-WASO-NAGPRA-

1311f; PPWOCRADN0-PCU00RP14.R50000).United States
Government Printing Office website: Retrieved from website:
http://www.gpo.gov/fdsys/pkg/FR-2013-06-17/html/2013-14362
.htm

Kanentiio, D. (2011, November 28). [Personal Communication].

Kanentiio, D. (2011, November 6). [Personal Communication].

Kanentiio, D. (2011, October 16). A rebirth for a sacred place on the
mohawk. *Times Union,* Retrieved from http://www.timesunion
.com/opinion/article/Arebirth-for-a-sacred-place-on-the-Mohawk-
2220932.php

Kanentiio, D. (2011, October 13). Iroquois regain sacred land at cohoes
falls. *Indian Time,* Retrieved from http://www.indiant
ime.net/story/2011/10/13/guest-editorial/iroquois-regain
sacred-land-at-cohoesfalls/042420122050746024368.html

Kerber, J. E. (2001). *Archaeology of the iroquois: Selected readings and research
sources.* (1st ed.). New York: Garland Publishing. Retrieved from
http://books.google.com/books?id=-Jb8MFIb6oC&pg=PA395
&lpg=PA395&dq=Skennenrahawi&source=bl&ots=0pvFyJ
CzPO&sig=tZ6m5uRg7loy_5BnGrr-nQ97uFQ&hl=en&sa
=X&ei=ic9iUtabDJLY9QToBo&ved=0CFcQ6AEwBw

Kings County New York Estate Files. (1866-1923). *Letters
of administration granted to petitioner, winifred moran.* Retrieved from
https://familysearch.org/pal:/MM9.3.1/TH-662-11300-3963-93
?cc=1466356&wc 7795098

Kings County N.Y. Surrogate's Court. (1866-1923). *Letters
of administration granted to petitioner, winifred moran.* Retrieved from
https://familysearch.org/pal:/MM9.3.1/TH-662-11300-3963-92
?cc=1466356&wc 7795098

Kings County N.Y. Surrogate's Court. (1866-1923). *Letters
of administration granted to petitioner, winifred moran.* Retrieved from
https://familysearch.org/pal:/MM9.3.1/TH-662-11300-3963
-86?cc=1466356&wc 7795098

Kings County N.Y. Surrogate's Court. (1866-1923). *Letters
of administration granted to petitioner, winifred moran.* Retrieved from
https://familysearch.org/pal:/MM9.3.1/TH-662-11300-3963
-83?cc=1466356&wc 7795098

Knickerbocker News. (1954, April 24). *Watervliet man found hanged.*
Retrieved from http://fultonhistory.com/Fulton.html

Knickerbocker News. (1964). *Fire escape plunge fatal.* Retrieved from
http://fultonhistory.com/Fulton.html

Lamere, C. (2001, February). *Colonial albany and rensselaerswyck.*
Retrieved from http://freepages.genealogy.rootsweb.ancestry
.com/~clifflamere/History/Albany-History.htm

Leadbeater, C. W. (1918). *A textbook of theosophy.* (3rd ed.). Los
Angeles: Theosophical Publishing House: American Branch.
Retrieved from http://books.google.com/books?id=7l9bAAAA

MAAJ&printsec=frontcover&source=gbs_ge_summary_r&cad=0

Livingston, R. (1689). *The schenectady massacre*. Retrieved from http: //www.digitalhistory.uh.edu/disp_textbook.cfm?smtID=3& psid=88

Madison County Times. (1942, December 25). *Muckland murder mystery solved two formally charged with murder*. Retrieved from: http://fulton history.com/

McColman, C. (2010). *The big book of christian mysticism: The essential guide to contemplative spirituality*. Charlottesville: Hampton Roads Publishing Co., Inc. Retrieved from http://books.google.com/books?id=zoO ojHybX-UC&printsec=frontcover&dq=christianmysticism&hl =en&sa=X&ei=vYBkUsTqKZKC9QTdtIFg&ved=0CEAQ6A EwBA

McGayhan, F., Stanislaus, M., & Whyte, M. (1911). *Order of the presentation*. Retrieved from http://www.newadvent.org /cathen /12397a.htm

Miraclehunter.com. (2013). *Vatican approved*. Retrieved from http:// www.marianapparitions.org/apparitions/Vaticanapproved

Moran, J. (1996, February 10). Police probe another death at st. colman's. *Daily gazette*. Retrieved from http://news.google.com /newspapers?nid=1957&dat=19960210&id=NHpGAAAA IBAJ&sjid=bOkMAAAAIBAJ&pg=6318,20361391996

Morris, J. (2011, December 31). [Personal Communication]

Morris, J. (2011, November 6). [Personal Communication]

Mother, L. (2012). *Algonquian history*. Retrieved from http://www.man ataka.org/page386.html

Myers, J. (1910). *The history of the city of watervliet, n.y., 1630 to 1910*. Retrieved from http://archive.org/stream/historyofcityofw00myer

New York State Board of Charities. (1906). *Annual report of the new york state board of charities*. (Vol. 2). Albany: J.B. Lyon Company. Retrieved from http://books.google.com/books?id=cCYrAAAAYAAJ &printsec=frontcover&source=gbs_ge_summary_r&cad=0

New York State Board of Charities. (1904). *Annual report of the new york state board of charities*. (Vol. 2). Albany: Oliver A. Quayle. Retrieved from http://books.google.com/books?id=IvoWAAAAYAA J&pg=PA713&lpg=PA713&dq=charities+%22rev.+william+ f.+sheehan%22+st.+colman+watervliet&source=bl&ots =tCXzKVxGG&sig=uEAkM4yh0t5pyDbIp_lgw7zlEe4&hl =en&sa=X&ei=bDuIUtTPDaW2QXapIC4Dg&ved=0CCsQ6AE wAQ#v=onepage&q=charities%20%22rev.%20william %20f.%20sheehan%22%20st.%20colman%20watervliet&f=false

New York State Library. (2013, April 22). *New york state history: Colonial period*. Retrieved from http://www.nysl.nysed.gov/scandocs/

colonial.htm

New York State Library. (2012, August 8). *Native American materials.* Retrieved from http://www.nysl.nysed .gov/scandocs/native american.htm

New York State Museum. (2002, April 1). *The bleecker map of rensselaerswyck - 1767 .* Retrieved from http://www.nysm.nysed. gov/albany/im/im1767.html

New York Times. (1994, February 11). *Court upholds murder charge if death follows a lesser plea.* Retrieved from: http://www.nytimes.com/ 1994/02/11/nyregion/court-upholds-murder-charge-if-death-follows-a-lesser-plea.html

New Zealand Tablet. (1909). *Irish news: cork - a remarkable coincidence.* Retrieved from http://paperspast.natlib.govt.nz/cgi-bin/papers past?a=d&d=NZT19090603.2.47&l=mi&e=-------10--1----2—

Pauls, E. P., & Tooker, E. (2008, March 06). *Northeast indian.* Retrieved from http://www.britannica.com/EBchecked/topic/177413/ Northeast-Indian

Pegels, C. C. (1962). *Philip john schuyler [1733-1804].* Retrieved from http://www.newnetherlandinstitute.org/history-and-heritage/dutch _americans/philip-john-schuyler/

Polk City Directory. (1941-1987). *Albany county, n.y. city directory: including Watervliet.* Boston, Mass., R.L. Polk & Co., 1943- R917.4743 POL (1941, 1942, 1943, 1944, 1946, 1947, 1948-1949, 1951, 1952, 1953,1954, 1959, 1960, 1961, 1962, 1963, 1964, 1967, 1968, 1971, 1972, 1973, 1974, 1975, 1976, 1977, 1979, 1980, 1981, 1987)

Pritchard, E. (2000). *The major alqonquin nations .* Retrieved from http://www.wilkesweb.us/algonquin/nations.htm

Ray, M., & Tikkanen, A. (2008, March 19). *Iroquois confederacy.* Retrieved from http://www.britannica.com/topic/294660/history

Regardie, I. (1971). *The golden dawn: A complete course in practical ceremonial magic .* (6th ed.). St. Paul: Llewellyn Publications. Retrieved from http://books.google.com/books?id=kXLAfCBj4boC&printsec =frontcover&dq=hermeticorderofthgoldendawn&hl=en&sa=X&ei =mZplUv7uNofo8gS_loBg&ved=0CDwQ6AEwAA

Reinfurt, M. (2013). *Our story.* Retrieved from http://www.parkerbros memorial.com/our_heritage.html

Rittner, D. (2012, March 18). For whom the bell tolls?. *Times Union.* Retrieved from http://blog.timesunion.com/rittner/for-whom-the-bell-tolls/2121/

Robbins, J. Department Of The Interior, National Park Service (2001). *Notice of inventory completion for native american human remains and associated funerary objects in the possession of the new york state museum, albany, ny.* (FR Doc. 01–24932). Retrieved from United States Government Printing Office website:http://www.gpo.gov/fdsys/pkg/FR-2001-10-04/pdf/0124932.pdf

Robertson Maloney, S. (2007, January 10). *Sex abuse investigations.* [Online community forum].Retrieved from http://factnet.org /vbforum/forum/religions-religious-sub-sects-and-religious-or spiritual-cults/christian-centered-groups/catholic-sects/9619 -sex-abuse-investigations

Robertson Maloney, S. (2003, December 16). *The throw away child.* Retrieved from http://www.Amazon.com/Throw-Child-Susanne-Maloney-Robertson/dp/1413700942

Sarudy, B. W. (2013, March 7). *Biography - american shaker founder "mother" ann lee 1736-1784.* Retrieved from http://b-womeninamerican history18.blogspot.com/2011/09/shaker-founder-mother-ann-lee -1736-1784.html

Schilling, V. (2012, October 5). *Brookfield renewable power donates 100 acres of sacred mohawk land to hiawatha institute for indigenous knowledge.* Retrieved from http://indiancountrytodaymedianetwork.com/ article/Brookfield-renewablepower-donates-100-acres-of-sacred-mohawk-land-tohiawatha-institute-for-indigenous-knowledge-137889

Scott, M. J. (1927). *Isaac jogues: Missioner and martyr.* (1st ed.). New York: P.J. Kennedy & Sons. Retrieved from http://www.heritagehistory. com/index.php?c=read&author=scottm&book=isaac&story =_front

Shovel, D. (1997, July 3). *Mahican history.* Retrieved from http://www .dickshovel.com/Mahican.html

Southworth, G. (1910). *Builders of our country.* (2nd ed.). New York: D. Appleton and Company. Retrieved from http://www.heritage history.com/?c=read&author=southworth&book=builders2&story =_front

Swantek, J. (2009). *Watervliet arsenal: A history of america's oldest arsenal.* (1st ed., pp. 435-36). Watervliet, New York: Watervliet Arsenal Public Affairs Office.

Stuart Rubin, N. (2006, June 12). The fox sisters: Spiritualism's unlikely founders. *History.net,* Retrieved from http://www.historynet.com/ the-fox-sisters-spiritualisms-unlikely-founders.htm

The Times Record. (1950, December 5). *Miss k.v. moran dies at residence, ill several days.* Retrieved from: http://search.ancestry.com/

The Times Record. (1944, January 7). *Former troy man electrocuted at sing sing prison.* Retrieved from: http://fultonhistory.com/

The Times Record. (1942, June 19). *Obituary.* Retrieved from:

http://fultonhistory.com/

The Times Record. (1942, June 16). *Obituary*. Retrieved from: http://fultonhistory.com/

The Troy NY Daily Times. (1929, April 13). *Find baby's body*. Retrieved from: http://www.fultonhistory.com/Fulton.html

The Troy NY Daily Times. (1915, March 29). *Watervliet: obituary*. Retrieved from: http://www.fultonhistory.com/Fulton.html

The Troy NY Daily Times. (1915, March 26). *Watervliet: obituary*. Retrieved from: http://www.fultonhistory.com/Fulton.html

The Troy Record. (2012, February 19). *Obituary: father dominic emery parillo*. Retrieved from: http://www.legacy.com

The Troy Record. (1961, September 1). *Obituary*. Retrieved from: http://www.fultonhistory.com/Fulton.html

The Troy Record. (1958, January 27). *Mrs. laliberte active in church circles, succumbs*. Retrieved from: http://www.fultonhistory.com/Fulton.html

The Troy Record. (1958, January 25). *Obituary*. Retrieved from: http://www.fultonhistory.com/Fulton.html

The Vatican. (1983). Code of canon law. (2nd ed.). Rome: Libreria Editrice Vaticana. Retrieved from http://www.vatican.va/archive/ENG1104/_PY.HTM

Troy Daily Times. (1908, June 27). *Golden jubilee*. pp. 1, 3.

Troy Daily Times. (1876, February 19). *Tired of Life*. Retrieved from http://fultonhistory.com/Newspaper18/TroyNYDailyTimes/Troy NYDailyTimes1876/TroyNYDailyTimes1876 - 0157.pdf

Troy Daily Times. (1858). *Brien rooney the west troy incendiary sentenced to death*. Retrieved from http://fultonhistory.com/Fulton.html

Troy Times. (1933 , July 19). *Painter, despondent*. Retrieved from http://www.fultonhistory.com/Fulton.html

Troy Whig. (1868, August 24). *Committed suicide*. Retrieved from http://www.fultonhistory.com/Fulton.html

Underhill, A. L. (1885). *The project gutenberg ebook of the missing link in modern spiritualism*. New York: Thomas R. Knox & Co. Retrieved from http://www.gutenberg.org/files/40485/40485-h/40485-h.htm

United States Catholic Historical Society., & Cahalan, J. E. (1911). *Historical records and studies*. (Vol. 6). New York: United States Catholic Historical Society. Retrieved from http://books.google.com/books?id=3Lc8AAAAIAAJ&pg=PA244&lpg=PA244&dq="rev.williamf.sheehan"necrology&source=bl&ots=uhicu63Xl0&sig

=GZSEGxU6Gc2XulJF_qDKFk1FEPU&hl=en&sa=X&ei=
RWVoUrqBJ8P7kQfQ7oCwAQ&ved=0CCkQ6AEwAA

Utica Daily Press. (1908, June 29). *Personal: Rev. william f. sheehan.* (1908,
Retrieved from http://www.fultonhistory.com/Processsmall/News
papers/UticaNYDailyPress/UticaNYDailyPress1908pdf/UticaNY
DailyPress1908-2858.pdf

White, J. T. (1892). *The national cyclopedia of american biography.* (Vol. 7).
New York: James T. White & Company. Retrieved from
http://books.google.com/books?id=0XZMAAAAYAAJ&pg=PA8
5&lpg=PA85&dq=kiliaenvanrensselaerbiography&source=bl&ots
=LnZGyQbwqs&sig=aOGmu983CHeTTFqgkGC0NjGlrcg&hl=
en&sa=X&ei=SO9hUtbpDo_K9gTluIEY&ved=0CFQQ6A
EwBjgK

ABOUT THE AUTHOR

Jill Marie Morris has studied art, design, and writing, and is the author of *207: A Personal Account of Love Paranormal Phenomenon and Demonic Possession (2011)*. She is also an accomplished artist, a freelance writer, and a 5th generation psychic medium. For more information, please visit: www.jillmariemorris.com.

Made in the USA
Charleston, SC
06 November 2014